The Transparency Paradox

The Transparency Paradox

Questioning an Ideal

IDA KOIVISTO

OXFORD
UNIVERSITY PRESS

OXFORD
UNIVERSITY PRESS

Great Clarendon Street, Oxford, OX2 6DP,
United Kingdom

Oxford University Press is a department of the University of Oxford.
It furthers the University's objective of excellence in research, scholarship,
and education by publishing worldwide. Oxford is a registered trade mark of
Oxford University Press in the UK and in certain other countries

First Edition published in 2022

Impression: 1

Published in the United States of America by Oxford University Press
198 Madison Avenue, New York, NY 10016, United States of America

British Library Cataloguing in Publication Data

Data available

Library of Congress Control Number: 2022933009

ISBN 978-0-19-285546-6

DOI: 10.1093/oso/9780192855466.001.0001

Printed and bound by
CPI Group (UK) Ltd, Croydon, CR0 4YY

To Oddvar

Acknowledgements

As I put the finishing touches to this book, I am struck by how the paradox of transparency in many ways relates to publishing a book such as this. Suddenly all the ideas slowly constructed and structured over years of hard work are now laid bare to the world to see. What you will read is, of course, very different from what I see when looking over my final manuscript. For me, its pages are filled with the memories of the spaces in which it was created and the people who helped and advised me on the way.

I wrote this book in New York, Florence, Helsinki, and Toronto, and these places have all added their own flavour to it. Although these influences cannot be reduced to anything clear and tangible, in this journey I have learned a lot about the multifaceted nature of my topic as well as about myself. I am eternally grateful to the many inspiring and encouraging people who have put their time and effort into helping me make this book as good as it can be. Sadly, not all of you can be mentioned by name here. However, I am confident in saying that with your help, I see transparency more clearly.

The seeds of this book set root during my research stay at New York University, where I had the privilege to delve into the world of globalizing law as well as legal theory. I especially wish to thank Rob Howse, Benedict Kingsbury, Richard Stewart, and Moshe Halbertal. In addition, I would like to thank warmly all my global fellows, most of all Zoran Oklopcic, Yaniv Roznai, Friedrich Rosenfeld, Luigi Nuzzo, Maria Adele Carrai, and Bilyana Petkova. At the European University Institute in Florence, Italy, I developed most of my theoretical ideas, a task made easier by all the amazing mentors and fellow Max Weber scholars there. My special thanks go to Deirdre Curtin, Dennis Patterson, Peter Szigeti, Florian Hertel, and Or Bassok.

I have produced most of my writing at my alma mater and current workplace, the University of Helsinki. I thank especially Susanna Lindroos-Hovinheimo and Toomas Kotkas for their invaluable input in reading through and commenting on my manuscript. I also wish to thank Olli Mäenpää, Päivi Leino-Sandberg, Riikka Koulu, and the people at the Legal Tech Lab, Jan Klabbers, Maarten Hillebrandt, and Panu Minkkinen—you all helped me more than you know. I especially want to thank Markus Dubber, the director of the Center for Ethics at the University of Toronto, for his invaluable encouragement and support.

Special thanks go to Sofia Sormunen for meticulous research assistance and Mark Shackleton for excellent proofreading. Heartfelt thanks also go to the team at OUP who did a wonderful job turning my manuscript into the book you hold today.

This work has been funded by grants and postdoctoral positions at the Academy of Finland, the Cultural Foundation of Finland, EUI and NYU. I wish especially to mention the funding from the Academy of Finland for the research projects 'Regulating Visibility—the Ideal of Transparency in Global Administrative Law', 'Transparency in the EU - From Reaction to Manifesto?' and 'Potential and Boundaries of Algorithmic Transparency'. Thank you all for believing in this project and in me.

Lastly, I thank my family and friends for their support and for putting up with my rants on transparency over the years. Most of all, I thank you, Trond, for being there and being you. I dedicate this book to our son, who was born soon after the submission of the manuscript of this book.

Table of Contents

PART I
THE OPACITY OF TRANSPARENCY

1
The Era of Transparency

Introduction: Why Transparency, Why Now?

Transparency has become the new norm.[1] A state should be transparent, institutions should be transparent, the market should be transparent, processes should be transparent, reasoning should be transparent, even the whole of society should be transparent.[2] The importance of transparency seems to be growing without interruption.[3] It has become a buzzword that transcends its old institutional habitat of the state. It may even be becoming a global norm.[4] For instance, Mark Fenster locates transparency 'among the pantheon of great policy virtues'.[5] Christopher Hood mentions 'the rise and rise of transparency',[6] and Anne Peters 'the transparency turn'.[7] Lars Thøger Christensen and Joep Cornelissen state that '[transparency] has become a taken-for-granted ideal and explanation of how society and its organizations must function'.[8] By supposedly enabling access to information and exposing the way in which power is exercised, transparency is celebrated as one of the cornerstones of liberal democratic government.[9]

Even beyond the context of governance, transparency talk is ubiquitous. Its demands seem to be constantly conquering new realms, forging a cultural

[1] This is indeed *expressis verbis* the case, for instance, in the International Monetary Fund (IMF). See Ida Koivisto, 'The IMF and the Transparency Turn' (2016) 25 Minnesota Journal of International Law 381 (hereafter Koivisto, 'Transparency Turn').

[2] Critically Byung-Chul Han, *The Transparency Society* (Erik Butler tr, Stanford University Press 2015); Gianni Vattimo, *The Transparent Society* (Polity Press 1992).

[3] Mikkel Flyverbom, 'Sunlight in Cyberspace? On Transparency as a Form of Ordering' (2015) 18(2) European Journal of Social Theory 168, 179 mentions of 'transparency evangelism'.

[4] Anne Peters, 'Towards Transparency as a Global Norm' in Anne Peters and Andrea Bianchi (eds), *Transparency in International Law* (Cambridge University Press 2013) 534 (hereafter Peters, 'Towards Transparency').

[5] Mark Fenster, 'The Opacity of Transparency' (2006) 91 Iowa Law Review 885, 888.

[6] Christopher Hood, 'Beyond Exchanging First Principles: Some Closing Comments' in Christopher Hood and David Heald (eds), *Transparency: Key to Better Governance?* (Oxford University Press 2006) 211 (hereafter Hood, 'Beyond Exchanging First Principles').

[7] Peters, 'Towards Transparency' (n 4) 534. Peters borrows the term from Aarti Gupta (Aarti Gupta, 'Transparency under Scrutiny: Information Disclosure in Global Environmental Governance' (2008) 8 Global Environmental Politics 1, 6).

[8] Lars Thøger Christensen and Joep Cornelissen, 'Organizational Transparency as Myth and Metaphor' (2015) 18(2) European Journal of Social Theory 132, 133 (hereafter Christensen and Cornelissen, 'Organizational Transparency').

[9] For critical analysis of that promise in the European Union (EU), see Deirdre Curtin and Albert Meijer, 'Does Transparency Strengthen Legitimacy?' (2006) 11 Information Polity 109.

The Transparency Paradox. Ida Koivisto, Oxford University Press. © Ida Koivisto 2022.
DOI: 10.1093/oso/9780192855466.003.0001

change.[10] It is hardly an overstatement to argue that we live in the era of transparency, the 'transparentocene'.[11] Conversely, 'the lack of transparency' instantly sounds ominous and condemnable in contemporary language. Transparency has gained an almost mythical status in modern society.[12] Although critical voices are proliferating—we can even talk about the emergence of critical transparency studies[13]—the background assumption of this book is that, thus far, 'the transparency turn' has occurred without sufficient conceptual analysis or critique. The underlying policy question is, thus, the soundness of the modern justificatory principles of governance.

Today, transparency is probably discursively stronger than ever. For example, Andrea Bianchi, one of the editors of the book *Transparency in International Law* (2013), mentions that 'I have never before experienced such unfaltering enthusiasm for a book proposal'. The research community as well as practitioners seem to have an endless thirst for transparency.[14] Arguably, the transparency craze has even intensified since 2013. It is not clear why this is the case.[15] What question does transparency answer? Why do we want transparency more than ever? And why now? Dominant discourses are interesting because they consolidate a certain conception of how things should be. Thus, the way in which words are used and how things are labelled are of crucial importance.

Let us undertake a thought experiment: What would happen if, in some imaginary regime, the legislation governing the release of government information

[10] Andrea Bianchi, 'On Power and Illusion: The Concept of Transparency in International Law' in Andrea Bianchi and Anne Peters (eds), *Transparency in International Law* (Cambridge University Press 2013) 1, 1 (hereafter Bianchi, 'On Power and Illusion'): '[Transparency] is recommended by psychologists to recover trust after infidelity; and it is increasingly imposed on banks and financial institutions. Non-transparent financial transactions, no matter how insignificant, by spouses may lead to a central banker's resignation. Medical practice leans dangerously towards unconditional forms of transparency: you may be unceremoniously told that you are going to die just for the sake of transparency (particularly vis-à-vis the physician's professional insurance!). Worldwide campaigns have been led in the name of transparency by not-so-transparent organizations, as was the case of WikiLeaks, against the abuse of power by States. Transparent portable phones present one of the most pressing research challenges for electronic gadget designers.'

[11] Emmanuel Alloa, 'Transparency: A Magic Concept of Modernity' in Emmanuel Alloa and Dieter Thomä (eds), *Transparency, Society and Subjectivity: Critical Perspectives* (Palgrave Macmillan 2018) 21.

[12] Christensen and Cornelissen, 'Organizational Transparency' (n 8) 132–49.

[13] As a token of this, for example, recent special issues on transparency have been published in the European Journal of Social Theory (2015) 18(2) and Cultural Studies ↔ Critical Methodologies (2014) 14(1). Sandrine Baume and Yannis Papadopoulos, 'Transparency: From Bentham's Inventory of Virtuous Effects to Contemporary Evidence-based Skepticism' (2018) 21(2) Critical Review of International Social and Political Philosophy 169 (hereafter Baume and Papadopoulos, 'Transparency: From Bentham's Inventory'); Ida Koivisto, 'Toward Critical Transparency Studies' (2019) 25(3) Res Publica 439.

[14] Bianchi, 'On Power and Illusion' (n 10) 2.

[15] See, for example, Michel Schudson, *The Rise of the Right to Know: Politics and Culture of Transparency, 1945–1975* (The Belknap Press of Harvard University Press 2015); Sandrine Baume, 'Publicity and Transparency: The Itinerary of a Subtle Distinction' in Emmanuel Alloa and Dieter Thomä (eds), *Transparency, Society and Subjectivity: Critical Perspectives* (Palgrave Macmillan 2018) 203.

(freedom of information acts (FOIA)) remained normatively untouched? All the information and documents would be as available as ever, and the restrictions on this availability would stay the same, but the name of the legitimating principle would be changed. The principle of transparency would be replaced with the principle of opacity, confidentiality, or secrecy. Under these conditions, the rules previously called the exceptions to transparency would now manifest the main rule of opacity. Correspondingly, the rules allowing information release would be conceptualized as exceptions to opacity, not transparency.

Would that legislation lose at least some of its legitimacy? I suspect it would. I argue that the general label has a halo effect: whatever is categorized under the canopy of 'transparency' sounds good. This is based on a peculiar assumption that transparency is good, regardless of what it means. Thus, transparency may be approached as a normative concept entailing a covert 'pro' attitude towards it, even when no assets are attributed to it.[16] Things would probably change if the principle of opacity became, for some reason, fashionable. That would, however, take time. First, the concept of opacity would need to gather an array of positive connotations in many different contexts. Secondly, transparency would lose its positive connotations and gather increasingly negative ones.

The entire motivation to write this book originates from the observation that legitimacy of different organizations is increasingly formulated in the vocabulary of transparency: whether there is enough of it, whether X or Y enhances it. On the one hand, the metaphorical authority of transparency is largely considered self-evident. Anyone who claims otherwise has the burden of proof. On the other hand, however, transparency is an ambiguous and context-dependent concept that lacks consensual definition. For example, Emmanuel Alloa singles out ten different meanings or narratives for transparency as an ideal:[17]

1) *Transparency as accessibility*: ensuring informational access to all citizens; implementing a 'right to know';
2) *Transparency as procedural fairness*: safeguarding due process to everyone involved;

[16] Normative or 'thick' concepts are concepts that not only contain descriptive power, but also a pro-attitude towards themselves. For instance, calling someone brave implies that being brave is desirable. Thus, they provide reasons for action. According to the *Oxford Dictionary of Philosophy* (2 rev ed, Oxford University Press, current online version 2014) <www.oxfordreference.com/view/10.1093/acref/9780199541430.001.0001/acref-9780199541430> accessed 16 July 2021, '[a] normative epistemology determines how you ought to conduct your cognitive life; a descriptive one only describes how people in fact do so. However, the distinction is not clear-cut in practice: according to the principle of charity the only way of interpreting what people do in fact think, is by assuming that by and large they think what they ought to think. The philosophy of social sciences is fraught with problems of distinguishing between fact and value.'

[17] Emmanuel Alloa, 'Transparency: A Magic Concept of Morality' in Emmanuel Alloa and Dieter Thomä (eds), *Transparency, Society and Subjectivity: Critical Perspectives* (Palgrave Macmillan 2018) 21, 31–32 (hereafter Alloa, 'Transparency: A Magic Concept').

3) *Transparency as accountability*: by making decisions available to the public, stakeholders are assumed to develop a sharpened sense of responsibility and enhanced accountability;
4) *Transparency as asymmetry reduction*: unlike secrecy, which typically privileges only a few, disclosure is held to re-establish a certain balance of power;
5) *Transparency as a public good*: when actions are placed under public scrutiny, the temptations of self-interest are reduced, if not removed;
6) *Transparency as rationalization*: making decision-makers give reasons for their actions leads to the improvement of rational behavioural standards;
7) *Transparency as truth-making*: by forcing people to speak out, falseness, deceit, and duplicity are dispelled;
8) *Transparency as moralization*: when everything is placed under constant visibility, people are compelled to act virtuously;
9) *Transparency as (self-)knowledge*: only a subject that knows about herself knows what she can count on and what she can account for;
10) *Transparency as authenticity*: things can be genuine and true to themselves only when nothing is withheld.

Depending on the context, each of these facets makes an appearance in this book, some more frequently than others. As an ideal, transparency cannot be reduced to one of its multiple facets. Nor are its intended consequences always taking place. On the contrary, transparency keeps on creating new meanings and requirements. Consequently, transparency can be seen, in Christopher Pollitt and Peter Hupe's words, as a 'magic concept'.[18]

According to Pollit and Hupe, magic concepts, used widely in governance parlance, have great rhetorical power. They are labelled by four main characteristics. First, they are broad in scope. They cover a large area of meaning. They may have many, potentially conflicting definitions, and they are connected to several other concepts. Second, they are normatively attractive. This means that their connotation is overwhelmingly positive. Correspondingly, it is difficult to be plausibly 'against' them. In part, this is due to their aura of 'modernity' or 'progressiveness'. This implies that previous conceptualizations may be flawed or obsolete (eg 'networks' replacing 'bureaucracy'). Third, they water down, obscure, or even deny conceptual opposites or traditionally conflicting interests or logics (eg democracy being contrary to efficiency). In this way, they imply consensus. Fourth, these concepts are both highly fashionable and popular. They are used by many practitioners and academics; they feature in numerous policy documents and academic writings. Thus, they are globally marketable.[19]

[18] Christopher Pollitt and Peter Hupe, 'Talking About Government: The Role of Magic Concepts' (2011) 13(5) Public Management Review 641 (hereafter Pollitt and Hupe, 'Talking About Government').

[19] Pollitt and Hupe, 'Talking About Government' (n 18) 642–43; see also Ida Koivisto, 'From Moral Rules to Individual Rights—and Beyond? The Institutionalization of Good Administration in Finland

Transparency meets the criteria of a magic concept; it is broad in meaning, it is extremely attractive normatively, it blurs conceptual opposites and is fashionable beyond compare.[20] Despite its magic qualities, however, transparency carries certain underlying assumptions. Therefore, instead of a self-evident public good, transparency should be approached as a naturalized ideology which, among other things, believes in visual metaphors, the power of a controlling eye, keeping power in check, distributing democratizable knowledge, the authenticity of communication, and conceptualizing opacities or concealment as exceptions.

When this ideology is adopted by those in power, it becomes a legitimating strategy. If we accept this assumption, the proliferation of transparency talk indicates that the legitimacy of power has become a more urgent concern than previously. Simultaneously, it creates and presupposes subjects ready to critique power when necessary; a greater demand for transparency implies a greater supply of it—or vice versa. In this book, these themes will be examined.

The Forerunners of Transparency

Apart from being a visual metaphor and a general legitimation strategy of power—both examined in detail in this book—transparency as a concept is embedded in law. It makes rules and exceptions but is not always reducible to rules even within law. Instead, it also forms a normative criterion to assess many legal rules and standards: does this or that rule enhance transparency? Are the rules themselves transparent? Although freedom of information acts have been around more or less from the 1960s on (with the important exception of the Nordic countries—the Freedom of Press Act in Sweden dates back to 1766), transparency has bloomed within and beyond the legal sphere to an unprecedented scope and in a novel way over the last thirty years or so. Transparency has become a meta-discourse. That said, transparency as such is not a novel ideal, although the extent to which it has become a globalizing, overarching ideal is novel. Against such a backdrop, it is surprising how little modern literature there is on the intellectual roots of the transparency ideal.[21]

and in Europe' (2018) 1 Förvaltningsrättslig tidskrift 71 (hereafter Koivisto, 'From Moral Rules to Individual Rights').

[20] See also Alloa, 'Transparency: A Magic Concept' (n 17) 29.

[21] Christopher Hood, 'Transparency in Historical Perspective' in Christopher Hood and David Heald (eds), *Transparency—Key to Better Governance?* (Oxford University Press 2006) (hereafter Hood, 'Transparency in Historical Perspective') is important in this regard. Also, Emmanuel Alloa and Dieter Thomä's (eds), *Transparency, Society and Subjectivity: Critical Perspectives* (Palgrave Macmillan 2018) contains chapters on this subject.

The emergence of transparency as an ideal—referring to purity of heart or soul—dates back all the way to Aristotle and in the Middle Ages to Augustine.[22] However, in the context of governing, the roots of transparency extend to the Enlightenment and, most importantly, to Jeremy Bentham's and Jean-Jacques Rousseau's thinking. In the spirit of the Enlightenment, they celebrated the victory of reason over religion, the establishment of civil rights and the demise of mythical or magical worldviews. They were after legitimation of power.[23] As Baume and Papadopoulos argue, the call for transparency (or publicity) emerged in political discourse at the end of the eighteenth century. Its advocates regarded it as a moral, legal, and political project. One of the key ideas was that a society could be transparent to itself.[24] Thus, transparency was never solely a legal project.

Although there is a long gap between the Enlightenment and the modern day, many ideas of that era have travelled to our contemporary conceptions of transparency. Christopher Hood names three strains of pre-twentieth-century ideas that can be identified as forerunners of the current transparency discourse: rule-governed administration, open and candid social communication, and ways of making society 'knowable'.[25] Here, I follow loosely Hood's three-pronged categorization.

When it comes to the idea of *rule-governed administration*, the most pronounced account is undoubtedly that in Max Weber's famous sociology of authority. In the simplest terms, rule-governed administration means that the governor or sovereign cannot rule according to his or her whims and personal preferences, and that all exercise of power should be based on legal norms and reason-based decision-making. Weber's idea of legal-rational authority begins with the idea that formally set rules, instead of tradition or charismatic authority, should constitute the cornerstone of governing.[26] This idea, however, cannot be attributed to Weber alone, to whom legal-formal rationality is primarily an ideal typical form of authority. Historically, the idea can be traced back to several independent sources.[27]

[22] Alloa, 'Transparency: A Magic Concept' (n 17) 21–55; Manfred Schneider, 'The Dream of Transparency: Aquinas, Rousseau, Sartre' in Emmanuel Alloa and Dieter Thomä (eds), *Transparency, Society and Subjectivity: Critical Perspectives* (Palgrave Macmillan 2018) 85; Jean Starobinski, *Jean Jacques Rousseau: Transparency and Obstruction* (University of Chicago Press 1988) (hereafter Starobinski, *Jean Jacques Rousseau*); Noreen Khawaja, 'Unbounded Confession' in Emmanuel Alloa and Dieter Thomä (eds), *Transparency, Society and Subjectivity: Critical Perspectives* (Palgrave Macmillan 2018) 105.

[23] Interestingly, the word 'enlightenment' refers to light, implying a preceding darkness attributed to mythical explanations of the world.

[24] Baume and Papadopoulos, 'Transparency: From Bentham's Inventory' (n 13) 169.

[25] Hood, 'Transparency in Historical Perspective' (n 21) 5–10. Obviously, the history of transparency could constitute an entire research project on its own. Here, my discussion attempts to be illustrative and contextual rather than comprehensive.

[26] For an overview, see Max Weber, *Economy and Society: An Outline of Interpretive Sociology* (G Roth and C Wittich eds, University of California Press 1978).

[27] Hood, 'Transparency in Historical Perspective' (n 21) 6. Hood mentions different forms reaching from ancient Athens and Sparta to Chinese legalists such as Shen Puhai, the Massachusetts constitution, and, later, nineteenth-century German Rechtsstaat thinking.

According to Hood, although this 'government by rule' thinking is typically associated with liberal democracy, this association is not watertight; transparency is not necessarily symmetrical with the liberal ideal. Different rulers and overseers tend to demand open and rule-governed processes from those they oversee while often claiming a cloak of confidentiality or privacy for their own functioning.[28] This starting point assumes that transparency takes the forms of rules and regulations or is closely associated to overseeing the adherence of rules. Alternatively, transparency can be an instrumental value to accountability: transparency should create structures of surveillance. I will analyse the different rationalities of transparency and their connection to democracy in more detail in chapter five.

The second forerunner of transparency in Hood's categorization is *open and candid communication*. In the era of the Enlightenment, the call for transparency was specifically targeted against opacity. It was associated with many undesirable things, such as injustice and unhappiness.[29] Michel Foucault notes that:

> a fear haunted the latter half of the eighteenth century: the fear of darkened spaces, of the pall of gloom which prevents the full visibility of things, men, and truths. It sought to break up the patches of darkness that blocked the light, eliminate the shadowy areas of society, demolish the unlit chambers where arbitrary political acts, monarchical caprice, religious superstitions, tyrannical and priestly plots, epidemics and illusions of ignorance were fomented.[30]

In general, opacity was connected to increasing disapproval of lies, pretence, hypocrisy, and other widespread cultural institutions considered theatrical or artificial. The culture of the 'mask' and the concomitant lack of authenticity were rejected, while the desire for just, natural, and expressive emotions—in contrast to court ethics—became new ideals.[31]

These issues were particularly a concern of Rousseau's: he abhorred inauthenticity. I delve into his utopia of transparency in more detail in chapter three. Here, it suffices to say that for Rousseau, transparency was the key component of authenticity and pureness of heart in all social action. He also brought this idea into the realm of government, although he remained somewhat ambiguous towards it. However, in *The Social Contract* and, in particular, his constitutional plans for

[28] Hood, 'Transparency in Historical Perspective' (n 21) 6; David Brin, *The Transparent Society: Will Technology Force Us to Choose Between Privacy and Freedom?* (Perseus Books 1998) 12; also, Koivisto, 'Transparency Turn' (n 1).

[29] Michel Foucault and Colin Gordon, *Power/Knowledge: Selected Interviews and Other Writings* (Harvester Wheatsheaf 1977) 146–65.

[30] Michel Foucault, 'The Eye of Power: A Conversation with Jean-Pierre Barou and Michelle Perrot' in Michel Foucault, *Power/Knowledge: Selected Interviews and Other Writings, 1972–1977* (Colin Gordon ed, Colin Gordon and others trs, Pantheon Books 1980) 153 (hereafter Foucault, 'The Eye of Power').

[31] Baume and Papadopoulos, 'Transparency: From Bentham's Inventory' (n 13) 170.

Poland, Rousseau argued that public servants should operate 'in the eyes of the public': a transparent society, according to his utopian view, would guarantee that nobody's private conduct could be veiled from public gaze. This would protect government from destabilizing intrigues and cabals.[32]

This brings us to the third forerunner of the modern transparency discourse, *ways of making society 'knowable'*. The ideal of knowability presupposes interested, knowledge-thirsty subjects. Therefore, transparency as a value can be associated with a new kind of citizenry. From the Enlightenment onwards, people have been constituted as subjects who have a right and a desire to know what is happening in society. If this was not the case, transparency as a governance ideal would not make much sense. This idea presupposes that such knowledge about society is possible and conceivable. Furthermore, it empowers people—informed by transparency—to keep power in check and accountable to the public.

In this respect, Bentham's work in particular is relevant. He had several ideas regarding transparency, publicity, and surveillance.[33] Bentham's transparency demands always had a political tone, unlike Rousseau's, whose point of departure was, in my view, more personal and interpersonal.[34] According to Hood, Bentham was the first to use the term 'transparency' in the governance context in the English language.[35] Although 'transparency' is predominantly used today, in Bentham's days this was not the case: 'publicity' was preferred.[36] As Baume and Papadopoulos explain, 'publicity' and 'transparency' have been historically close, yet are separate in scope. Publicity was more dominant in political discussions, whereas transparency referred more to people's acts and speeches, intentions or thoughts.[37]

[32] Hood, 'Transparency in Historical Perspective' (n 21) 6–7; Jean-Jacques Rousseau, *The Social Contract and the Discourses* (first published 1762, G D H Cole ed, Dent 1988); Jean-Jacques Rousseau, *The Government of Poland* (first published 1772, W Kendall tr, Hackett Publishing Co 1985) 154; Jean Starobinski, *Jean Jacques Rousseau* (n 22).

[33] These were discussed in 'Of Publicity' and were first published in *Tactique des assemblées Législatives* (Jeremy Bentham, *Tactique des Assemblées législatives* (J. J. Paschoud 1816). See also Baume and Papadopoulos, 'Transparency: From Bentham's Inventory' (n 13) 173.

[34] See also Dilip Parameshwar Gaonkar and Robert J McCarthy, 'Panopticism and Publicity: Bentham's Quest for Transparency' (1994) 6(3) Public Culture 547, 570 (hereafter Gaonkar and McCarthy, 'Panopticism and Publicity') and Foucault, 'The Eye of Power' (n 30) 152: 'According to Foucault, Bentham shares Rousseau's dream of "a transparent society, visible and legible in each of its parts, the dream of there no longer existing any zones of darkness, zones established by the privileges of royal power or the prerogatives of some corporation, zones of disorder". Yet their dreams are not the same. Rousseau dreamed that each individual regardless of his social location might see the whole of society and converse with his fellow citizens on the basis of a prereflective consensus of hearts. Bentham's version of transparent society, however, is galvanized by "an apparatus of total and circulating mistrust." Bentham notes in the Panopticon: "Each comrade becomes an overseer".'

[35] Hood, 'Transparency in Historical Perspective' (n 21).

[36] Sandrine Baume, 'Publicity and Transparency: The Itinerary of a Subtle Distinction' in E Alloa and D Thomä (eds), *Transparency, Society, Subjectivity: Critical Perspectives* (Palgrave Macmillan 2018) 204–05 (hereafter Baume, 'Publicity and Transparency'): As Baume shows using Google Books Ngram Viewer, transparency is increasingly preferred over publicity in the wake of the 2000s.

[37] Baume and Papadopoulos, 'Transparency: From Bentham's Inventory' (n 13) 170–71.

Interestingly, however, publicity included the same metaphorical dimension now vested in transparency. It was to expose what was inaccessible to scrutiny by the public eye: '"publicity [means]—exposure—the completest exposure of the whole system of procedure—whatever is done by anybody, being done before the eyes of the universal public" (Bentham 1962b, p. 8). Like transparency, the force of publicity was equated with the force of light: "the light of publicity shining in full splendour" (Bentham 1962b, p. 75).'[38] I will examine this metaphorical dimension more closely in chapter two.

That said, the term 'transparency' also made sense in referring to the knowability of society. It had a specific illustrative power. Bentham's major sources of inspiration were optics and mechanics, although, as Baume argues, he rarely uses the term 'transparency' in its metaphorical meaning in comparison to the word 'publicity'.[39] In Bentham's time, Isaac Newton had recently used transparency to discover the laws of optics. His work suggested that the natural world could be governed by the law of mechanics. Bentham applied those ideas and developed moral mechanics that could be implemented in transparent architecture and management.[40] To that end, Bentham famously argued that, 'I do take it as an undisputable truth, and a truth that is one of the corner-stones of political science—the more strictly we are watched the better we behave.'[41] Bentham thus associated transparency with inspectability.

In his pamphlet *Panopticon or the Inspection House* (1791), Bentham extended the idea of inspectability to prisons and, through analogy, to government. He declared that:

> jealousy is the life and soul of government. Transparency of management is certainly an immense security; but even transparency is of no avail without eyes to look at it. Other things equal, that sort of man whose conduct is like to be most narrowly watched, is therefore the properest man to choose.[42]

According to Gaonkar and McCarthy, Bentham's strategy for regulating the behaviour of legislators is indeed like his strategy for conducting the behaviour of prisoners.[43] As discussed later in this book, Michel Foucault adopted this idea in a comprehensive manner to structure his views on disciplinary power. Throughout

[38] ibid.

[39] Baume, 'Publicity and Transparency' (n 36) 206.

[40] Vincent August, 'Theorie und Praxis der Transparenz. Eine Zwischenbilanz [Theory and Practice of Transparency. A Preliminary Synthesis]' (2018) 21(76) Berliner Blätter 129.

[41] Jeremy Bentham, *The Collected Works of Jeremy Bentham*. Writing on the Poor Laws, vol 1 (Michael Quinn ed, Oxford University Press 2001) 277.

[42] Jeremy Bentham, *Panopticon: Postscript: Part II: Containing a Plan of Management for a Panopticon Penitentiary-house* (T. Payne 1791) 40.

[43] Gaonkar and McCarthy, 'Panopticism and Publicity' (n 34) 550.

Bentham's extensive work on government and the principles thereof, the idea of transparency or publicity remains a consistent theme.

Here, it is neither possible nor desirable to go through the entire intellectual history of transparency. However, it is important to be aware of the historical circumstances that allowed the lack of transparency to be coined as a societal problem and the normative—political, moral, and legal—debates on transparency to emerge. These discourses were reacting to the reality at the time, being closely connected to the ideology of the Enlightenment and the emergence of liberal-democratic society and its core ideals. As Hood puts it: 'it is hard to identify any institutional line of continuity from Bentham and Rousseau to the present day, and transparency seems to be an idea that has been reinvented after having been left aside, like some of other Bentham's ideas'.[44]

As we can see, transparency as a present-day governance ideology has a familiar undertone to it. Many of the original justifications for transparency are still relevant today. However, one should not jump to hasty conclusions based on the described fragments of intellectual history. On the one hand, as Foucault has shown, the history of ideas does not necessarily follow a clear line of development; rather, it is characterized by interruptions and breaks.[45] On the other hand, as Hood argues, neither the word 'transparency' nor many of the modern doctrines it may refer to are an invention of the twentieth century.[46]

What Is This Book About?

Critical Appraisal of Three Overarching Themes

This book is about questioning the omnipotence of transparency. To that end, I will unpack the ideal of transparency and show how it cannot fulfil its promise. I will argue that the modern call for transparency exposes something of our political imagination. We live in the age of transparency, and this cannot but have manifold implications. To explore these implications, I have chosen three overarching themes that I will elaborate throughout this book. They relate both to the basic functional mechanism of transparency and its current topicality as a globalizing norm. These themes are, in a way, modern versions of the presented forerunners of transparency.

First, *rule-governed administration* is the baseline for approaching transparency as a governance ideal—how has transparency become normatively so attractive in

44 Hood, 'Transparency in Historical Perspective' (n 21) 19.

45 cf also David Pozen, who claims that transparency in America is undergoing an 'ideological drift'. David Pozen, 'Transparency's Ideological Drift' (2018) 218 The Yale Law Journal 100.

46 Hood, 'Transparency in Historical Perspective' (n 21) 11.

and around law and legal discourse? Although transparency is a traditional principle in public law—especially in Nordic legal culture and, through its influence, in the EU—there is more to it than the traditional understanding implies. As mentioned, the desire to write this book was initially motivated by the observation that, notwithstanding its legal basis, much normative material—soft law, policy papers, codes of conduct, academic research with a normative agenda—has been starting to require transparency without being exactly binding. Although transparency requirements are no longer restricted to matters of public law, public law seems to be becoming more popular as an ideal for legitimating power.[47] This could hardly be possible without transparency's long roots in democratic theory.

When it comes to public law as a modern emblem of rule-governed administration, two seemingly opposed megatrends seem to exist: fragmentation and convergence. By fragmentation I mean two things. First, the meaning of international and transnational governance has increased over recent decades. However, the different transnational players involved do not form a clear system or hierarchy. In consequence, it is hard to decipher the entirety of transnational governance. In addition to international organizations and non-governmental organizations, these players include networks and private-public hybrid regimes. These regimes may even collide with each other.[48] Second, public administrations, even in national settings, function increasingly in private law forms when carrying out their tasks. This makes it difficult to delineate public administration from business, as contracts, for example, are frequently used within both realms. In this context, traditional bureaucratic governance often appears dated.

Convergence has the opposite goal and effect. It denotes recent attempts to use public law as a moral vocabulary. Today even diffuse transnational power, described above, is easily labelled as 'administration'. For example, the proliferation of these different players is referred to as 'the emergence of global administrative space'. In this sense, convergence is a reaction to fragmentation. This is followed by normative attempts to place procedural rules on (public) global 'administration'. This is, most prominently, the main ambition in the debate on global administrative law.[49] In addition, a more unified set of administrative law principles has proven desirable. In particular, the principles of good administration are seeking

[47] Megan Donaldson and Benedict Kingsbury, 'Ersatz Normativity or Public Law in Global Governance: The Hard Case of International Prescriptions for National Infrastructure Regulation' (2013) 14 Chicago Journal of International Law 1.

[48] Fragmentation may lead to competing or conflicting regimes. Andreas Fischer-Lescano and Gunther Teubner, 'Regime-collisions: The Vain Search for Legal Unity in the Fragmentation of Global Law' (2004) 24(4) Michigan Journal of International Law 999; Martti Koskenniemi and Päivi Leino, 'Fragmentation of International Law? Postmodern Anxieties' (2002) 15 Leiden Journal of International Law 553.

[49] Benedict Kingsbury, Nico Krisch, and Richard Stewart, 'The Emergence of Global Administrative Law' (2005) 68 Law and Contemporary Problems 15.

common ground in Europe[50] and maybe even globally.[51] This duality of inputs—fragmentation and convergence—can be summarized thus: public law is 'out' when referring to hierarchy or bureaucratic arrangements of power, and 'in' when framing procedural justice and legitimacy.[52]

Thus, as is the case today, the rule-governed administration creates a powerful undercurrent for the desirability of transparency. Transparency is a salient part of that procedural megatrend. Transparency is, as mentioned, a normatively attractive concept. Thus, proliferating transparency talk and regulation may indicate the reconfiguration of global power. As the roots of the transparency ideal are both in creating a public space for critical reasoning and the inspectability of power, something signals that power is escaping from both democratic checks and the legal avenues of making, at least seemingly, the exercise of it visible. This implies, as mentioned, that the traditional exercisers of unequal power, states, are no longer the only targets of transparency requirements. This raises certain questions. To what extent are public and private spheres converging? What are the implications of transparency principles conquering new realms?

Secondly, *open and sincere communication*: I will argue that transparency as a socio-legal ideal primarily contrasts with secrecy discursively. This opposition may be at least partially illusory. The main assumption is, quoting Andrea Bianchi, that 'what secrecy does overtly, transparency may do surreptitiously'.[53] That is to say; transparency does not mean the lack of concealment, it means regulating visibilities. As argued, framing or labelling something as 'transparency' gives those practices a sheen of legitimacy, regardless of how they do or do not work. An important aspect here is *the human face of transparency*. I argue that the way in which transparency works as a legitimating principle is a corollary of control, impression management, and the avoidance of losing face.

As a more general cultural trend, there seems to be growing resentment towards inauthenticity. This might stem from the incremental demise of strongly predisposed societal roles and the neoliberal call for 'being truly oneself', regardless of the immediate expectations of conformity. This is, of course, paradoxical and potentially an illusion. The requirements of 'being yourself' or 'being authentic' are challenging for several reasons. First, they presuppose an authentic self to be exposed, a requirement whose problematic nature is easy to detect in the postmodern world. Secondly, these requirements make authenticity a norm; one *must* be what one is. This seemingly emancipating idea, however, diminishes the individual freedom of

[50] Jürgen Schwarze, 'The Convergence of the Administrative Laws of the EU Member States' (1998) 4(2) European Public Law 191; Ulrich Stelkens and Agnė Andrijauskaitė (eds), *Good Administration and the Council of Europe: Law, Principles, and Effectiveness* (Oxford University Press 2020).

[51] Daniel C Esty, 'Good Governance at the Supranational Scale: Globalizing Administrative Law' (2006) 115(7) Yale Law Journal 1490.

[52] Koivisto, 'From Moral Rules to Individual Rights' (n 19) 74.

[53] Bianchi, 'On Power and Illusion' (n 10) 19.

choosing one's identities, or, alternately, leads to an over-inclusive conception of 'self'. Thirdly, even if there was a 'true self' to be exposed, its fully fledged functioning would be impossible. We live as a society, and we need to restrict our impulses and desires in the name of peace and harmony. These caveats aside, I argue that the desire for authenticity, as problematic as it is, also buttresses the quest for transparency today.

Thirdly, *the knowability of society*—I am examining the phenomenology of governance as a corollary of transparency practices. I am asking what the relationship is between how governance is and how it appears to be. What are the connections between the beholder, her perceptions, and the representation of the target? Or can these be separated to begin with? These questions are largely of a philosophical nature. They question our ability to access the reality of governance through transparency practices.

The knowability of society is as burning a question today as it was during the inception of transparency discourse. In the era of the internet, we have access to more information than anyone could ever have dreamed of just a couple of decades ago. However, ultimately, the knowability of society is a phenomenological question. What can we know, through transparency practices or regardless of them, about what is happening around us? How can we know what is happening in the chambers of power? How can we successfully navigate through phenomena such as fake news, alternative facts, and post-truth politics? How much can we control the nature and amount of information we are giving out about our own lives, often unbeknownst to us? These questions guide my discussion.

The visibility of power is, in a way, a secondary question regarding the idea of rule-governed administration. Namely, we cannot be sure whether those who govern although bound by legal rules and principles, adhere to those rules. We cannot know unless we see. The dynamic of trust and distrust is one of the basic dramas of transparency today. Keeping power in check by watching how it operates is still something we are assumed to desire. Yet, for various reasons, we often cannot trust what we see.

The Main Argument: The Truth-Legitimacy Trade-off

What is new in this book? The simple answer is this: its argument and approach. It aims to answer the following questions: What is the problem to which transparency is the solution? Why do we use the metaphor of transparency specifically? How does law regulate the visibility of governance? Is first-hand knowledge about governance possible? Thus far, a fundamental critique of the functioning logic of transparency has not been conducted in a comprehensive manner, although valuable points of critique are increasingly raised (cf the emergence of critical transparency studies). However, the need for this kind of critique is urgent, as transparency has rapidly come to denote a self-evident virtue in the modern world. The mainstream narrative of transparency promises legitimacy: when we can witness with our own eyes what is happening in the chambers of power, we can control it and, when needed, change it, even overthrow it.

The main objective of this book is to question that narrative, which in its quest for legitimacy, utilizes the vocabulary and rationality of truth. Although I discuss many interrelated themes to construct a solid account, in the end, my argument is simple: I argue that transparency cannot simultaneously provide 'truth' and legitimacy. Instead, it is labelled by either-or-logic, which is here referred to as the truth-legitimacy trade-off. In simplest terms, the truth-legitimacy trade-off means that *against its promise, transparency may provide either truth or legitimacy, but not legitimacy through access to truth.* Although transparency specifically couples the ideas of truth and legitimacy, I argue the opposite: they are often mutually exclusive.

As I will explain, if we want transparency to create legitimacy, we want—probably unbeknownst to ourselves—transparency to be planned and controlled. We want the information release to be attentive to the receiver. However, this controlled nature of transparency is necessarily selective: it can be argued that the person or the organization releasing information in the name of transparency has the motive of managing impressions so that potentially embarrassing or otherwise sensitive information stays hidden. I argue that this logic also applies to institutions. Institutions and humans as their agents have a face to uphold.[54] Therefore, through controlled, legitimacy-inducing transparency we can only access sanitized, filtered, mediated truth. In the context of governance, these transparency practices often follow a legal script.

However, if we want the unfiltered truth about governance, this can be done only through unauthorized exposure or legal transparency practices whereby no impression management can play a role. This is something which is mythically recognized as an allegory of revealed nakedness and the shame resulting from it. In institutions, information leakages provide an illustrative example. This transparency, in turn, cannot create immediate legitimacy as the control of disclosure is lacking. We see more than we are intended to see. This excess, this 'too much information', shows how much of the inner workings of people or institutions needs to stay hidden to uphold certain faces, personas, appearances—and legitimacy.

Arguing that the truth-legitimacy trade-off is the deep structure of transparency as a governance ideal is the main contribution of this book. I elaborate the building blocks of this argument throughout the book and examine it as an independent theme in the concluding chapter nine.

[54] cf Leopold Ringel, 'Unpacking the Transparency-secrecy Nexus: Frontstage and Backstage Behavior in a Political Party' (2019) 40 Organization Studies 705; Mikkel Flyverbom and Juliane Reinecke, 'The Spectacle and Organization Studies' (2017) 38(11) Organization Studies 1625, 1631.

The Approach and Structure of the Book

The Approach of the Book

The book aims to contribute to critical transparency studies literature from the perspective of law. To execute this scholarly mission, a legal approach is, however, insufficient. As Richard Sherwin argues, 'when law marries visual culture their joint offspring requires new academic partners, including media and cultural studies, art history, cognitive psychology, psychoanalysis, and neuroscience'.[55]

Similarly, I am adopting various, partly overlapping approaches: conceptual analysis, law, social and political theory, cultural and media studies, and some concepts and approaches from semiotics and social psychology.

Some might call this choice intellectual eclecticism. Although this statement may be fair, eclecticism cannot be equated with contingency; all the applied approaches are chosen to illuminate some thus far unnoticed or under-theorized aspect of transparency. From a legal point of view, we could perhaps call the chosen approach a cultural study of law. In Paul Kahn's words, it 'seeks to bring to self-consciousness those background structures of meaning that are always already in place and which make possible the particular regulatory schemes over which we argue'.[56]

In that sense, it is about examining the sub-consciousness of our legal thought, its societal, social, and even anthropological assumptions of meaning. Conversely, this means that the book will not engage in a doctrinal approach or suggest any normative agendas. Neither does it build on the analysis of empirical material. This is a conscious choice made to serve the intellectual goals of the book.

Thus, this book is not a traditional law book, although it discusses law. For better or for worse, the very questions of truth, reality, illusion, knowledge, and their social implications form the undertow of the book. This book is both inspired by the idea of revealing the 'truth' behind the façade—making transparency transparent—and the consciousness of the impossibility of such a revelation. This dialectical starting point underpins both the discussion in the book and the nature of the scholarly intervention it attempts to make. It has roots in the 'depth metaphor'. As Moshe Halbertal argues:

> our ontology and epistemology is, so to speak, in a grip of the 'depth metaphor.' We distinguish between the apparent and the real, the internal and the merely

[55] Richard K Sherwin, *Visualizing Law in the Age of the Digital Baroque: Arabesques and Entanglements* (Routledge 2012) 3.

[56] Paul Kahn, *The Cultural Study of Law: Reconstructing Legal Scholarship* (University of Chicago Press 1999) 92.

> external. Our epistemology is grounded in such a picture. We 'discover' or 'uncover' the 'underlying' assumption, the 'depth of the matter' and so on.[57]

As scholars, we want to reveal, enlighten, and emancipate, to excavate the truth hiding underneath a deceitfully neat surface of appearance. Ontologically and epistemologically, this presupposes a vertical understanding of truth: the non-apparent truth is more fundamental than the apparent one. It thus covertly privileges the non-apparent essence of things over their manifestations in the apparent. However, this assumption that 'the truth is down there'[58] is in tension with the perspectivist idea of 'truth is in the eye of the beholder', or at least that it crucially depends on a chosen perspective.[59] As a rule, we intuitively seem to subscribe to both ideas, the vertical and horizontal multitude of truths, and potentially some principle of ranking them.[60] In this book, both perspectives are present.

The Structure of the Book

In its entirety, the book is a compact theoretical account of the hidden functioning logic of the ideal of transparency, and the challenges that modern society poses on it. The book is organized in three parts, consisting of three chapters each, reflecting on the three overarching themes of the study. The structure is designed

[57] Moshe Halbertal, *Concealment and Revelation: Esotericism in Jewish Thought and Its Philosophical Implications* (Princeton University Press 2007) 155.

[58] This approach is both epitomized and complicated by Michel Foucault in his archaeological and genealogical projects. As Gordon (Neve Gordon, 'On Visibility and Power: An Arendtian Corrective of Foucault' (2002) 25 Human Studies 125) notes, 'according to Foucault discursive practices do not conceal a hidden reality; they are neither a facade for immoral practices nor do they produce false interests. Foucault's genealogical method, Hubert Dreyfus and Paul Rabinow point out, suggests that the "very project of finding a deep meaning underlying appearances may itself be an illusion, to the extent that it thinks it is capturing what is really going on"' (Hubert Dreyfus and Paul Rabinow, *Michel Foucault: Beyond Structuralism and Hermeneutics* (Second Edition with an Afterword by and an Interview with Michel Foucault, University of Chicago Press 1983) 181.

[59] Perspectivism is famously attributed to the philosophical writings of Friedrich Nietzsche. Slavoj Žižek, for one, approaches the necessary perspectivist appearance of reality with the term *ideological anamorphosis*. Slavoj Žižek, *The Plague of Fantasies* (Verso Books 1997) 97–104.

[60] Christensen and Cornelissen, 'Organizational Transparency' (n 8) 134: 'Reality, according to modern thought, is usually out of sight, concealed, so to speak, "behind" the scene. Through the use of reason and rationality, the promise of modern thought is to move the spectator behind the "curtain", to uncover the truth behind its fancy façades and seductive appearances and eventually emancipate the individual from the superstitions and repressions of authoritative regimes (Nisbet, 1966). Hegel's distinction between *Schein* and *Wesen*—a distinction reproduced in the works of Marx—represents the modern ideal of revealing and exposing the truth concealed by the glittering images of the world. Likewise, Weber's description of modern society as "disenchanted" (inspired by Schiller's notion of the "de-divinization" of the world) described modernity as a secularized society in which scientific knowledge is valued higher than faith and where processes of "rationalization" replace ancient beliefs with naturalist scientific explanations. Modernity, thus, represents the goal of absolute (self-)transparency—a goal reflected in positive science and notions of open and unrestricted information (see e.g. Vattimo, 1992).'

to build incrementally and systematically the overarching argument of what I, as mentioned, call the truth-legitimacy trade-off.

Part I, 'The Opacity of Transparency', discusses the conceptual points of departure of the book. In particular, it delves into the themes of vision, visibility, and ocular-centricity that transparency necessarily presupposes. In this introductory chapter at hand, 'The Era of Transparency', I have outlined the overall theme of the book. Why should we be interested in transparency, and why now? The chapter describes the theme, scholarly intervention, and research context of the book. Chapter two, 'Transparency as a Medium', is about the theoretical foundations of the study. It concentrates on the questions of why we use the term transparency when we refer to the 'see-ability' or 'knowability' of abstract things that typically lack physical appearance. Chapter three, 'The Eye of the Beholder', is about the different modalities of gaze. What is the meaning of the viewer in transparency? I argue that the viewer can affect the object viewed and is thus not a passive recipient of information, but the gaze can result in different outcomes depending on its arrangement.

Part I thus aims at demonstrating how transparency itself is a more complicated concept than one might think; in many ways its own quality remains opaque. It grapples in particular with the theme of the knowability of society. In particular, it discusses the ways in which transparency can provide truth by eye witnessing: is seeing a superior way of knowing? This discussion is essential for laying the foundations for my argument about the truth-legitimacy trade-off. More accurately, it discusses the structural assumptions of the truth-transparency nexus, necessary to the mentioned trade-off: what kind of truth can transparency provide? In the first part, I will show how the bias towards seeing for oneself may prevent us from seeing how visibilities are deliberately constructed.

Part II, 'The Promise of Transparency' focuses on the ways in which transparency is used as a value judgement in social and societal life: in interpersonal relations, in relation to power, and interwoven in law. At the core of this part is the question: Why is transparency a good thing? To answer this, transparency will be discussed as a governance ideal, with its own promises and perils. Chapter four, 'Transparency and Social Life', concentrates on transparency as a moral concept. I show that transparency is not an unalloyed good, but it also has a negative connotation, referring to unwanted or unauthorized exposure. This duality of connotations accentuates the performativity of transparency. Chapter five, 'Transparency and Power', is about the positive and institutionalized connotation of transparency. The chapter discusses unequal power relations as the precondition of the transparency ideal. Chapter six, 'Transparency and Law', concentrates on investigating how the promise of transparency is translated into legal arrangements and their shadows, if you will.

Part II is important in constructing the other premise of the truth-transparency trade-off, the legitimacy-transparency nexus. As I am going to argue, the premise that transparency leads to legitimacy needs to be examined critically. In this part of the book, I show the pitfalls of this premise, as the legitimacy that transparency can offer necessitates performativity. All of the above-mentioned overarching themes are relevant in this part: the open and candid communication in particular in chapter four, the rule-governed administration in chapters five and six, and the knowability of society in all of them, most of all in chapter five. With different accents, the chapters in this part demonstrate the theoretical foundations that the often-unarticulated promise that transparency creates legitimacy depart from.

Part III, 'The Reality of Transparency', discusses the contemporary societal developments that pose challenges to the promise of transparency for both truth and legitimacy. It delves into the ways in which transparency has become a virtual synonym of legitimacy outside its traditional usage. At the same time, paradoxically, its potential to deliver truth is diminishing in our increasingly digitalized society. Chapter seven, 'The Discursification of Transparency' delves into the implications of transparency having become a normative ideal with no legal guarantees. I suggest that the new fashionableness of transparency has partially broken the transparency-democracy conjunction. In chapter eight, 'The Future of Transparency: From Representation to Simulation?' the theme is governance phenomenology: What happens to the truth that transparency promises in a digitalized world? The discussion peaks at questioning whether the reality principle, the performativity of transparency, and the crumbling of the reality principle can coexist in the digitalized society. Chapter nine, 'The Truth-Legitimacy Trade-off', concludes the book by bringing the different threads of transparency together and summarizing the main arguments.

Part III thus reflects the ambition to expand the purely structural analysis of transparency. If the first part reflects the truth-transparency nexus and the second one the legitimacy-transparency nexus, the third one examines the bafflement that results from their contradictory points of departure. In other words, I discuss the simultaneous developments of the spread of transparency discourse, and its decreasing power of representation. In that sense, it reflects all of the mentioned overarching themes of the book and shows what kinds of intellectual sacrifices their simultaneous fulfilment can require. That is why I have called this book *The Transparency Paradox*.

2
Transparency as a Medium

Approaching Transparency as a Concept

In the first, introductory chapter, I discussed some fragments of transparency's evolution as a governance ideal. I argued that we are living in the age of transparency and that cannot but have a multitude of ramifications in our contemporary societies. In this chapter, I adopt a different point of view: conceptual instead of temporal.[1] I delve into the realm of language, metaphors, ocularcentricity, and visual semantics.[2] This is necessary because we often demand transparency, and bemoan the lack of it, without pondering the implications of the concept. What is transparency, exactly? What is so amazing about it?

According to the *Oxford English Dictionary*, transparency is 'the quality or condition of being transparent; perviousness to light; diaphaneity, pellucidity' and 'that which is transparent; a transparent object or medium'. Hence, in its literal meaning, transparency refers to an optical condition or an arrangement that is inherently material. To have a bearing, transparency needs light, the power of illumination. Otherwise, it remains a mere affordance. It further presupposes a person who is watching something that is located on the other side of a transparent object—like looking through a window—or assessing the optical quality of an object. It thus allows us to see through. However, in discourses of governance and power, transparency is mostly used metaphorically to refer to practices *as if* they were transparent. For example, we seldom physically look at abstractions such as power, as I will explain later. That said, the literal meaning of transparency is also one of its functioning mechanisms as a governance ideal. In both cases, transparency relies on the power of vision.

In this chapter, I suggest that the metaphoric nature of transparency is not haphazard. On the contrary, the very optical feature of seeing through allows the metaphorical or analogical use of the concept.[3] As mentioned, the literal meaning of transparency was also Bentham's inspiration—he was interested in optics. However,

[1] See also a previous a version of this chapter: Ida Koivisto, 'The Anatomy of Transparency: The Concept and its Multifarious Implications' (2016) Max Weber Programme 2016/09 Working Paper <http://hdl.handle.net/1814/41166> accessed 22 June 2021. Additionally, chapters one and three are partially based on this publication.

[2] Jan Teurlings and Markus Stauff, 'Introduction: The Transparency Issue' (2014) 14(1) Cultural Studies ↔ Critical Methodologies 3, 6 (hereafter Teurlings and Stauff. 'The Transparency Issue').

[3] See Colin Rowe and Robert Slutzky, 'Transparency: Literal and Phenomenal' (1963) 8 Perspecta 45.

The Transparency Paradox. Ida Koivisto, Oxford University Press. © Ida Koivisto 2022.
DOI: 10.1093/oso/9780192855466.003.0002

the belief in the illustrative power inherent in the materiality of transparency is not shared by everyone. For example, David Heald argues that 'transparency as a physical construction carries symbolic power quite apart from its metaphorical use in discourse about the ways in which government, business and public affairs should be conducted'.[4] I question this separation and argue that transparency's symbolic power—based on its characteristics as a physical phenomenon—and its metaphorical use are deeply intertwined.[5]

As mentioned, transparency today can be considered a normative concept, or even a magic concept. It is hard to be against it. It has a positive halo, regardless of how it is defined. Nonetheless, the desirability of seeing through is not self-explanatory, but requires careful analysis. Why do we wish to see through it, regardless of what there is to see? How can we see through? What are the mechanisms that underpin it?

In this chapter, I establish the conceptual basis for the entire book. The following chapters thus reflect, develop, and contextualize the conceptual tools that I introduce in this chapter. For this undertaking to work, I approach transparency as a concept that has material, metaphoric, and symbolic dimensions. More accurately, I argue that we can best understand the paradoxical nature of transparency as a socio-legal ideal if we also regard transparency as a medium beyond the immediate material meaning of the word. Transparency as a medium is inconspicuous, but it can be detected if one knows how to look. To that end, I will analyse the characteristics of transparency as a medium.

The chapter is organized as follows. First, I discuss transparency as a metaphor with the help of conceptual metaphor theory, and further, I discuss the different variants of the transparency metaphor. Second, I describe how transparency oscillates between visual and verbal practices. Third, I introduce one of the key concepts of this book, icono-ambivalence, which labels the mediating character of transparency as a governance ideal. Fourth, I discuss another important concept, the hand at work, which refers to the human involvement in mediation, and is important in understanding icono-ambivalence. Fifth, I analyse the implications of using the transparency concept specifically: is there a danger of essentialism? Lastly, I summarize the chapter and argue that due to its metaphorical character, transparency has proven to be superior to other similar concepts.

[4] David Heald, 'The Varieties of Transparency' in Christopher Hood and David Heald (eds), *Transparency—Key to Better Governance?* (Oxford University Press 2006) 25.

[5] Alloa argues that when it comes to different aspects of transparency, there is more to them than just a vague family resemblance. Emmanuel Alloa, 'Transparency: A Magic Concept of Modernity' in Emmanuel Alloa and Dieter Thomä (eds), *Transparency, Society and Subjectivity: Critical Perspectives* (Palgrave Macmillan 2018) 32 (hereafter Alloa, 'Transparency: A Magic Concept').

The Transparency Metaphor

To Understand Is to See

As mentioned, it is not self-evident why we would wish to see through, regardless, what there is to see. To answer that question, and to diagnose the functional mechanism of transparency as a metaphor, some basic ideas from conceptual metaphor theory are helpful. The point of departure in conceptual metaphor theory is the following question: how do metaphors shape our thinking and language? It thus goes beyond treating metaphors as mere tropes or figurative speech but argues that they rely on deeply rooted cognitive mechanisms. George Lakoff and Mark Johnson's influential book *Metaphors We Live By* (1980, 2003) concentrates on addressing and proving this idea: 'Do we systematically use inference patterns from one conceptual domain to reason about another conception domain?'

In brief, the authors' answer is yes. According to them, our thinking largely utilizes analogy, reasoning based on similarity. Thus, as mentioned, the theory's main idea is that metaphors are not merely a matter of figurative speech as they are traditionally understood.[6] Instead, they relate to cognitive functions. As Lakoff and Johnson argue, 'since much of our social reality is understood in metaphorical terms, and since our conception of the physical world is partly metaphorical, metaphor plays a very significant role in determining what is real for us'.[7] Strikingly, metaphors and our conception of reality are profoundly intertwined.

According to conceptual metaphor theory, our very thinking is partly structured by the metaphoric form. Certain conceptual metaphors govern basic abstract ideas. It is important to note that what makes them 'conceptual' or 'cognitive' is their pre-linguistic nature. This means they are a type of the deep structures of different metaphors that do not necessarily feature as such in quotidian language. Instead, they structure speech by making linguistic metaphors comprehensible. One structured concept is restructured by another.

In order to couple two different ideas metaphorically, there needs to be a so-called source domain and a target domain of meaning. The source domain stands for the more concrete phenomenon, whereas the target phenomenon is the more abstract one. Subsequently, some features of the source domain are analogously attributed to the target domain. This is reflected in the choice of words and the

[6] On metaphors in philosophy, see, for instance, Marga Reimer and Elisabeth Camp, 'Metaphor' in Ernerst Lepore and Barry C Smith (eds), *The Oxford Handbook of Philosophy of Language* (Clarendon Press 2006) 845–46 (hereafter Reimer and Camp, 'Metaphor'): metaphor is a trope or figure of speech, where a 'figure of speech' is a non-literal use of language. What distinguishes metaphor from other tropes such as irony, metonymy, synecdoche, hyperbole, and meiosis? According to a standard definition, a metaphor is 'a figure of speech in which one thing is represented (or spoken of) as something else'.

[7] George Lakoff and Mark Johnson, *Metaphors We Live By* (University of Chicago Press 2003)146 (hereafter Lakoff and Johnson, 'Metaphors We Live By').

particular rationalities they embody, like LOVE IS A JOURNEY, TIME IS MONEY, ARGUMENT IS WAR, THE MIND IS A MACHINE. In these examples, 'journey', 'money', 'war', and 'machine' form the source domains and 'love', 'time', 'argument', and 'the mind' the target domains. Many abstractions are so overarching and multifaceted that one conceptual metaphor is incapable of capturing all their aspects. In these cases, many conceptual metaphors are needed to illustrate them. However, they do not form a coherent taxonomy. Some conceptual metaphors may suggest conflicting ontologies even when pointing to the same abstraction (such as IDEAS ARE PEOPLE, IDEAS ARE FOOD).[8]

Discerning abstract concepts occurs through different techniques of analogous reasoning called 'mapping', and using 'images schemes' and 'experimental gestalts'.[9] They function as methods of juxtaposing different spheres of meaning. In addition, these mappings are further reflected in our language and action. Moreover, according to Lakoff and Johnson, these metaphorical mappings are not purely contingent or arbitrary in nature. Instead, they are based on our bodily experiences of the world: 'experiences in which the two conceptual domains are correlated and consequently establish mappings from one domain to another'.[10] This gives a metaphor the trait of universalism, even though it is debatable to what extent conceptual metaphors are language-specific.[11] In addition, the danger of essentialism may emerge; it is hard to verify whether every human being really shares the same cognitive structures and concomitant cognitive metaphors, regardless of their cultural background, level of education, and intellectual capacity.

The entire theory in all its sophistication cannot be discussed here. However, we now know enough to approach transparency from its point of view. The question is: can we detect a conceptual metaphor that would make 'transparency' an apt linguistic metaphor? In other words, which conceptual metaphor, if any, allows transparency to appeal to us?

Following Lakoff and Johnson, transparency is probably based on the conceptual metaphor UNDERSTANDING IS SEEING.[12] This can be argued since 'seeing'

[8] Conceptual metaphors are categorized into different groups according to their structural characteristics, such as ontological (eg ideas are entities and words are containers), orientational (eg more is up, good is up, etc) and structural metaphors (eg time is money, saving time).

[9] According to Mark Turner, not only concepts or metaphors but also so-called small spatial stories, kinds of skeletal schemata which make larger narratives understandable, have their basis in our cognitive system. They are semantically very rudimentary, such as 'catch a ball', 'throw a rock', 'sit in a chair', 'pet a dog', 'take a drink from a glass of water'. Much of our thinking consists of projecting these schemes onto different situations (parapoligal projection; image schemas). Mark Turner, *Literary Mind* (Oxford University Press 1996) 15–17 (hereafter Turner, 'Literary Mind').

[10] Lakoff and Johnson, 'Metaphors We Live By' (n 7) 246–47.

[11] ibid, 247. It seems there are both universal metaphors and those subject to cultural variation. In addition, at 145: 'Much of cultural change arises from the introduction of new metaphorical concepts and loss of old ones. For example, the Westernization of cultures throughout the world is partly a matter of introducing the TIME IS MONEY metaphor into those cultures.'

[12] This can be put into the category of structural (activity) metaphors. Christensen and Cornelissen share the view of the foundational metaphor of transparency to be 'understanding is seeing', or, as they

transcends its literal meaning. It also has wider cognitive implications. On a linguistic level, it appears in sentences such as 'I *see* what you mean'; 'let me *point out* something to you'.[13] When a gaze, even metaphorically, can reach its target uninhibitedly, understanding presumably follows. Hence, as an ideal type, transparency allows us to see and, subsequently, to understand. I argue that this is the basic cognitive underpinning of transparency as a linguistic metaphor.

However, it is important to note that although metaphoric structures make abstractions more discernible, they are inevitably simplifications. Love is not a journey but a complex compound of emotions, thoughts, desires, social norms, and expectations. Nor do we always understand when we see: even if I can see the sun in the sky, I do not 'understand' it.[14] Indeed, the whole notion of understanding is loaded with philosophical questions. The implicit 'like' needs to be postulated: love is (like) a journey, time is (like) money. In that sense, a conceptual metaphor is a condensed simile.[15] In the following, I will examine transparency as a linguistic metaphor more closely.

The Window and the Flashlight Variants of the Transparency Metaphor

As explained, transparency can be argued to derive its attractiveness from the conceptual metaphor of 'understanding is seeing'. Therefore, transparency makes an apt linguistic metaphor: it promises visibility, clarity, understanding; it promises that things will make sense. How exactly does it promise this in our language? How does transparency enable understanding through seeing—or seeing through

put it, 'seeing is knowing'. Lars Thøger Christensen and Joep Cornelissen, 'Organizational Transparency as Myth and Metaphor' (2015) 18(2) European Journal of Social Theory 132, 133.

[13] Lakoff and Johnson also use transparency as an example of a linguistic metaphor based on the cognitive metaphor of UNDERSTANDING IS SEEING: 'That is a remarkably transparent argument' or 'Your argument has no content at all—I can see right through it.' Lakoff and Johnson, 'Metaphors We Live By' (n 7) 104.

[14] Christina Garsten and Monica Lindh de Montoya, 'In Retrospect: The Play of Shadows' in Christina Garsten and Monica Lindh de Montoya (eds), *Transparency in a New Global Order: Unveiling Organizational Visions* (Edward Elgar 2008) 283–86; Jean Comaroff and John Comaroff state: 'The more literally we believe in the axiom "to see is to know" the more haunted we are by what hovers beyond the edges of the visible.' Jean Comaroff and John Comaroff, 'Transparent Fictions; or, the Conspiracies of a Liberal Imagination: An Afterword' in Harry G West and Todd Sanders (eds), *Transparency and Conspiracy: Ethnographies of Suspicion in the New World Order* (Duke University Press 2003) 288. See also Slavoj Žižek, *The Plague of Fantasies* (Verso Books 1997) 131.

[15] This idea—metaphors being 'compressed' or 'abbreviated' similes—was apparently already presented by Aristotle; see Reimer and Camp, 'Metaphor' (n 6) 851. However, as Reimer and Camp state, the idea of a metaphor as a condensed simile might also be suitable for so-called non-cognitivist theories of metaphor. Here, metaphors are not considered to include any specific cognitive element. Instead, they emphasize the effectiveness of the metaphor, its ability to deliver a message. Reimer and Camp, 'Metaphor' (n 6) 857.

understanding, for that matter? To answer this, we need to take a closer look at how the linguistic metaphor of transparency operates. In the following, I will argue that transparency as a metaphor has, in fact, two main variants, which I call the window variant and the flashlight variant. Depending on which variant we use, a different understanding of transparency's potential effect follows.

Let us start with the window variant, which is, perhaps, the more obvious of the two. It is easy to understand based on the literal meaning of transparency: a window is, no doubt, typically transparent, or at least translucent. A window is an architectonic arrangement in a building or a construct of another kind, made of glass or another transparent medium.[16] With no window, I cannot see what is happening, but with a window I can. From the outside, I can see what it is happening inside the building; from the inside, I can see what is happening outside. This visibility is specifically designed. It lets light in and visibility out, without letting heat or cold in or out. According to the window variant, metaphoric transparency is like a window. By looking through it, reality is visible to us, and, in the best-case scenario, is also understandable.

That said, the window variant may prove unsatisfying for accessing a visual representation of reality. A window does not do much. It is static, it is limited, it is immobile. Andrea Bianchi enumerates a list of puzzling questions that the window variant fails to answer. The whole array is worth quoting here: 'Do I have a clear view if I look through a clean window? What if my view is blurred? Is what I see reality or just a mental representation of what I expect to see? Does it make a difference whether the window is open or closed? Is transparency equivalent to nothingness? What if the outside is dark or if the sun is shining? Would what I see then not be different? To what extent could different types of window glass alter my perception of what I see? Is standing behind a perfectly transparent window equivalent to standing outside? Is what I see dependent also on the position in which I am behind the window? By moving a few inches either side or by turning my eyes up or down, left or right, what I see can be remarkably different.'[17]

It is easy to notice how imperfect the window variant is. It provokes several questions and leaves them unanswered. At the same time, however, it has proven surprisingly powerful, maybe partly due to its very simplistic nature. It is easy to understand with the help of the literal meaning of transparency. The promise of transparency can be seductive. Nonetheless, it neither addresses the beholder's capacity to interpret what she sees nor the target's capacity to manipulate its representation. In that sense, transparency is neutral and passive, which are, of course,

[16] See eg Hans Krause Hansen, Lars Thøger Christensen, and Mikkel Flyverbom, 'Introduction: Logics of Transparency in Late Modernity: Paradoxes, Mediation and Governance' (2015) 18(2) European Journal of Social Theory 117, 118.

[17] Andrea Bianchi, 'On Power and Illusion: The Concept of Transparency in International Law' in Andrea Bianchi and Anne Peters (eds), *Transparency in International Law* (Cambridge University Press 2013) 1, 9.

the very values attributed to it. It just allows the gazer and its object to meet visually, it does not promise good or predict bad. Indeed, it is hard to think of anything more neutral and passive than a window. I will return to the capabilities of the beholder in the next chapter.

However, the passivity of transparency is not self-evident. In some contexts, the window variant is replaced with or accompanied by a flashlight variant. According to the flashlight variant transparency is a tool for illumination rather than allowing visibility to emerge as it is. The flashlight variant means that by directing a beam towards certain areas, it illuminates them while leaving other areas in darkness.[18] Technically, the window variant does this too. It also allows only certain visibilities. That said, the window variant remains more static than the flashlight, which presupposes someone who directs the beam and deliberates on what is worth seeing.[19] Instead of creating a certain visible yet immobile area, the flashlight variant actively creates visible objects by illuminating them.

This understanding of transparency is visible in language. As already mentioned, both transparency and light belong to the same visual vocabulary.[20] In addition, literally understood, transparency also needs light to have significance. Without light, transparency does not matter. Informed by this, it is hardly surprising that transparency is associated with light-related slogans. For example, US Supreme Court Justice Louis Brandeis famously said that 'sunlight is the best disinfectant'.[21] The founder of WikiLeaks Julian Assange uttered 'lights on, rats out'.[22]

In both slogans, light has the power to purify what has gone bad or corrupt. As a metaphor, light is associated with truth and purity, like transparency, thus connecting transparency to the cultural and historical meanings and connotations of light.[23] Light is not just an antonym of darkness but is culturally preferred. Light is

[18] Teurlings and Stauff, 'The Transparency Issue' (n 2) 6: 'Each tool that renders one thing visible also contributes to the invisibilization of something else, either by systematically (and necessarily) leaving certain matters out or just by distracting the attention from other facts and interrelations.'

[19] Eviatar Zerubavel argues that 'by figuratively *spotlighting* certain issues and events while downplaying or even completely ignoring others, they in effect shape our collective sense of relevance, thereby basically determining what we attend and inattend to' (emphasis in original). Eviatar Zerubavel, *Hidden in Plain Sight: The Social Structure of Irrelevance* (Oxford University Press 2015) 70.

[20] See also Vincent August, 'Theorie und Praxis der Transparenz. Eine Zwischenbilanz' in Maren Heibges (ed), *Transparenz: Schlüsselbegriff Einer Anthropologie der Gegenwart* (Berliner Blätter 79/2018) 129, 132 (hereafter August, 'Theorie und Praxis der Transparenz. Eine Zwischenbilanz').

[21] Louis Brandeis, *Other People's Money and How the Bankers Use It* (Frederick A Stokes Company 1914) <https://louisville.edu/law/library/special-collections/the-louis-d.-brandeis-collection/other-peoples-money-by-louis-d.-brandeis > accessed 22 June 2021. Amitai Etzioni, 'Is Transparency the Best Disinfectant?' (2016) 18(4) The Journal of Political Philosophy 389.

[22] Alex Gibney, 'We Steal Secrets: The Story of WikiLeaks' (Documentary Film, Jigsaw Productions, Global Produce, Focus World 2013).

[23] Light is also a powerful metaphor, typically referring to truth. Sean Cubitt, Daniel Palmer, and Nathaniel Tkacz, 'Introduction: Materiality and Invisibility' in Sean Cubitt, Daniel Palmer, and Nathaniel Tkacz (eds), *Digital Light* (Open Humanities Press 2015) 7, 17: 'The light of God, of reason, of science, of truth: light's metaphorical power is undimmed by the material practices in which it is embroiled.' See also Jon Ippolito, 'The Panopticon is Leaking' in Sean Cubitt, Daniel Palmer, and Nathaniel Tkacz (eds), *Digital Light* (Open Humanities Press 2015) 204, 204–05): 'Of course, Euroethnic culture has inherited from Enlightenment metaphysics a deep-seated sense that light is the emblem of truth,

good, darkness is bad. Dieter Mersch argues that the key metaphor of 'light', and particularly the 'light of reason', reveals the influence of Platonism and Christian theology in the history of transparency. They both associate darkness with the diabolical, in the sense of *dia-bolon*, that which is in the way. In theology, the rhetoric of light refers to divine qualities such as purity and innocence.[24]

In the context of rationalism and the Enlightenment, however, light adopts a somewhat different connotation. As Mersch argues, it takes on a cold and relentless form. The light of reason permeates even the darkest corners, unmasking them, bringing to light things which would have better remained covered. This mercilessness undercuts the sheer positive ethos of light, as light everywhere and above all else produces its own opposition. In so doing, it confronts the spirit of the Enlightenment with its own ambiguities. Thus, light not only 'shines' but also divulges; it does not distinguish the things worthy of being made visible from those which are banal and had perhaps better stay out of sight.[25]

Mersch's account considers the light of reason to be absolute, and this absoluteness makes it its own antonym. However, if we approach the metaphor of light in a more specific usage, as a flashlight variant of transparency, this absoluteness becomes relative. Unlike the window variant, the flashlight variant accentuates the intentionality, temporality, and purposefulness of transparency.[26] Something is actively made visible in practice, instead of being allowed to be visible in theory. Something in darkness is consciously brought into the light.

Both variants of the transparency metaphor, the window and the flashlight, can be argued as bases for the conceptual metaphor of 'understanding is seeing'. The most apparent distinctive parameter between the two is the activity of the created visibility, and the power and value attributed to light. Nonetheless, neither of these variants features in legal and policy discourses *per se.* Rather, they function through analogous ways: transparency is 'the ability to look clearly through

rather than a biological contingency. As René Descartes stated, "Whatever is revealed to me by the natural light … cannot in any way be open to doubt" [1641] 1904: 38). Even today, despite the fundamental transformations in physics over this period, our language betrays our debt to Descartes' legacy. Web designers aim to attract a lot of "eyeballs" to a Website, to maximize its "visibility". "Watchdogs" press governments to enact "sunshine" laws to guarantee "transparency". The closer we look at our dependence on the metaphor of light as truth, the more we will see a political expediency hidden beneath it.' René Descartes, 'Meditation Three' in Charles Adam and Paul Tannery (eds), *Oeuvres de Descartes*, vol 7 (J. Vrin [1641] 1904) Quoted in *The Stanford Encyclopedia of Philosophy*. <http://plato.stanford.edu/entries/descartes-epistemology/> accessed 22 June 2021.

[24] Dieter Mersch, 'Obfuscating Transparency' in Emmanuel Alloa and Dieter Thomä (eds), *Transparency, Society, Subjectivity: Critical Perspectives* (Palgrave Macmillan 2018) 259, 261 (hereafter Mersch, 'Obfuscating Transparency').

[25] ibid.

[26] cf Mikkel Flyverbom and Oana Brindusa Albu, 'Organizational Transparency: Conceptualizations, Conditions, and Consequences' (2019) 58 Business and Society 268, 273–75.

the windows of an institution'.[27] I have never seen demands for more windows or more flashlights. More transparency, however, is a frequent outcry. Therefore, the described variants could be considered tools for analysis. They have the potential to illustrate questions of the intentionality of transparency. I will discuss the intentionality of transparency in depth in chapter four.

How Can We Approach Transparency as a Medium?

Thus far, I have described and analysed some aspects of the transparency metaphor. I argued that the choice to call the metaphor 'transparency' is not haphazard but is based on its literal meaning. As explained, transparency refers to allowed or created—and not spontaneous or natural—visibility. This is not, however, all there is to it. Besides distinguishing the literal and metaphorical meanings of transparency, and the different variants of the metaphor, we need to make another distinction: the signifier must be separated from the signified. This means transparency is a word, a signifier, consisting of a group of letters, and a signified, a visual phenomenon, the things to which the word 'transparency' alludes. This distinction is also necessary for understanding the way in which transparency works as an ideal.

If we approach transparency as a signified, we must step outside the world of language. This is, of course, paradoxical: how can we talk or write about transparency beyond its verbal representation, without language? We cannot. That is why we must approach this theme indirectly, through the avenue of visual representation. We can assume that in many contexts, transparency operates like images. When it comes to receiving accurate information on reality, we seem to privilege nonverbal visual information over verbal. We often ask for 'a picture, or it did not happen', say that 'a picture is worth a thousand words', or demand 'do not take my word for it, see for yourself'. Seeing with one's own eyes is connected to immediate, firsthand knowledge of reality. In Morris's words, vision is privileged in our society and our sensorium.[28] Understanding is, indeed, seeing.

This privileging of visual information may lead us astray, however, without us even noticing. This is because we easily take images as icons, meticulous mimicry of reality, whereas words are a system of conventional signs, that is symbols.[29]

[27] Monica Den Boer, 'Steamy Windows: Transparency and Openness in Justice and Home Affairs' in Veerle Deckmyn and Ian Thomson (eds), *Openness and Transparency in the European Union* (European Institute of Public Administration 1998) 91, 105.

[28] Errol Morris, *Believing is Seeing: Observations on the Mysteries of Photography* (Penguin Books 2011) 92 (hereafter Morris, 'Believing is Seeing').

[29] This vocabulary of semiotics is based on Charles Peirce's well-known categorization of different signs. He divides signs into indexes, which refer indirectly, using a sensory cue, to its object (eg smoke is an index of fire); icons, which resemble their objects (eg a portrait of a person); and symbols, conventional signs (eg words). See Charles Peirce, *Collected Writings*, vol 8 (Charles Hartshorne, Paul Weiss, and Arthur W Burks eds, Harvard University Press 1958); Albert Atkin, *Peirce's Theory of Signs* (Edward

Images and pictures seem to derive their authority from reality itself, whereas words need more interpretation and decoding. Hence, words, written or spoken, seem to be perceptually more deceitful than images. A word's mimetic power is always more indirect than that of an image.[30] As Jean Baudrillard puts it, pictures are a substitute for the real through signs.[31]

Is this the reason why visual information is so valuable to us? Is it because understanding is seeing, but it is not insignificant what we see—a picture, a scenery, or a text? The semiotic categorization of images and words seems to be unconscious. We attribute disparate propositional merits to words and images regarding their power to represent reality. However, the verbal and the visual are overlapping and intertwined phenomena. The visual filters into the realm of the verbal and the iconic into the symbolic. On the one hand, when we talk or write with words that allude to eyesight, the verbal and visual intersect. By so doing, we refer to understanding: 'I *see* what you mean.' On the other hand, we need vision to read, for example, a text, which is a verbal composition of ideas.

Despite our reliance on the visual, we struggle with the reliability of visual information. Our sensory capacities are limited, and the scope of visibility is easily manipulated.[32] If we fail to recognize this, we are vulnerable to naïve realism, an uncritical reliance on appearances.[33] Images may be deceitful, distorted, out of context, photoshopped, or otherwise unreliable: to use Morris's example, an elephant may be cropped out of the image, unbeknownst to us.[34] We can never be sure about the level of human manipulation in visual representation, even in the case of photography.[35] As David Brin puts it, '[p]hotography ceases to be our firm anchor

N Zalta ed, *The Stanford Encyclopedia of Philosophy* 2010) <https://plato.stanford.edu/entries/peirce-semiotics/> accessed 22 June 2021.

[30] See Walter Benjamin, 'On the Mimetic Faculty' in Walter Benjamin (ed), *Reflections. Essays, Aphorisms, Autobiographical Writings* (Edmund Jephcott tr, Schocken Books 1986) 333, 336: 'In this way, language may be seen as the highest level of mimetic behavior and the most complete archive of nonsensuous similarity: a medium into which the earlier powers of mimetic production and comprehension have passed without residue, to the point where they have liquidated those of magic.'

[31] Daniela Carpi, 'Crime Evidence: "Simulacres et Simulations", Photography as Forensic Evidence' in Leif Dahlberg, Klaus Stierstorfer, and Daniela Carpi (eds), *Visualizing Law and Authority: Essays on Legal Aesthetics* (Walter de Gruyter 2012) 253, 254; Jean Baudrillard, *Simulacra and Simulation* (Sheila Glaser tr, University of Michigan Press 1994).

[32] Ida Koivisto, 'Transparency in the Digital Environment' (2021) 8(1) Critical Analysis of Law 1, 1–3.

[33] Richard K Sherwin, *Visualizing Law in the Age of the Digital Baroque: Arabesques and Entanglements* (Routledge 2012) 40 (hereafter Sherwin, 'Visualizing Law'): 'That is how naïve realism works. It insists that it is enough to understand (or think we understand) what we see on the screen. No reflection is required when common sense tells us that the visual truth of the matter is self-evident. But the meaning of an image always goes beyond what it depicts. Visual truth, like visuality itself, is a construct.' Teurlings and Stauff, 'The Transparency Issue' (n 2) 6.

[34] Morris, 'Believing is Seeing' (n 28) 65–67.

[35] Bruno Latour, 'What is Iconoclash?' in Bruno Latour and Peter Weibel (eds), *Iconoclash: Beyond Image Wars in Science, Religion, and Art* (MIT Press 2002) (hereafter Latour, 'What is Iconclash?'). Further elaborated by Sherwin, 'Visualizing Law' (n 33) 36.

in a sea of subjectivity'.[36] To what extent can we rely on our eyes? Bruno Latour refers to the dual attitudes towards images with the term *iconoclash*: it stands for the recurrent oscillation between belief in and suspicion of the representation of an image. In our digitalized world, this uncertainty deepens. Naïve realism and postmodern scepticism form an ongoing dynamic. I will come back to this topic in chapter eight.

How exactly does this relate to transparency? It does so through the idea of the signified, the visuality to which transparency points. We could also use the terms intension and extension. At first glance, transparency appears to be an avenue to reality, a mere facilitator, and at the same time nothing in itself.[37] However, transparency embodies a peculiar rationality that differs from purely visual representation. It is best described through metaphoric illustrations: transparency is not visibility itself, it enables visibility; it is not a photograph, it is the optimal lighting for a photograph; it is not a film, it is the screen; it is not the play, it is the stage; it is not the content, it is the platform; it is a signifier whose signified varies. It is meant to enable visibility, and yet it is not meant to be visible itself. When transparency is taken as an ideal, it leads to the curious idolatry of (seeming) nothingness. This, however, may be an illusion. A facilitator is not insignificant. As I argue in this chapter, transparency can be interpreted as a medium (cf above: transparency as 'that which is transparent; a transparent object or medium'), though a very inconspicuous one.

The idea of transparency as an inconspicuous medium is well voiced by Clare Birchall: '[t]ransparency (. . .) is an invisible discourse because its mediation is obscured by its status as a cultural signifier of neutrality. It is seen as not having a particular quality in and of itself but as, rather, merely the invisible medium through which content is brought to our attention, into the visible realm.'[38] In a corresponding way, Emmanuel Alloa states that 'transparency symbolizes a medium without qualities, a cultural signifier which stands for the absence of any form of symbolic or non-symbolic intervention'.[39] Thomas Docherty associates transparency with its at least seeming immediacy: 'The essential thing about transparency is not just that it reveals the inside of something; rather, the essence of transparency is that it does this immediately. That is to say, transparency is related to the

[36] David Brin, *The Transparent Society: Will Technology Force Us to Choose Between Privacy and Freedom?* (Perseus Books 1998) 29. See also Morris, 'Believing is Seeing' (n 28) eg 58: 'The concepts of naturalness, authenticity, and posing are all slippery slopes that when carefully examined become hopelessly vague.'

[37] Clare Birchall, 'Introduction to "Secrecy and Transparency": The Politics of Opacity and Openness' (2011) 28 Theory, Culture and Society 8: 'But why the rush to acquire [transparency]? After all, it's not a thing in itself. In a sense, it's nothing at all, merely the absence of concealment.' Byung-Chul Han, *The Transparency Society* (Stanford University Press 2015) 40: 'Neither truth nor symbolic appearance are see-through. Only emptiness is entirely transparent.'

[38] Clare Birchall, 'Radical Transparency?' (2014) 14(1) Cultural Studies ↔ Critical Methodologies 77, 81–82.

[39] Alloa, 'Transparency: A Magic Concept' (n 5) 37.

immediacy of the moment: it literally takes no time at all to see what is going on inside something or inside someone's head.'[40] In summation, transparency is 'mediated immediacy'.[41]

Indeed, it is not always easy to observe the way in which media represents its object, or whether a medium can be seen as a medium at all. As Mattijs van de Port argues, a mirror, for example, is very difficult to categorize in this respect: 'Responding to [photographs and portraits] by saying something like "that is not a flattering photograph of me" or "the likeness of the portrait is striking" is perfectly possible. Not so with one's mirror image: it makes no sense to say that one's mirror image is "not very flattering" or "absolutely striking." What's more, it is very difficult to conceive of one's mirror image as an image at all. Just go to the nearest mirror and try for yourself: you will not succeed to look at your face as if it were an image. All that you will see is you yourself.'[42] And yet, a mirror image is exactly that: an image, it is two-dimensional and necessarily reflects the qualities of the medium. For example, we easily fail to notice that the mirror image is inverted along its vertical axis.[43]

Similarly, transparency promises to be a disinterested messenger between the 'real thing' or the 'thing in itself' and the representation. We do not say: 'this thing is accurately delivered through transparency'. No, we assume that transparency creates direct access to its object, the thing in itself. Hence, we are not supposed to see transparency itself, but through it, with the help of it.[44] However, media are not invisible, harmless, or automatically objective, as already implied. The fact that we may not pay attention to the medium does not mean that we could not see it if we knew how to look: for example, we recognize the breach of the norms of TV as a medium when the so-called fourth wall is broken, and the actor addresses the viewer. By this very violation of the norm—a norm we did not necessarily know that we knew—the peculiarity of that medium may become apparent.

Thus, a medium implies the conscious showing or constructing of its object: it implies selection, highlighting, omission, and following the conventions of the medium. Even if transparency just showed how things are, this showing is necessarily partial at best. It may also alter the very nature of the object shown.[45] When we

[40] Thomas Docherty, *Confessions: The Philosophy of Transparency* (Bloomsbury Publishing Plc 2014) 74.

[41] Alloa, 'Transparency: A Magic Concept' (n 5) 36; see also Mersch, 'Obfuscating Transparency' (n 24) 267: 'Every mediation modifies, influences and transforms the mediated, because it "mediates" the mediated through itself, thus making its mark on it. The mediated has its own form of otherness.'

[42] Mattijs van de Port, '(Not) Made by the Human Hand: Media Consciousness and Immediacy in the Cultural Production of the Real' (2011) 19(1) Social Anthropology 74, 76–78 (hereafter van de Port, '(Not) Made by the Human Hand').

[43] Patrick Stokes, 'Kierkegaard's Mirrors: The Immediacy of Moral Vision' (2007) 50 Inquiry 70, 77.

[44] Sherwin, 'Visualizing Law' (n 33) 84.

[45] Mark Fenster approaches transparency as communication. As such, it is essentially mediated: it is 'excessively simplified and thus is blind to the complexities of the contemporary state, government information, and the public'. Mark Fenster, 'Transparency in Search of a Theory' (2015) 18(2) European Journal of Social Theory 150, 150.

see with the aid of a tool, the tool becomes part of what we see. Is the medium, as Marshall McLuhan famously coined it, ultimately the message?[46] If we approach transparency as a medium and take that idea seriously, we must concede that transparency is not neutral. It neither is the message itself nor does it become part of the thing it shows. This leads us to ask: how does transparency as a medium allow us to see its object when it comes to abstractions such as governance?[47] I will discuss this in the following.

Icono-ambivalence

We have now established that one of transparency's core complexities is its nature both as a verbal and visual phenomenon, or as 'mediated immediacy'. It can be approached as a medium, albeit an abstract and peculiar one. It is hard to say to what extent transparency is a construction, a result of conscious efforts, and to what extent it is something that takes place spontaneously. As Teurlings and Stauff note, '[t]he meaning of the word transparency oscillates between something that is and something that needs to be created'.[48] What are the dynamics of this oscillation?

Transparency functions in two registers of abstraction. It refers to the visual organization of seeing through (signified1), the literal meaning of seeing through (signifier1), and transparency as a metaphor (signifier2) for access to reliable information (signified2). I will examine this aspect of transparency further, discussing how these different registers of abstraction create some of the basic characteristics of transparency as mediated immediacy. The underlying question is, as Martin Jay puts it: how can we make abstractions visible?[49] In the context of governance, this mediated immediacy or visibility of abstraction can be formulated in the following

[46] Marshall McLuhan, *Understanding Media: Extensions of a Man* (MIT Press 1964) 7: 'The instance of electric light may prove illuminating in this connection. The electric light is pure information. It is a medium without a message, as it were, unless it is used to spell out some verbal ad or name. This fact, characteristic of all media, means that the "content" of a medium is always another medium. The content of writing is speech, just as a written word is a content of print, and print is the content of the telegraph. If it is asked, "What is the content of speech?," it is necessary to say, "It is an actual process of thought, which is in itself nonverbal."' Even though McLuhan's conception of the medium is, according to some critics, too over-inclusive and reductionist, in the context of this study it helps to address an important question: what it the message of transparency as a medium apart from the content it may deliver? Jean Baudrillard in *Simulacra and Simulation* (University of Michigan Press 1994) 33 writes: 'The medium itself is no longer identifiable as such, and the confusion of the medium and the message (McLuhan) is the first great formula of this new era. There is no longer a medium in the literal sense: it is now intangible, diffused, and diffracted in the real, and one can no longer even say that the medium is altered by it.'

[47] cf Mikkel Flyverbom, 'Transparency: Mediation and the Management of Visibilities' (2016) 10 International Journal of Communication 110 (hereafter Flyverbom, 'Transparency: Mediation and the Management of Visibilities').

[48] Teurlings and Stauff, 'The Transparency Issue' (n 2) 3–10.

[49] Martin Jay, *Downcast Eyes: The Denigration of Vision in Twentieth-Century French Thought* (University of California Press 1994) 95.

way. As an ideal, transparency is an *icono-ambivalent* phenomenon. I mean that transparency is simultaneously both suspicious towards images or other consciously created representations and reliant on them. This will be specified in the following.

Ambivalence means endorsing two—at least seemingly—contradicting values. Wanting to have one's cake and eat it is a classic emblem of ambivalence. This holds true in the case of transparency. On the one hand, transparency is ideologically *iconoclastic*. This means hostility towards images and representation; those only hinder the true visibility of the object and distort reality. Therefore, the iconoclastic ideology of transparency attempts to strip from governance all kinds of obfuscating veils: secrecy, appearances, and concealment. It promises to allow governance itself to emerge in its pure essence before the eyes of the viewer. As Baume and Papadopoulos state, '[t]ransparency, viewed as the absence of a veil, not only denotes a lack of concealment but also connotes cleanliness and the desire to show things in their purity'.[50] In that sense, this iconoclastic aspect is suspicious of mediation and craves immediacy. Following this reasoning, the transcendence of governance could take care of its own representation so long as the impediments blocking its visibility for the viewer were removed.

On the other hand, transparency is also *iconophilic*, and necessarily so. Iconophily means love for or acceptance towards images and representation. If iconoclasm is the ideological aspect of transparency, iconophily is its unescapable practicality. In many cases, there is nothing to show or to emerge without conscious effort and constructs. There is no spontaneous way for an abstraction to reveal itself. Instead, the mimicry of reality typically involves a conscious agent; images or other representations rarely emerge *ex nihilo*, as I will show in the next section.[51] Therefore, transparency needs to rely on images, metonymically understood: illustrations, statistics, performances, and reports, etc—conscious, constructed appearances, mostly falling into the category of *documents*. Ultimately, it needs to rely on people and their mimetic abilities, their capabilities to 'capture' the essence of governance by communicating it to the public.

Different constructs are thus forms by which governance may manifest itself. It is debatable whether governance has a transcendent appearance beyond those constructs. To quote Gary Watt, 'the image of a thing is usually contrasted with the thing itself; the image of a thing is said to be reflective, representative, reproductive or mimetic of the thing rather than identical to it. And yet the image of a thing can

[50] Sandrine Baume and Yannis Papadopoulos, 'Transparency: From Bentham's Inventory of Virtuous Effects to Contemporary Evidence-based Skepticism' (2018) 21(2) Critical Review of International Social and Political Philosophy 169, 172.

[51] cf Hans Krause Hansen, 'Numerical Operations, Transparency Illusions and the Datafication of Governance' (2015) 18(2) European Journal of Social Theory 203, 204. As Hansen argues, 'it is by means of signs we can represent people, objects and relationships, with implications for those who take the authority of the representations for granted and for those who contest it'.

sometimes be the most reliable knowledge we have of the thing. Sometimes we lack the capacity to see the thing itself, because the thing itself is too abstract or too profound or too remote. In such cases we might have to settle for a flame-cast shadow on the wall of the cave or an image reflected in a mirror in the dark.'[52] Thus, in order to appear, governance inevitably needs mediation, and this mediation takes the form of constructs. Governance is too abstract to appear as a thing in itself, or at least in its totality.[53]

How do we know that these iconophilic representations are loyal to their unseen object? Is a document reliable? If the object indeed has no visual makeup to imitate, can we talk about loyal imitation (mimesis) of the object at all? Following Sherwin, it may be helpful to make a conceptual distinction between mimesis1 and mimesis2. According to him, mimesis1 is the standard meaning of the concept, in the sense of 'good images are accurate copies'. In the case of governance, however, mimesis1 is rarely available, as I will discuss later. Is it in fact possible to make an accurate copy of an abstraction?

The answer is that we also need mimesis2, which has a different approach to representation than making copies. Representation then becomes performative. As Sherwin explains, 'the economy of the sublime, of appearance as event (let's call it mimesis2), insists upon a very different ground of truth than accurate imitation. Symbolic or iconic truth coincides with what the image reveals in our encounter with it. This kind of phenomenological exchange in the face of the iconic image is more akin to a performance. Something happens. The image brings something (perhaps some form of being) into a clearing, created within the space of the image, for the gaze to encounter.'[54]

Because mimesis2 cannot imitate, it needs to communicate a believable relation between its object and its observer. If mimesis1 copies, mimesis2 attempts to deliver the idea of the thing represented. How do these representations subject to mimesis2 manifest themselves? We can approach them as performances (I will return

[52] Garry Watt, 'Law Suits: Clothing as the Image of Law' in Leif Dahlberg, Klaus Stierstorfer, and Daniela Carpi (eds), *Visualizing Law and Authority: Essays on Legal Aesthetics* (Walter de Gruyter 2012) 23, 23.

[53] Carpi analyses the meaning of pictures, stating that: 'Pictures are a "mise en scène" of communication: instead of producing meaning they fade away in the very act of producing reality. Images, while pretending to portray the real and fix reality, in generating models of a real, as Baudrillard would say, end up effacing reality itself: "it is dangerous to unmask images, since they dissimulate the fact that there is nothing behind them." However, not all images mimic reality in a concrete sense, they may illustrate abstractions instead. These can be called "aniconic images".' Daniela Carpi, 'Crime Evidence: "Simulacres et Simulations", Photography as Forensic Evidence' in Klaus Stierstorfer and Daniela Carpi (eds), *Visualizing Law and Authority* (Leif Dahlberg ed, De Gruyter 2012) vol 4, 253, 254. As Sherwin describes, 'Aniconic images may present themselves as visual, but they actually point toward the unseen. The authority of an aniconic image derives from an invisible source.' I also consider necessary performativity a version or an interpretation of iconophily—an image (of governance) may be interpreted as a frozen image, a still picture of a performance. Sherwin, 'Visualizing Law' (n 33) 16.

[54] Richard K Sherwin, 'What Authorizes the Image? The Visual Economy of Post-Secular Jurisprudence' in Desmond Manderson (ed), *Law and the Visual: Transitions and Transformations* (University of Toronto Press 2017) 334.

to this in chapter four), or as *aniconic images*. According to Sherwin, these are images which do not attempt to mimic the visual makeup of the thing depicted. In fact, the representable thing does not have a makeup to mimic: it is an abstraction. Thus, aniconic images do not, and cannot, resemble its object.[55] Instead, they are illustrations: they attempt to create a visual form for something which naturally lacks it. In Sherwin's words, the authority of an aniconic image derives from an invisible source.[56]

What does this kind of representation mean in practice? For example, databases and algorithmic calculations produce images which point to abstract phenomena, naturally unfit for mimetic, iconic representation. As Sherwin puts it, they activate our senses as if we were perceiving objects and events in real life. For instance, functional magnetic resonance imaging (fMRI) may appear as a brain alight in neural electric activity. However, despite this appearance, it is neither a photograph nor an x-ray. Instead, it is a computational construct based on complex data sets and cues of water molecules in the blood circulation of the brain. A specific computer program translates this data into visual imaging, which looks as if the brain was lighting up in colours.[57] Mimesis2 is thus necessarily at play in the iconophilic side of transparency, although its representations cannot point to something spontaneous or natural, but to social constructs and conscious human activity.

Interestingly, this idea of mimesis2 is even traceable in the word 'diaphaneity', the Greek equivalent of transparency. As Alloa argues, 'whatever appears (phainestai) in sense perception appears through (dia) something else, which does not so much appear in itself; rather, it lets something else appear. In the case of vision, any element that yields this quality will be called "diaphaneous", inasmuch on the one hand, it lets the gaze through (dia), and on the other, it brings about or generates (dia) the visible object for the case.' Thus, as Alloa summarizes, diaphaneity means, on the one hand, the permeable quality of a medium that spatially lets the vision through (translucidity) and, on the other, the productive quality of a medium that allows (causally) something to come into view (generativity).[58] Transparency can thus function as a medium of mimesis2, which simultaneously is the very core of the icono-ambivalence of transparency. The promise of mimesis1 becomes relational to mimesis2.

The icono-ambivalence of transparency is thus based on these two sides: iconoclasm, on the one hand, and iconophily, on the other. It results in a specific doubt: we can never be sure of the quantity and quality of mediation in transparency. This further raises an array of questions: How can we know when transparency needs constructions to make its object appear, when is non-intrusion required? When

[55] Sherwin, 'Visualizing Law' (n 33) 16.
[56] ibid.
[57] ibid.
[58] Alloa, 'Transparency: A Magic Concept' (n 5) 35.

can we trust governance to take care of its own representation, when does it need iconophilic practices? When are we talking about mimesis1, when about mimesis2? When is transparency mediated, when is it immediate? Is it ever immediate? How can it be mediated or is it just illustrated? As Teurlings and Stauff put it, 'All too often, the visible is equated with an unmediated access to reality, but of course each medium that visualizes is a mode of representation.'[59]

These doubts resemble something that van de Port calls *the chagrin over mediation*, discontent over the fact that mediation is 'all we have' to render present the world of our imagination. That is to say, our dependence on media seemingly prevents us from knowing 'the real thing', the thing in itself. Perhaps this very chagrin also underpins our knee-jerk reaction to 'kill the messenger', when bad news is delivered. Paradoxically, as van de Port notices, the anthropological truism that realities are culturally constructed does not prevent people—even anthropologists—from behaving as though this was not the case.[60] Mediation thus always produces a fiction of premediated existence.[61] Seeking the truth beyond mediation seems to be a very human desire. By promising iconoclastic immediacy, the ideology of transparency utilizes this quest.

The Hand at Work

In the context of iconophily, the generative component of transparency, or mediation, can be approached obliquely, following Bruno Latour's concepts. In his theorizing on iconoclash, Latour uses the enigmatic expression of 'the hand at work'. 'The hand at work' is a metonym of human influence or interference in a picture. Something is done to make a picture come about. As this may sound self-evident, the hand at work conversely implies that not all pictures are man-made. Some have emerged spontaneously. The latter condition is called *acheiropoieta* in Greek, 'made without hands'.

The original meaning of *acheiropoieton* is religious. It refers to certain Christian icons, typically depicting Jesus or the Virgin Mary, which are claimed to have come into existence without human contribution, miraculously.[62] An example of an (allegedly) acheiropoietic image would be the Shroud of Turin, a picture of Jesus that emerged on a cloth without human influence. The implication is that an image which has come about without 'the hand at work' is more valuable than one made by man. In acheiropoietic images, transcendence reveals itself without human

59 Teurlings and Stauff, 'The Transparency Issue' (n 2) 6.

60 van de Port, '(Not) Made by the Human Hand' (n 42) 74.

61 William Mazzarella, 'Culture, Globalization, Mediation' (2004) 33 Annual Review of Anthropology 345, 357.

62 For more examples of spontaneous icons, see van de Port, '(Not) Made by the Human Hand' (n 42) 78–79.

mediation, which is unreliable. As Latour puts it, if one were able to show that these icons had been made by 'a humble human painter', this would be 'to weaken their force, to sully their origin, to desecrate them'.[63]

Van de Port widens the meaning of acheiropoieta from images and icons to the human body. He argues that in religious settings, the human body can serve as a medium of acheiropoieton. Illustrative examples of acheiropoieta represented in the human body would be stigmata or speaking in tongues.[64] They are phenomena of non-human origin—they are, according to religious explanations, a divine intervention which uses the human body as its platform or medium of generative expression.[65] Indeed, as van de Port notes, to be aware of the role of mediation is to be aware of human agency. This, in turn, may undermine the conceptualization of the divine as that which transcends the human imagination.[66]

Latour also talks about the hand at work and acheiropoieta more abstractly in order to describe the basic structure of iconoclash, the oscillation between belief in and suspicion of images. His definition is worth quoting at length here: '[w]e can define iconoclash as what happens when there is uncertainty about the exact role of the hand at work in the production of a mediator. Is it a hand with a hammer ready to expose, to denounce, to debunk, to show up, to disappoint, to disenchant, to dispel one's illusions, to let the air out? Or is it, on the contrary, a cautious and careful hand, a palm turned as if to catch, to elicit, to educe, to welcome, to generate, to entertain, to maintain, to collect truth and sanctity?'[67] The hand at work can do many things.

Thus, according to Latour, the hand at work is not always a metaphor of construction or even mediation; the hand can also destroy, enhance, or diminish certain features, and even alter its object altogether. This goes well with the idea of human interference in general. Not all human interference is concoction or construction. On the one hand, it can be a sincere attempt to mimic reality or an attempt to translate the unseen into a human, understandable form (mimesis2). On the other hand, however, it can be a self-serving distortion of reality: it may be biased, false, or partial.

Indeed, recognizing these many things that the hand at work can do precisely constitutes the suspicion towards it. What is the exact input of the hand? We cannot be sure. Do we thus need to settle with an invisible hand and give up our fantasies of acheiropoietic representations of the unseen? As Mitchell puts it, the dream of immediacy is a direct result of the awareness of mediation. As soon as we recognize the medium for what it is, '[it] constructs a corresponding zone of immediacy,

[63] Latour, 'What is Iconoclash?' (n 35) 19.
[64] van de Port, '(Not) Made by the Human Hand' (n 42) 79–82.
[65] Latour, 'What is Iconoclash?' (n 35) 16.
[66] van de Port, '(Not) Made by the Human Hand' (n 42) 78. See also Matthew Engelke, 'Text and Performance in an African Church: The Book "Live and Direct"' (2008) 31(1) American Ethnologist 76.
[67] Latour, 'What is Iconoclash?' (n 35) 19.

of the unmediated and transparent, which stands in contrast with the medium itself'.[68] We encounter the chagrin over mediation again.

Would acheiropoietic images be more reliable than those made by a human hand, then? If we approach images in general as a product of a conscious agent (cf religious icons), the logic of depiction changes. Acheiropoietic images have not come about because a human wanted to depict an object, but because the object itself wanted to be depicted. It wanted to be seen, perhaps by only certain people, to deliver a message. It means that the unseen is intervening in the world of the visual. The danger of manipulation is diminished, as no agent with an agenda is involved. At the same time, however, it means that that image is not necessarily designed for humans to understand; it may appear as unfathomable noise, understandable only to a consecrated few. What, for example, do stigmata *mean*? Indeed, the implications may be myriad, and not many of them can be discussed here. However, the idea of acheiropoieta leads us to ask whether governance 'wants' to be seen? Or is its premediated existence only a fiction?

It is important to remark that the hand at work has a standing both in the iconophilic and iconoclastic aspects of transparency. When it comes to iconophily, the effect is more evident. We can assume that governance cannot form acheiropoietic images but is reliant on people (or at least on their initiative) and their mimetic capacities to represent governance in visual or verbal forms, their ability to *document*. The accuracy of this documentation is, of course, necessarily limited because, in most cases, mimesis1 is not available: good copies are not possible. I will discuss documentation more in chapter six. However, the effect of this hand is not restricted to the iconophilic aspect. In the iconoclastic aspect, transparency is based on the idea of showing. This, in turn, alludes to removing obstacles that block the desired visibility. Someone is opening the curtain, lifting the veil, directing the beam, leaking secrets—someone who has both the interest and the capability to do so. Again, a hand at work, this time debunking, as Latour puts it.

Relatedly, van de Port discusses the aesthetics of transparent things—such as plexiglass objects (eg a see-through telephone exposing its technology to the viewer)—and couples it with an alternate road to immediacy. He argues that transparency, not mystification, is the keyword in this context. Rather than hiding, denying, or naturalizing the medium with this created transparency, a medium can be revealed as what it is, in its human-made, technically put-together fashion. This plexiglass aesthetics, as he calls it, calls attention to the technology of the mediation process, and thus to the inescapable human involvement in all mediation.[69]

Van de Port continues that there are interesting performative equivalents of this aesthetic. For example, take Brechtian theatre, with its constant disruptions of the

[68] William T J Mitchell, *What Do Pictures Want? The Lives and Loves of Images* (University of Chicago Press 2005) 214.

[69] van de Port, '(Not) Made by the Human Hand' (n 42) 84.

stage illusion and its instructions to the audience to remain critical and not give in to suspicion and disbelief.[70] However, van de Port fails to recognize the very mediatedness of the created 'plexiglass' transparency itself, both its materiality and performativity, and thus fails to notice the second-order medium that transparency can make. In this very way, transparency—seemingly only exposing another medium—has the potential to make us oblivious to the subtle human hand at work. When it exposes another medium—like the technology of a phone or even the way in which documents are made in governance—its own mediumness is easy to miss.

Regardless of how we think of the hand at work in transparency, what we are encountering is, in van de Port's words, the cultural production of the real. These are the rhetorical, performative, and aesthetic practices through which people seek to upgrade the reality calibre of the stories-they-live-by.[71] Although we cannot reach the thing in itself, but only the representation of some kind of accuracy, we are trying to make the distance between the two shorter: even though we cannot reach the really real, we can, perhaps, reach something more real than before.

In line with this, the entire binary language of transparency is symptomatic. It builds on questions of credible/incredible, true/untrue, and real/unreal, thus revealing three things: its hidden value judgments or ideological bias (true is better than untrue); its denial of the real as a continuous variable (can there be degrees of realness?); and its persistent yet futile chagrin over mediation (the language of transparency does not make any sense unless we pose the question of the medium). In other words, it reveals its icono-ambivalence.

Transparency Essentialism or Contingent Signifiers?

As this book builds on conceptual analysis, a few words on the potential blind spots of this approach are necessary. The fact that transparency is used metaphorically, and that metaphor is used strategically, does not and cannot fully colonize its literal meaning. How do we deal with the fact that transparency is optical, material, concrete, and technical, as well as symbolic, metaphorical, mythical, social, historical, ideological, political, and legal? Are we talking about features of actual things and arrangements or merely conceptual contingencies and homonymy?

Undeniably, transparency is a word, and in that sense, semiotically, a symbol. As such, it is the most mediated of signs—more so than an index (eg smoke is an index of fire) or an icon (eg a portrait is an icon of the person it depicts). As a metaphor, it is, however, based on a cognitive analogy. This analogy stems from transparency's meaning as an optical, physical condition that enables a gaze to meet its target. Paradoxically, it simultaneously escapes all obfuscating mediation, although it is

[70] ibid.
[71] ibid, 75.

based on mediation by definition; otherwise, we could simply talk about visibility ('mediated immediacy'). That is why transparency can form a metaphor in the first place: metaphors link a concrete meaning to abstract phenomena. In so doing, they help to make sense of things which may lack physical form and easily elude comprehension. This was discussed above.

This duality of operational mechanisms makes transparency peculiar. Consequently, an important question follows. How can we know when transparency is filtered by symbolic mediation and when it is, at least seemingly, direct, immediate, free from any distortion (icono-ambivalence)? As mentioned before, this is the watershed between the visual and the verbal. When are we talking about the signifier and when the signified? What is the meaning of the specificity of the signifier 'transparency' or is it entirely contingent? Quite close to these themes come questions of the intension and the extension of the transparency concept.

Although I use the term transparency here almost solely, other conceptualizations are possible. In the context of governance, we can also talk about publicness, publicity, the right to know, access to knowledge, freedom of information, openness, etc. If, however, we choose to talk about transparency and argue for the peculiarity of its rationality, are we stepping into an essentialist trap? By this I mean the assumption that transparency would always and necessarily be also an optical arrangement, however it is defined. When do we talk specifically about transparency rather than the aforementioned concepts based on family resemblance? Do we always inevitably refer to its optical connotation? Would it be the same to say that if we talk metaphorically about openness, for example, we would also always accept its spatial or haptic connotation, the possibility of stepping into some predefined space?

Let us look at the other option. We could also adopt the contingent signifier approach, or the attitude of Humpty Dumpty in Lewis Carrol's classic *Through the Looking Glass*: '"When I use a word," Humpty Dumpty said, in rather a scornful tone, "it means just what I choose it to mean—neither more nor less."' This is the argument, a 'nice knock-down argument' as Humpty Dumpty puts it, which strips any word of denotation, of its conventional meaning. If we apply this to the case of transparency, one could argue that there is no point in tracing some primary or core meaning of transparency in natural language or in any specialized context, for we could replace it with any word whatsoever so long as we could somehow identify its scope in the physical or conceptual world.

I would suggest that we should neither underestimate nor overestimate the choice of the term. It is true that in many instances, transparency could quite easily be replaced with some other word. That said, the history of the metaphor of transparency speaks for its peculiarity and non-contingency. Sandrine Baume analyses this especially in relation to the notion of publicity. She argues that the 'multifunctionality' of the term transparency constitutes an appeal that publicity does not have. That is to say, the appeal of transparency lies in its capacity to absorb multiple virtues or aspirations, such as clarity, consistency, sincerity, pureness, truthiness, and efficiency.[72] This is peculiar to magic concepts, as earlier explained.

Correspondingly, transparency should be able to protect us from various problems and vices, like tyranny, ignorance, arbitrariness, and inefficiency. Due to this, Baume argues, in the second part of the eighteenth century, transparency became a political, moral, and legal project, which it continues to be. Baume claims that to achieve such a huge ambition, the metaphor of transparency was better equipped than that of publicity; transparency has broader lexical fields associated to it than publicity.[73] In a similar vein, August argues that from its very inception, transparency in its materiality proved to be a great source of association power. The visual nature of the transparency metaphor inspired social orders organized in a similar way to rationalize communication.[74] Thus, historically, neither essentialism nor the contingent signifier approach is warranted. Transparency is not the only obvious choice, but it has proved to have better qualifications than its immediate rivals.

If we look at the question from a social theory point of view, we can find more motivations to try to combine the two approaches or to show their false binary nature. That is to say, transparency's special nature can also be recognized through a broader notion of visibility in society. To that end, Andrea Brighenti's reasoning in his book *Visibility in Social Theory and Social Research* (2010) is helpful. Instead of transparency, he discusses visibility as a category, thus adopting a more general approach. He aspires to complicate our understanding of visibility as a binary, on/off phenomenon. He specifically seeks to avoid determinism and essentialism. Hence, he presents visibility as a phenomenon which is inherently ambiguous. Its meaning depends on context and complex social, technical, and political arrangements, which could be called 'regimes' of visibility.[75] As transparency falls undeniably into the field of the visible (or the ocularcentric, to be more precise), his analysis is pertinent in many ways.

Following Brighenti's reasoning, the relationship between essentialism and contingency may be more multifaceted that one might assume. Namely, Brighenti rejects the semantic split between the literal meaning, referring to the immediate sensory realm, and the metaphorical, symbolic meaning of the visible, communicated via the media.[76] He argues that visibility is simultaneously socio-technical or optical and bio-political or cultural in nature. Visibility is socio-technical because it concerns linkages and mediations that occur in a realm in which ideas and

[72] Sandrine Baume, 'Publicity and Transparency: The Itinerary of a Subtle Distinction' in Emmanuel Alloa and Dieter Thomä (eds), *Transparency, Society, Subjectivity: Critical Perspectives* (Palgrave Macmillan 2018) 221.

[73] ibid, 219–21.

[74] August, 'Theorie und Praxis der Transparenz. Eine Zwischenbilanz' (n 20) 134.

[75] Andrea Mubi Brighenti, *Visibility in Social Theory and Social Research* (Palgrave Macmillan 2010) 3 (hereafter Brighenti, 'Visibility in Social Theory and Social Research').

[76] ibid, 186.

material forces coexist. This socio-technical realm infiltrates the material world. Simultaneously, visibility is also necessarily bio-political because it concerns the populations and subject positions therein. As Flyverbom argues, transparency is a matter of socio-material mediation and visibility management.[77]

Yet, it is not clear what kind of work transparency as a medium can perform. As Brighenti notes, the struggles and controversies over visibility are neither merely optical nor merely cultural. Instead, visibility constitutes a kind of *social optics.* Struggles and controversies reshape pre-existing visibilities and may even question the dominant regime of visibility. They revolve necessarily around the tight conjunction between the political, the technological, and the social. Therefore, as Brighenti maintains, the notion of visibility we need is not one that naively conflates invisible things with non-existing ones. This claim would lead us to a reductionist ontology.[78] It seems that a pure distinction between optical (cf essentialist) and metaphorical (cf contingent) transparency may be unwarranted and potentially even dangerously misleading. There are indeed many bridges between the two modes of rationality.

Summing Up: From the Literal to the Metaphorical—and Back

In this chapter, I have departed from the idea that we live in an ocularcentric world, one in which vision is the most important of all the senses. Psychologically, perhaps even anthropologically, we are intrigued by the visual field.[79] By virtue of this, seeing seems to be self-authenticating.[80] We tend to privilege our visual observation (firsthand knowledge) over what is told to us (secondhand knowledge). To a suspicious person we might say: do not just believe what you are told, see for yourself. Vision is even mythically coupled with truth; somehow, truth is epitomized in the ineffable, whereas words and explanations are less reliable. Transparency's metaphorical power derives from this premise.

Informed by this ocularcentricity, I discussed some of the theoretical preconditions of the transparency ideal. I broke down its general metaphorical functionality and argued that transparency is closely linked to vision as a sense. I argued that the metaphor of transparency is so powerful because it is derived from the conceptual

[77] Flyverbom, 'Transparency: Mediation and the Management of Visibilities' (n 47) 113; Michael Ananny and Kate Crawford, 'Seeing Without Knowing: Limitations of the Transparency Ideal and Its Application to Algorithmic Accountability' (2018) 20 New Media and Society 973.

[78] Brighenti, 'Visibility in Social Theory and Social Research' (n 75) 39–40.

[79] Turner, 'Literary Mind' (n 9) 12–13. See also Sherwin, 'Visualizing Law' (n 33) 11: 'There is something authentic, something grounding and sublimely transformative in our experience of the visual, as well as something deadening, reductive, flat, and sensationally hollow, as baroque culture manifestly demonstrates.'

[80] Sherwin, 'Visualizing Law' (n 33) 43: '[Common sense belief] seeks no extrinsic warrant; it needs no reasons in its behalf. This is why we say, "Seeing is believing," or "The thing speaks for itself." '

metaphor of 'understanding is seeing'. On a linguistic level, I argued, the transparency metaphor works as two different variants: the window and the flashlight. These two variants differ in how static or dynamic they depict the created visibility.

I discussed the meaning of transparency both as a verbal and a visual practice and its characteristics as an inconspicuous medium. Although transparency privileges direct see-ability over mediation, paradoxically it is a form of mediation itself. At first glance, it appears a mere facilitator of visibility, 'the cultural signifier of neutrality'. However, as a medium, transparency builds on curious epistemological commitments. As I have argued, media not only expose but also create part of the object seen. We do not only see things made visible by transparency, we also see the created transparency itself in the form of the practices labelled 'transparency'.[81]

I argued that transparency may lead to fostering naïve realism, uncritically believing that what can be immediately seen is true. The question of naïve realism goes back to the separation of the verbal and the visual. As Sherwin argues, 'words are obviously constructed by the speaker and thus are immediately recognized as abstractions. A word is unlikely to be mistaken for a window. By contrast, photo-realistic photographs, videos, film, as well as digital re-enactments can appear to be caused by the outside world, as if untouched by human mediation or authorial interpretation.'[82] Images seem to hold more truth in themselves than words by deriving their content directly from the reality they depict.

I explained that when we talk about transparency as a governance ideal, it has an icono-ambivalent logic: it oscillates between iconoclastic and ionophilic practices. Transparency functions both *as* transparency and *as if* transparency. These two forms of transparency involve different amounts and forms of mediation. It is 'torn between "hard" and "soft" meanings, essentialist connotations and constructivist qualifiers'. Icono-ambivalence makes us suspicious. We can seldom be sure how and to what extent the hand at work is at play (cf chagrin over mediation: iconoclash). Is transparency made with or without hands? When is the hand at work, and what does it do? Does it mimic, does it manipulate, does it omit, does it expose, does it conceal? Can governance even form acheiropoietic images; can it appear to the viewer without human interference, spontaneously? These questions are quintessential because they reveal the basic problem of transparency: we cannot really know to what extent we can access the 'truth' of governance, and its acheiropoietic image.

I discussed how abstractions are barely physically visible through transparency. When transparency is taken as a metaphor, it loses its innocence, its described neutrality, as a mere material phenomenon. In most cases, transparency becomes a construct, and can imitate its object only through mimesis2, performative

[81] Rogers Brubaker and Frederick Cooper, 'Beyond "Identity"' (2000) 29 Theory and Society 1; quoted in Steven Lukes, *Power: A Radical View* (2nd edn, Palgrave Macmillan 2005) 118.

[82] Sherwin, 'Visualizing Law' (n 33) 60.

imitation. As Alloa and Thomä argue, 'the metaphoric level of the notion seems to strangely mirror its literal meaning: the perfectly transparent window is one which completely diverts the attention from itself. The less we see the window-pane, the more we see through it.'[83] However, the meaning of actual visibility lingers; the constructive function does not fully occupy its meaning and functionality. Transparency is a visual and verbal phenomenon alike.

To conclude, as I have presented in this chapter, transparency as a concept has a specific appeal that is superior to its competitors. Therefore, it has been able to form a normatively attractive linguistic metaphor, suggesting immediacy when in fact mediation is at play. I argued that this goes back to the conceptual metaphor of understanding is seeing. Thus, transparency is simultaneously literal and metaphorical, verbal and visual, symbolic and iconic, revelatory and constructive. Noticing this multitude of modalities is the essential precondition for understanding the way in which transparency can work as a governance ideal.

[83] Emmanuel Alloa and Dieter Thomä, 'Transparency: Thinking Through an Opaque Concept' in Emmanuel Alloa and Dieter Thomä (eds), *Transparency, Society and Subjectivity: Critical Perspectives* (Palgrave Macmillan 2018) 3.

3
The Eye of the Beholder

Transparency and Seeing as an Object of Knowledge

As explained in the previous chapter, as a medium, transparency builds on particular assumptions in which visual and verbal elements on the one hand, and revelatory and constructive elements on the other, intersect. These assumptions have so far remained undertheorized if not unnoticed in current theorizing on transparency. Hence, the description of the inherent functioning logic of transparency has remained incomplete.

However, more follows concerning the visual semantics of transparency. In addition to the structural characteristics of transparency as a peculiar medium, its usage needs to be addressed. Namely, to have any bearing, transparency needs eyes to look through it—and at it. It requires someone who utilizes the possibility of seeing the visibilities it offers; otherwise, the mediating character of transparency makes no sense. Mediation implies an addressee. As mentioned earlier, Bentham claimed that 'even transparency is of no avail without eyes to look at it'.[1] Similarly, Tsoukas argues that transparency inevitably presupposes a subject: transparent to *whom*?[2] In this chapter, the goal is to continue the discussion on visual semantics that transparency presupposes, but from a partially different perspective than in the previous one. Who is looking through, and what are the potential effects of this looking? In other words, the questions of a gaze are at the heart of the discussion here.

Talking about a gaze and a beholder also means talking about vision more generally. Vision as an activity is important even though it often goes unnoticed. In everyday life, we do not pay much attention to it. Much of it seems to be unconscious. At the same time, as explained, the activity of vision also flourishes in language in an abstract sense. This was discussed in the previous chapter: besides observing, vision also carries the promise of understanding. When we talk about understanding, we often use language with visual meanings: to see, to look, to illuminate, to enlighten, to introspect, etc.[3] Visual metaphors, transparency among

[1] Jeremy Bentham, *Panopticon: Postscript: Part II: Containing a Plan of Management for a Panopticon Penitentiary-house* (London 1791).

[2] Haridimos Tsoukas, 'The Tyranny of Light: The Temptations and the Paradoxes of the Information Society' (1997) 29 Futures 827, 834.

[3] Martin Jay illustrates this strikingly by using twenty-one visual metaphors in one paragraph: glance, demonstrate, focus attention, vigilant, keeping an eye, illuminating, insight, mirroring, perception, outlook, point of view, speculation, imagination, blinded, inspect, introspect, prospect, foreseeable,

The Transparency Paradox. Ida Koivisto, Oxford University Press. © Ida Koivisto 2022.
DOI: 10.1093/oso/9780192855466.003.0003

them, are so powerful, because they create a promise of seeing, understanding, and possibly also accepting. According to conceptual metaphor theory, understanding *is* seeing. That is probably why it is so hard for us to understand invisible phenomena such as gravity, electricity, or consciousness. We must believe that they exist because their effects are very real, but at the same time they are hardly discernible. They do not succumb to mimesis1.

This chapter builds on the previous discussion of transparency as a medium and the production of reality it entails. This time, however, the focus is on the beholder herself and the effects of a gaze, enabled by transparency, the human production of meaning through visual and as such, nonverbal means. Without a beholder who is interested in using the medium of transparency, be it an iconoclastic or iconophilic aspect, transparency becomes futile. It remains a possibility, an affordance, or an opportunity. Whatever sceneries transparency would provide to be seen would have no bearing. Here, the effects of seeing are of interest both regarding the beholder, the subject, that is, as well as the object of the gaze. To that end, we need to look at seeing and vision more closely.

I will now discuss the meaning of reciprocity of gazes as a default condition of transparency. Although vision as an object of knowledge underpins and enables my discussion in the following, I am not, however, discussing human physiology. Rather, I am interested in the effects of a gaze meeting its object, mediated through transparency. My hypothesis is that the single most important effect of a gaze is its transformative potential. Namely, apart from registering an object, a gaze may change it.[4] I will name and analyse four different types of gaze: the observing, the revelatory, the transforming, and the projecting gaze. I will conclude that even though transparency would seem like a static organization of visibility, the way in which we use it by gazing makes the object look different.

This chapter is organized in the following fashion. First, I discuss the reciprocity of gazes, following in particular Rousseau's fantasy of transparency, and ask: How does the ideal of transparency change if reciprocity is lost? As I shall argue, this reciprocity is problematic in many ways. I then move to analysing different modalities of unilateral gazing. Thus, second, I address the observing gaze and the revelatory gaze. How can the eye meet its target and falsify the apparent? Third, I delve into the transforming gaze, which has the potential to alter its object. Fourth, I introduce the idea of the projecting gaze: can we trust our eyes or are the visibilities that transparency provides reflections of our own mind? Lastly, I summarize the

dimmed, synopsis, *lecture optique*. Martin Jay, *Downcast Eyes: The Denigration of Vision in Twentieth-Century French Thought* (University of California Press 1994) 1 (hereafter Jay, 'Downcast Eyes').

[4] Mikkel Flyverbom and Oana Brindusa Albu, 'Organizational Transparency: Conceptualizations, Conditions, and Consequences' (2019) 58 Business and Society 268, 273–75.

chapter and argue that the power of gazing is understood in an implicit but specific way in the ideology of transparency.

Transparency, Mediation, and the Reciprocity of Gazes

In current transparency debates, the meaning of the beholder has been left largely untheorized. Instead, the discussions revolve around the affordance and assumed effects of transparency: the created visibility is highlighted, whereas the different varieties of gazes and gazing as an activity in general have been left in the margins. Visibility is assumed to create a welcome matrix for control, critique, and change, utilized by well-informed and engaged citizens. I shall come back to this idea later in this book.

I claim, however, that the particular arrangement of visibility is of crucial importance. Namely, transparency as created visibility has two important caveats. First, transparency cannot determine how the beholder interprets what she sees. For example, she may look closer, turn away, ignore, or take a quick glance. A gaze can do a plethora of different things.[5] Second, the continuity of the gaze plays an important role. A sudden look has a very different effect on its object than continuous staring or monitoring. As a rule, the longer the gaze lasts, the more probable it is that the object—if it is a conscious agent—will change its presentation, due to or regardless of the perceived gaze. Thus, we must also consider the position and power of the beholder. We must delve into the theme of vision.

I acknowledge that the whole theme of vision as an object of inquiry deserves an intellectual history of its own. Vision and its meaning are recurrent themes in philosophy. Although I am not delving into that vast field *per se*, it is important to notice a certain moment in the general rendering of vision. It could be called the emergence of a meta-level understanding of vision. As Crary explains, in the aftermath of Kant, instead of being a privileged way of knowing, vision has become an object of knowledge itself. From the beginning of the nineteenth century onwards, the beholder gains increasing attention. This can be contrasted with the approach in which vision is analysed merely as a mechanism of light and optical transmission or as a function of the physiology of the human body.[6]

In other words, after this Kantian turn, vision has lost some of its transcendental privilege. It has become a function of our ocular system. This turn roughly coincided with the first blueprints of transparency as a governance ideal. It can

[5] Andrea Mubi Brighenti, *Visibility in Social Theory and Social Research* (Palgrave Macmillan 2010) 2: 'There are so many ways and styles of perceiving, seeing, beholding, looking at, viewing, descrying, glancing, catching sight of, glimpsing, spotting, watching, inspecting, detecting, noting, noticing, recognising, scrutinising, making out, picking out, setting eyes on, peeping and spying.'

[6] Jonathan Crary, *Techniques of the Observer: On Vision and Modernity in the Nineteenth Century* (MIT Press 1990) 70.

be hypothesized that this emergence of vision as an object of knowledge has also affected Bentham's endeavours to instrumentalize the gaze as a means of control. Indeed, for Bentham, transparency was meant to represent 'a new mode of obtaining power of mind over mind' in the Panopticon.[7]

In public discourse, transparency is often treated as a one-way phenomenon, similar to the way Bentham sees it. Something is transparent to someone. However, in a literal or material sense, transparency allows visibility in both directions.[8] What does it mean, then, if both simultaneously have the role of beholder and object? This question presupposes, of course, that the object of the gaze is a human and not a document, for example, or some other inanimate object.

The reciprocity of gazing could even be regarded as a default condition in our social life. This becomes apparent when we think of the opposite alternative, namely when unilateral gazing is considered rude. Conversely, in order for unilateral gazing to be justified, specific institutional arrangements that serve a particular purpose are required, such as recognizing a perpetrator in a row of suspects, or watching a performance. It is important to remember that transparency is, as argued in chapter two, a medium, albeit an inconspicuous one. Although transparency is often considered to mean specifically a lack of mediation, it is not the arrangement of an immediate encounter. In that sense, it is a third agent in the relationship between the beholder and the object of a gaze.[9] Thus, if we know how to look, we do not only see through transparency, but we can also see transparency itself. This paradox implies that reciprocity and mediation in transparency seem to form a tense relationship. The question raised is whether the immediacy of visibility is enabled or obstructed via transparency practices.

Rousseau recognized these tensions between transparency and mediation in his utopia of total transparency.[10] It is worth taking a close look at Rousseau's utopia, as it makes the potential and the problems of the reciprocity of transparency evident. For him, transparency was primarily a metaphor of thoughts and actions, extending from interpersonal relations to politics. In other words, transparency was not only used descriptively, but also as a moral judgement, as I shall argue in the next chapter.

As Schneider puts it, Rousseau wanted to submit modern society to the laws of transparency and sincerity, a desire that is visible both in his political and in

[7] Emmanuel Alloa, 'Transparency: A Magic Concept of Modernity' in Emmanuel Alloa and Dieter Thomä (eds), *Transparency, Society and Subjectivity: Critical Perspectives* (Palgrave Macmillan 2018) 40 (hereafter Alloa, 'Transparency: A Magic Concept'); Jeremy Bentham, *The Panopticon Writings* (Miran Božovič ed, Verso Press 1995) 31.

[8] cf David Heald, 'The Varieties of Transparency' in Christopher Hood and David Heald (eds), *Transparency: The Key to Better Governance?* (Oxford University Press 2006).

[9] Alloa, 'Transparency: A Magic Concept' (n 7) 36.

[10] Jean Starobinski, *Jean-Jacques Rousseau: Transparency and Obstruction* (University of Chicago Press 1988) (hereafter Starobinski, 'Jean-Jacques Rousseau').

his autobiographical confessions.[11] In Rousseau's utopia, transparency would be an omnipresent condition. Everyone in a society could communicate with each other immediately and effortlessly, directly from heart to heart. This is to say, communication would take place without obstructing language or other systems of symbols.[12] Rousseau thus considered language—regardless of what was expressed with it—an impediment rather than an avenue to sincere communication. Language was in any case a form of mediation and thus prone to distortion, unlike in the direct mind reading that Rousseau preferred. This goes well with the analysis in the previous chapter: words are more easily recognized as symbols than visual representation, and hence it is visual representation rather than words that is generally taken as a window to reality.

However, also for Rousseau the paradox of transparency, its mediated immediacy or its icono-ambivalent character that is, was at least tacitly recognized. This was particularly the case in his autobiographical writings. As Alloa explains, in Rousseau's view transparency needed both to be something natural or spontaneous and something which needed to be actively created. On the one hand, Rousseau claims that: 'In the whole course of my life one has seen that my heart, transparent as crystal, has never been able to hide for an entire minute a slightly lively feeling that has taken refuge in it.'[13] On the other, however: 'I would like to be able to render my soul transparent to the eyes of the reader in some fashion, and to do so I seek to show it to him under all points of view, to clarify it by all lights, to act in such a way that no motion occurs in it that he does not perceive so that he might be able to judge by himself about the principle which produces them.'[14] Rousseau thus considered his soul or heart was both naturally transparent and something that needed to be made so.

Rousseau's resentment towards inauthenticity—which he particularly attributes to theatricality—becomes evident in his *Lettre à d'Alembert sur le théâtre* (1758), which regards the potential establishment of a theatre in Geneva. Rousseau thought that the representation and dissimulation that theatre provided should be replaced with a less pretentious form of entertainment, namely a festival. In a way, theatre creates a vertical relation between the performers and spectators, which, in turn, Rousseau considered an impediment for reciprocal transparency. Festivals

[11] Manfred Schneider, 'The Dream of Transparency: Aquinas, Rousseau, Sartre' in Emmanuel Alloa and Dieter Thomä (eds), *Transparency, Society and Subjectivity: Critical Perspectives* (Palgrave Macmillan 2018).

[12] Starobinski, 'Jean-Jacques Rousseau' (n 10).

[13] Alloa, 'Transparency: A Magic Concept' (n 7) 38–39; Jean-Jacques Rousseau, *The Confessions and Correspondence, Including the Letters to Malesherbes: The Collected Writings of Rousseau*, vol 5 (Christopher Kelly tr, Christopher Kelly, Roger D Masters, and Peter G Stillman eds, University Press of New England Hanover 1995) 375 (hereafter Rousseau, 'The Confessions and Correspondence').

[14] Alloa, 'Transparency: A Magic Concept' (n 7) 38–39; Rousseau, 'The Confessions and Correspondence' (n 13) 375.

would break the actor-spectator bond and make everyone equal.[15] As Rousseau puts it, 'But what then will be the object of these spectacles? What will be shown in them? Nothing, if you please. With liberty, wherever abundance reigns, well-being also reigns. Plant a stake crowned with flowers in the middle of a square; gather the people together there, and you will have a festival. Do better, yet; let the spectators become the spectacle to themselves; make them actors themselves; do it so that each sees and loves himself in the others so that all will be better united.'[16]

At festivals, Schneider explains, all citizens would change completely and carry themselves to an excess of transparency. There would be no medium left between heart and eye or heart and tongue. Communication with no words would be the condition of their becoming transparent.[17] According to Jay's interpretation, Rousseau understood, nevertheless, that this utopia could never be totally fulfilled. Rousseau thought that a man could not be the source of his own light. This incapability led inevitably to the condition of linguistic mediation. Thus, the role of signs was to interfere with the pure reciprocity of gazes and transparency of hearts. Yet, Rousseau fantasized about the restoration of natural, primitive language in which the alienation of impersonal signs could be overcome. That would, allegedly, remove the conventional obstacles of total transparency. He also argued that music would form an additional pure form of immediacy that would directly reach the hearts of the listeners. Hence, other senses would help vision in abolishing the impediments of transparency.[18]

In Rousseau's utopia, transparency is thus portrayed as unimpeded immediacy free from mediation.[19] It that sense, using my own terminology, this kind of transparency is crucially iconoclastic. Reciprocity is its main functional requirement. It is built on a suspicion towards words (cf chagrin over mediation) and a romantic idea of completely effortless and personal communication between people. As Schneider contends, Rousseau thought that the origin of language was the origin of the theatre of society, which would also be the end of natural transparency. The destructive power of language would be cross-cutting and pervasive: in society,

[15] Manfred Schneider, 'The Dream of Transparency: Aquinas, Rousseau, Sartre' in Emmanuel Alloa and Dieter Thomä (eds), *Transparency, Society and Subjectivity: Critical Perspectives* (Palgrave Macmillan 2018) 92–97 (hereafter Schneider, 'The Dream of Transparency').

[16] Jean-Jacques Rousseau, *Politics and the Arts: Letter to M. d'Alembert on the Theatre* (Allan Bloom tr, Cornell University Press 1968), 126; Schneider, 'The Dream of Transparency' (n 15) 93.

[17] Schneider, 'The Dream of Transparency' (n 15) 93–94.

[18] Starobinski, 'Jean-Jacques Rousseau' (n 10) 88–90; Jay, 'Downcast Eyes' (n 3) 92.

[19] Jay, 'Downcast Eyes' (n 3) 92–93: 'Unlike the theater with its division between spectators and actors, the festival was a model of total participation. Whereas the theater trafficked in illusion and pandered to the senses, the festival provided a healthy moral experience in the open air. Rather than a mere representation—Rousseau was Platonic in his hostility to aesthetic as well as political representation—the festival was pure presence, an end in itself, a communion of souls without anything to mediate between them. Thus, the festival, most strikingly presented in the wine harvest in *La nouvelle Heloise*, had its counterpart in the patriotic community expressing the General Will developed in *The Social Contract*.'

in love, in politics, in child education, language as a medium would put an end to transparency.[20]

On the one hand, this approach presupposes transparency to be a technical term that allows mutual gazes to both encounter and communicate. Transparency is a technical term in a very specific sense, however: it is necessarily nonverbal and visual. Otherwise, language could not be so detrimental to natural transparency as it is portrayed in Rousseau's thinking. On the other hand, transparency is manifested as an ideology or morality of immediacy; transparency is desirable. Transparency becomes a normative concept. Thus, in Rousseau's world, the emphasis is on the demolition of power. This horizontal transparency would be radical to the extent to which everyone could read each other's thoughts, a kind of deep and effortless unity of people. A pre- or non-lingual form of communication is considered more authentic and reliable than a linguistically mediated one. Anachronistically, psychoanalytical implications concerning suspicions about the symbolic order can be detected; there seems to be a wish to return to the pre-lingual, symbiotic relationship between a mother and a child, in which the mother is able to fulfil all the needs of the child, who cannot express his or her needs.[21]

As implied earlier, this primary horizontality of transparency is not foreign to Rousseau's political thought. In fact, it underpins it: the ideal of total transparency is filtered into Rousseau's major concept of political philosophy, *volonté générale*, the general will.[22] The general will is the one that needs to be voiced by democratic assembly voting. However, the general will does not mean majority rule. This epistemic peculiarity (how can we know what the general will is?) indeed presupposes some form of mind-reading that transcends the forms of verbal communication.[23] However, as discussed above, unintended transparency like that would be psychologically and socially highly problematic. After all, we do value our mental privacy.

How is this Rousseauan utopia relevant to the discussion of the beholder and her object? As explained, in Rousseau's world, transparency is the condition which enables us to communicate without words, from heart to heart if you will. In that sense, people would be mutually transparent to each other. In this context, the main contribution of this idea is in making the meaning of the reciprocity of gazes visible as a precondition of mutual, equal transparency that would be free from all negative conditions. Conversely, without reciprocity there is no equality, no

[20] Schneider, 'The Dream of Transparency' (n 15) 94.

[21] Compare Noreen Khawaja, 'Unbounded Confession' in Emmanuel Alloa and Dieter Thomä (eds), *Transparency, Society and Subjectivity: Critical Perspectives* (Palgrave Macmillan 2018) 122.

[22] Schneider, 'The Dream of Transparency' (n 15) 93.

[23] Compare Schneider, 'The Dream of Transparency' (n 15) 94: 'The festival functions as a *tabula rasa*. The citizens celebrate the release from the theater of society and the end of all representation. The true republic, based on the *volonté générale*, makes all theater and theatric communication disappear. Spectators turn into actors, and the difference between representatives and represented citizens fades. At the same time, they are actors in politics and observe of their own actions. Nonetheless their observation is not from outside, since everyone is reading in the transparent heart of the other.'

mutual sharing, no balance of information. However, the reciprocity of gazes is an untenable ideology in current transparency practices. As I will argue in detail in the next chapters, these practices build necessarily on unequal visibility. In the following, I analyse different modalities of gazes in which this inequality becomes apparent by enabling the different visibilities to emerge.

The Observing and Revelatory Gazes

Primarily, to gaze at something means authenticating the existence of an object in the world. Secondarily, a gaze recognizes its nature or quality, its essence: What is it? What is it like? What is it made of? It is also possible to argue an opposite order: essence comes first. Philosophically, this is a chicken and an egg problem: How can we identify the existence of something without simultaneously identifying its nature, its essence? Without attempting to answer that question, we can hypothesize that an object exists notwithstanding its gazer, and therefore, a gaze may merely observe it. The human brain is hard-wired to bringing this to the extreme, intuitively assuming that outside the gaze there is nothing. This is, of course, an illusion that our brain feeds us.[24]

In fact, the question of what we can know, or sense, is subject to hundreds of years of philosophical inquiry extending from Plato all the way to modern cognitive psychology and behavioural economics, Cartesian solipsistic anxiety being its most famous example. I acknowledge this rich theorizing, but I will not delve into that. Instead, my goal is more modest: to analyse gazes with different effects.

To that purpose, I call a gaze which merely identifies its object *the observing gaze*. This quality makes it a prerequisite for all other categorizations: by looking, a gazer notices something existing or happening in the world. Importantly, the observing gaze is spontaneous, and it lacks conscious intentionality. By conscious, I mean that intentionality may also be unconscious. Our brain is constantly filtering visual information and allows only a fraction of it to enter our consciousness. Thus, intentionality can be argued to direct the gaze, but this intentionality may elude our attention.

The observing gaze aspires to deliver reliable information of our surroundings; it helps us navigate in the world. We see our surroundings, we see people, objects, landscapes. We can see dangers and avoid them, we can see all kinds of desirable things and pursue them We can rely on the world to be approximately as we see it. Otherwise, functioning in daily life would be almost impossible. This makes sense, since the very observing gaze is necessary for the metaphor of transparency to

[24] Daniel Kahneman discusses this in his famous book, *Thinking, Fast and Slow* (Farrar, Straus and Giroux 2013).

function as it does. For understanding to be seeing, that seeing needs to be trusted as a default condition.

This observational element can be a necessary precondition for a more particular type of gaze, which I call *the revelatory gaze*. By that I mean a gaze which not only observes its object, but, by this observing, also falsifies its immediate appearance. It is the gaze of the iconoclastic aspect of transparency. What does this mean? The epithet 'revelatory' gives a hint. It presupposes concealment or at least a curated appearance, which in the form of the revelatory gaze is broken down, penetrated, or abolished. In that sense, the revelatory gaze observes an object that is not designed or desired to be seen, at least by that gazer, in that particular surprising way.

The revelatory gaze resembles something called *anagnorisis*, a term that Aristotle introduces into his *Poetics*. Anagnorisis means a moment of sudden revelation which precedes the turning point in a play.[25] It is thus a moment of truth whereby ignorance or false consciousness is transformed into knowledge. For example, a stranger will be recognized as a familiar person, or suddenly the correct state of affairs is understood. Anagnorisis often precedes a change in the main character's life, in comedy to happiness, in tragedy to unhappiness (*peripeteia*, 'reversal'). In Sophocles's drama *Oedipus Rex* (ca. 428 BC), anagnorisis takes place when Oedipus finally realizes that he has killed his father and married his mother.[26]

If we compare the idea of the revelatory gaze with anagnorisis, both thus mean that the immediate appearance of things is proven wrong. Just by gazing, the multilayered nature of the visual realm is revealed: things are not as they seem, and the gazer cannot ignore this change of perception without sacrificing her intellectual honesty. Things are different before and after the sudden gaze, which can have an effect both on the gazer and the object. However, anagnorisis is a term in literature and as such is accompanied by the dramatic structures of a play. The revelatory gaze, in turn, needs no such turning points in the life of the gazer. That said, change in the perception of the world is unavoidable. I will return to the effects of the sudden gaze in the next chapter.

Unlike the observing gaze, an emancipatory component underpins the revelatory gaze, although this emancipation may not be desired and can cause pain (eg Oedipus's realization). If unexpected, the revelatory gaze can be deeply undesired for both the gazer and the object; it can even be traumatic. Namely, the revelatory gaze may be either intentional or unintentional. It can be investigative (secret surveillance; intelligence), when the exposure is intended and pursued, and the

[25] Aristotle, *The Poetics of Aristotle* (Samuel H Butcher tr, The Project Gutenberg 2008) 9. Aristotle defined anagnorisis as 'a change from ignorance to knowledge, producing love or hate between the persons destined by the poet for good or bad fortune'. For different definitions, see John MacFarlane, 'Aristotle's Definition of "Anagnorisis"' (2000) 121(3) The American Journal of Philology 367.

[26] The Editors of Encyclopaedia Britannica, 'Anagnorisis literature' (article added 1998, modified by Emily Rodriguez 2016, Britannica) <www.britannica.com/art/anagnorisis> accessed 24 June 2021.

anagnorisis, the falsification of the apparent, is expected to take place; or it can be accidental, when the gazer does not anticipate the revelation (eye-witnessing a crime; opening a door which was supposed to be locked). This is precisely what makes the revelatory gaze peculiar, and what distinguishes it from a mere observation.

However, intentional or not, the revelatory gaze requires to remain undetected in order to create a revelation. Even if not intended, the consequence is a disclosure of the concealed. That said, it needs to presuppose at least a certain suspicion towards appearances. Furthermore, the revelatory gaze has temporal implications. A revelation would not be possible if the gaze were not sudden and surprising. This is because otherwise the object—itself or in the control of a conscious agent—could be prepared to be revealed and act accordingly. Thus, the revelatory gaze cannot be continuous unless it is simultaneously hidden, functioning unbeknownst to the object or its agent. In a way, this makes the revelatory gaze repressive.

The Transforming Gaze

As argued, to complete the analysis of transparency's effects, we need to consider the position of the beholder. This was already discussed with the revelatory gaze. I argue that this is not all there is to it: a gaze can affect its object in a different way just to reveal its unfiltered essence. In Garsten and De Montoya's words, 'the gaze of transparency does something to that which is being observed, monitored and made legible'.[27] A gaze which does exactly that I call *the transforming gaze*. It makes its object react to the gaze, and follow its implicit orders and preferences. It is a gaze of power. The analysis of the transforming gaze is important for the democratic rationality of transparency and its preventive mechanism. I will discuss these themes in chapter five.

The transforming gaze is not only about seeing but also crucially about being seen. This experience of being seen is also pertinent in the case of the revelatory gaze, as presented. However, as argued, in that case the gaze is unexpected, hidden, or sudden in the sense that the object of the gaze does not have time to adjust. The object is found as it is. This is not true in the case of the transforming gaze. Its object forms a relation with the gazer. As a rule, the object may or may not see the gazer, but she knows that she is, or can be, seen. The transforming gaze is not possible without the object's awareness of its existence, or at least of its potentiality.

In psychology, the awareness of a gaze is also referred to as the Hawthorne effect or the Watching Eye effect. The main idea is that we act differently—more

[27] Christina Garsten and Monica Lindh de Montoya, 'In Retrospect: The Play of Shadows' in Christina Garsten and Monica Lindh de Montoya (eds), *Transparency in a New Global Order: Unveiling Organizational Visions* (Edward Elgar 2008) 284.

pro-socially—if we are being watched than if we are not. Bentham's words, mentioned previously, also mirror this: 'the more strictly we are watched the better we behave'.[28] Even a mere picture of an eye may suffice to bring about the effect. The gazer remains unseen or otherwise in the position in which he cannot be controlled, whereas the object may be seen all the time. This awareness of the gaze constitutes the principal difference between the revelatory and the transforming gaze.

Building on Bentham, Foucault has most famously theorized the logic of the transforming gaze, and the power embedded in it. Becoming an object of such a unilateral, controlling gaze may have a profound effect on its objects. As mentioned in the first chapter, the transforming gaze is most famously explored by Foucault in *Discipline and Punish* (1975), which builds on the Benthamite idea of surveillability. However, Foucault's conception is more overarching: he approaches the transforming gaze as a metaphor of a particular kind of power. This power is often called panopticism or the panoptic modality of power. Even though the panoptic modality of power is discussed and analysed almost *ad nauseam* in social theory, politics, and law, for the sake of clarity, it is still worth describing briefly here.

The panopticon, the all-seeing prison, creates an apt metaphor for the functioning of the preventive function of transparency, which I will discuss in chapter five. The panopticon's architecture is peculiar. It is a ring-shaped building, consisting of multiple cells on various floors. In the middle there is a central tower, which allows visibility into each of the cells. In the tower, a guard can see the inmates of every cell if he chooses to. The catch is that the inmates do not know whether or when they are being watched. This lack of knowing is the whole idea of the panopticon.[29] When the object is aware that she might be subject to a gaze at any time, she starts to behave as if she were being watched all the time. That is to say, she internalizes the all-seeing gaze and starts to transform her own behaviour accordingly. At the same time, actual surveillance becomes unnecessary. The gaze becomes hypothetical, even fictive, and pre-emptive. As such, it decreases deviant behaviour. That exactly is its idea—discipline that becomes self-discipline.[30]

In Foucault's thinking, the gaze is transformative in a particular way: it normalizes. This normalization departs from the assumption that the object internalizes the real or assumed expectations of the gazer.[31] To do so, the object needs to have at least an idea of those expectations to pursue them. However, it is important to recognize that for Foucault, the object of a gaze is individual subjects, whereas the gazer represents power. The panoptic gaze is thus an efficient way of making obedient subjects. Acknowledging this, I will use the idea of the panoptic

[28] Jeremy Bentham, *The Collected Works of Jeremy Bentham: Writing on the Poor Laws*, vol 1 (Michael Quinn ed, Oxford University Press 2001) 277.

[29] Jeremy Bentham, *Panopticon; or, The Inspection-House* (Dodo Press 2008) 3–18.

[30] Michel Foucault, *Discipline and Punish: The Birth of Prison* (Penguin Books 1991).

[31] ibid.

gaze more liberally. In fact, I argue that for the sake of argument, it can applied the other way around, namely for exploring the ways in which subjects gaze power. To my understanding, this was also the way in which Bentham understood the power of gazing.

In the case of transparency, the transforming gaze thus requires different arrangements than the revelatory gaze. Unlike the revelatory gaze, the transforming gaze is not based on a similar kind of unexpected disclosure. Instead, it is a matter of control before disclosure. In order to work, the transforming gaze requires such arrangements, either literally or symbolically, so that the scope of the controlled self-reporting becomes either futile or impossible. This is to say, the object must be in conditions in which its actions can be directly monitored, as the saying has it, the object is in a fishbowl.

Glass walls or ceilings in public buildings would make an illustrative example of this fishbowl transparency: as mentioned, glass works as a primary metaphor. As Fisher puts it, 'as with the use of transparency in public administration, the early use of glass was underpinned by the two assumptions ... a) the normative hope that transparency will make life and society better and b) that transparency is largely a physical process of making things visible'.[32] These assumptions still seem valid: transparency is good and making things visible would underpin this goodness. When the operations of the governor can be made visible in real time, no self-reporting would be necessary.[33] We can see its operations immediately. However, such literal visibilities may not communicate much, as they may merely reveal something as unimpressive as people sitting in their offices. I will discuss this theme in chapter six.

In addition to direct and immediate monitorability, the transforming gaze can also have more subtle and indirect implications. In addition to physical appearances and performances, it can even extend to the process of documentation, in other words, icono-genesis, although admittedly, the process of documentation is hardly visually very impressive or informative. The transforming gaze would extend to the way in which the writer would picture the assumed reader of the document. If the created documents became public later, their writer could not ignore this upcoming publicity and its effects. This is to say, the writer would make those documents such that the expectations of the potential reader were met. In other words, she would write them using such utterances and information that the author expects that the gazer would want to read and approve them.

However, here again, the danger of naïve realism becomes evident: the mere visuality of an event and the mimetic representation of it in the form of picture,

[32] Elizabeth Fisher, 'Exploring the Legal Architecture of Transparency' in Padideh Ala'i and Robert G Vaughn (eds), *Research Handbook of Transparency* (Edward Elgar 2014) 59, 60.

[33] For an empirical research on the 'civilizing effect' of transparency, see Daniel Naurin, *Deliberation Behind Closed Doors: Transparency and Lobbying in the European Union* (European Consortium for Political Research Press 2007).

film, or text makes transparency a construct (the iconophilic aspect of transparency). Transparency as a medium always includes some element of planning and assessment of its potential consequences, in other words, the hand at work. For instance, a video recording does not expose itself. Instead, it is uploaded, and probably also edited. Even if this were not the case, the camera at least captures certain parts of the performance worth filming and leaves out other parts. However, if we follow the idea of the panoptic modality of power, the object of a gaze must behave as if it was being watched and even recorded all the time. This is to reduce deviance.

The paradox of the transforming gaze is, thus, that it cannot encounter the object as it is; there is no anagnorisis, no revelation. Instead, it makes the object or its agent act in a way that requires internalizing at least the assumed expectations of the gazer. In a way, this very gaze creates its object. If we did not know about its existence, the gaze would be observing or revelatory instead. Transparency in the form of the transforming gaze is a form of power, namely the power of the gazer to make a change in its object.

The Projecting Gaze

Thus far, I have considered the gazer potent in her gazing. In other words, the gaze has appeared pure from external or internal, potentially disturbing, influences. The gaze has reached its object either with or without constructed transparency arrangements. Regardless of whether the aim is revelation or control, the power of a gaze has not been questioned. It was considered potent in affecting its object. Nevertheless, it is important to notice that it is not self-evident that the gazer sees what he thinks he sees. As mentioned, our sensory capabilities are necessarily limited, and our consciousness easily biased.

Seeing is not just a physical but also a mental, cognitive activity. As Zerubavel notes, 'The capacity of our sense organs far exceeds our mental capabilities, and as such, looking at something does not guarantee that we will notice it'.[34] Centuries earlier, Francis Bacon stated something similar: 'The mind of man is far from the nature of a clear and equal glass, wherein the beams of things should reflect according to their true incidence, nay, it is rather like an enchanted glass, full of superstition and imposture, if it be not delivered and reduced.'[35] What our eyes see and what reaches our consciousness are thus two different things. Therefore, we need to address the following question: To what extent do we see the object itself or at least such a representation that we are intended or allowed to see, and to what

[34] Eviatar Zerubavel, *Hidden in Plain Sight: The Social Structure of Irrelevance* (Oxford University Press 2015) abstract.

[35] Francis Bacon, *The Advancement of Learning and New Atlantis* (Arthur Johnston ed, Clarendon Press 1974) 127.

extent something we create by ourselves, something we want, expect, or fear to see? What is the meaning of the gazer herself? What is the effect of the 'enchanted glass'? What and how do we want to see?

Even if we could see something, we do not necessarily want to see it. We might either look away or see something we can see or choose to see. Although I have argued that transparency builds on the cognitive metaphor of 'understanding is seeing', the opposite way of approaching the issue is also possible. As Morris argues, we do not form the beliefs which guide the way we see. Rather, our beliefs often determine what we see. In consequence, Morris contends, believing is seeing, and not the other way around.[36] Our beliefs thus affect our sensorium. We often project our own ideas and beliefs upon visual information; we do not have access to visual experience that would not include our own attitude towards it.

Consequently, we can have different concerns towards visual information. Sherwin singles out various anxieties provoked by the proliferation of visual images. In my view, these anxieties can extend to the views enabled by transparency. For example, Sherwin mentions the Matrix effect, the fear of moving from dream world to dream world in an infinite hall of mirrors. In addition, he distinguishes several other effects: 'the Medusa effect: the fear of being frozen in an other's gaze; or the Narcissus effect: the fear of being swallowed (or drowned) in the image (that stares back); or the Pygmalion effect: the fear associated with the fantasy of bringing the image to life as an autonomous being (and perhaps joining it in a virtual world unto itself); or, finally, the Tantalus effect: the fear of the image as cruel catalyst—a force that stokes desires it can never fulfill'.[37] We cannot be sure that the object of the gaze remains passive: it may stare back, and by that staring affect us.

As said, the capacity of our sense organs exceeds our conscious mental capabilities. That is to say, looking at something does not guarantee that we will notice it, make sense of it, or do justice to it. Instead of arguing that we could not visually reach the object by looking at it—although this holds true in a certain sense regarding the transforming gaze, as presented—I argue that sometimes the gazer may project her own impressions onto the object. Therefore, I call this kind of gaze *the projecting gaze*. Not only does the representation reflect the object's essence but the gazer interprets its meaning. We cannot be sure of the tricks that can be played on our mind.

Bianchi, as mentioned previously, asked 'Is what I see reality or just a mental representation of what I expect to see?'[38] Or, as Sherwin puts it, 'Are we looking

[36] Errol Morris, *Believing is Seeing: Observations on the Mysteries of Photography* (Penguin Books 2011) 93.

[37] Richard K Sherwin, *Visualizing Law in the Age of the Digital Baroque: Arabesques and Entanglements* (Routledge 2012) 45 (hereafter Sherwin, 'Visualizing Law').

[38] Andrea Bianchi, 'On Power and Illusion: The Concept of Transparency in International Law' in Andrea Bianchi and Anne Peters (eds), *Transparency in International Law* (Cambridge University Press 2013) 1, 9.

as if through a window, at something actual? Or must the image we see be deconstructed, or decoded, in order to get at that which exists outside the mind?'[39] Thus, no matter how much intentional or unintentional transparency there is, the gazer cannot be reduced to a mechanical perceiver. As argued, the image or representation of another kind may change the observer. The inverse was partly presented in the case of the transforming gaze. As this may be counterintuitive as such, it holds some interesting ramifications. Namely, the object of a gaze can appear different to the viewer for various reasons; it is not always a matter of projection. Instead, in addition to the beholder's projections and interpretations, the difference may stem from the essence of the object itself, as I will clarify in the following.

First, if we subscribe to the idea of perspectivism as a general epistemological attitude, the position of the gazer, in the sense of the spatial location, is of crucial importance. For instance, if we look at an abstract statue, it looks different from every angle, each of which is equally true. The object just appears different, and is probably intended to do so. Perspectivism as a general epistemology indeed does not exclude different interpretations; however, it cannot and will not distinguish the correct interpretation from the others. In this sense, it is a totally democratic mindset. It builds on the situatedness of a gaze. Postmodern thought is loosely based on the notion of situatedness in which the existence of universal truths is questioned. At the same time, whatever our understanding of an object would be, it could not trump any other view. Another question is whether some comprehensive view is possible, and if so, is it desirable?

Second, the object itself can be such that it is intended to create or deliver a message only from a certain point of view. In a sense, it makes that message esoteric; or it distinguishes exoteric and esoteric meanings of the object. This does not mean that the object would not be comprehensible from other angles, could not communicate a disparate, more obvious message, or that it could not otherwise be subject to different interpretations. It is not opposed to perspectivism but is rather a particular reading of it. Instead, the object 'looks back' at the observer, delivering a distinct message from a certain specific direction. In art, this phenomenon is called *anamorphosis*. It means a distorted reflection that is understandable only from a certain vantage point or by using a certain device. Anamorphic pictures are used in art from the early Renaissance onwards.

The best-known anamorphic painting is probably Hans Holbein the Younger's *The Ambassadors* (1533). In it, two men—the ambassadors—are depicted in a standing position with a detailed still-life. In the forefront, in front of the still-life and between the men, there is a skull motif, which, orthogonally looked at, cannot be recognized as a skull. Rather, it resembles some abstract pattern on the floor. However, viewed from an oblique direction, the skull becomes a *memento mori* or

[39] Sherwin, 'Visualizing Law' (n 37) 16.

vanitas symbol, whereas the other motifs in the painting become skewed. In that way, the painting delivers a radically different message depending on the vantage point.[40] Thus, anamorphosis is a specific form of artistic expression. It indirectly states that the obvious or the exoteric differs from the esoteric, and that the medium or the vantage point enabling the deciphering of the esoteric message is, in fact, an essential part of the picture.

In philosophy, the concept of anamorphosis is used in a more abstract, metaphorical sense. For instance, writers such as Jacques Lacan, and, building on Lacan's thinking, Slavoj Žižek, have used the concept to account for certain dimensions of human understanding and the dynamics of the psyche.[41] In Žižek's view, our projections of reality are necessary because they constitute, not distort, our very reality. However, unlike in art, there seems to be no 'obvious' or exoteric picture to be grasped to which the anamorphic, back-gazing part or esoteric meaning would be subordinate. Thus, by anamorphosis, Žižek means a vantage point from which an individual can understand reality. This is essential because if reality were approached orthogonally, it would not be capable of expressing itself at all. In other words, a perspective is mandatory; there is no view from nowhere. One needs to look awry.[42]

The idea of anamorphosis as a peculiar avenue to reality poses some epistemological challenges. Does anamorphosis contradict the perspectivist idea of truth, or is it a different way of formulating it? Does it presuppose that there is a 'truer truth' out there, regardless of the perspectivist interpretations, which, however, are not accessible without our fantasy-like projections? If we follow Žižek, the answer would be negative. We are capable of perceiving reality only through our own fantasies and perspectives, no other kind of reality is available or conceivable to us. Whether that perceived reality is 'objective' does not really matter. The 'objective' reality would be just fog with no shape or meaning.

Stating this, however, could undermine the very possibility of other types of gaze (discussed above). If we always perceive reality through an anamorphic way, does that mean that we cannot 'reveal' truth or transform the object with our gaze? Is there any other reality than the one composed in our mind? This line of interpretation is certainly possible. However, this could also lead to an ultra-individualistic conception of reality, with little room for shared views. We would be doomed to solipsism, with no interest in societal participation, as there would be no common interests to be furthered. Consequently, a radically anamorphic conception of reality would make the entire idea of transparency futile. Why would we call for it,

[40] Sherwin, 'Visualizing Law' (n 37) 33–34. Sherwin argues that 'When a change in perspective brings the blurred skull into view, the normative register of the work completely shifts (from worldly values to transcendental ones).'

[41] Slavoj Žižek, *For They Know Not What They Do: Enjoyment as a Political Factor* (Verso Books 2008).

[42] ibid, xxvii.

why would we care for it, if it did not carry the promise of seeing reality freed from our fantasies, ignorance, and misconceptions?

I acknowledge that Žižek's idea of our quintessentially anamorphic view of reality may be incommensurable with the other described gazer positions. True, we all have our unique interpretation of reality, which at least to some extent is different from that of others. This is why the idea of a projecting gaze makes sense in the first place: not only does our gaze affect its object, but we might project things onto reality which actually reside in our mind. Although strictly speaking all observations are products of our mind, I would maintain that as social animals we need to rely on some approximation of a common reality. If that were not the case, we could not really form groups and societies, and we would struggle to live as a community. Therefore, talking about a revelatory or a transforming gaze still makes sense. Although we might have different interpretations of what we see—like ink stains in the Rorschach test—we would still share some elements of a common reality. We would still agree on the ink stain being the object of interpretation.

Summing Up: What Is the Effect of the Gaze?

In this chapter, I have argued that gaze matters. Transparency can have a bearing only if we assume that there are eyes to look through it—and at it. Although transparency is an icono-ambivalent phenomenon, building on both revelatory and constructive mechanisms, visual authentication is sustained as its deep structure. Transparency promises reliable information; and seeing with one's own eyes seems to be the most reliable way of knowing. Immediacy is what is first and foremost pursued with transparency.

However, regardless of the ideal of immediacy, mediation is and cannot but be at the heart of transparency (cf 'mediated immediacy'). Its mediated nature entails suspicion, which was previously referred to as the chagrin over mediation. This is to say, the more mediation there is, the more the hand is at work. More room for impression management logic means less direct access to 'the real thing'. The emergence of this chagrin was exemplified by Rousseau's utopia of transparency, which—unlike the modern conceptions of transparency—is based on the reciprocity of gazes. According to Rousseau's utopia, people would be transparent to each other: communication without words forms the epitome of optimal transparency and the purity of hearts, as words, a form of mediation that is, would obscure this immediate purity. However, to the extent that the gaze is unilateral rather than reciprocal, transparency is doomed to be theatrical. It cannot represent the allegory of a festival, which Rousseau preferred.

Whether reciprocal or unilateral, transparency relies on a gaze. A gaze is a tacit but irreplaceable component of transparency, and it makes the relational nature of transparency visible. Without a gaze, transparency is merely an affordance. To examine the dynamic between transparency and its user, I analysed four different modes of gazes with different effects. The idea was to show that even if transparency appears static or neutral, and importantly, legitimacy inducing, the way in which it is used may have different impacts on its object. To illustrate this, I distinguished observing, revelatory, transforming, and projecting gazes. Each of these gazes has a different impact on its object.

The observing gaze merely acknowledges the existence of its object. It is the least dramatic. The revelatory gaze is otherwise similar than the observing gaze, except for its debunking effect. It falsifies an apparent state of things. It can be either intentional or unintentional. It 'sees through' the apparent. The transforming gaze, for its part, has the potential to change its object in a more controlled manner. It does so by constant monitoring or at least with a possibility of such monitoring. As a result, the object is pressured to meet the actual or imagined expectations of the gazer. The projecting gaze makes its object by imagining it. Its relation to the actual essence of the object is complex. The perception received through it is at least partially based on the viewer's own hopes, fears, or individual perceptions of one kind or another. On the other hand, the object may well enable many, equally defensible interpretations.

I argue that all of the gazes discussed above can be understood as playing a role in governance transparency. The observing gaze makes the other gazes possible. The revelatory gaze underpins involuntary transparency and transparency vigilance, which will be discussed in detail in the following chapters. The transforming gaze makes the panoptic or 'fishbowl' transparency understandable. It is the functioning logic behind the democratic rationality of transparency. This kind of transparency aligns with the self-interest of the object of the gaze by sustaining one's status in a community. It diminishes the danger of being exposed and losing face, as I will explain in the next chapter.

The projecting gaze may make an appearance in two ways. First, it may be argued that it is always at play, as we cannot but filter the perceived reality through our anamorphic point of view. Second, seen less comprehensively, it may be a matter of the crumbling of the seeing-as-understanding-bond. The more complex and esoteric the information and representations become in modern society, perhaps in the form of highly specialized expert information, the more projection and interpretation there can be.[43] We do not always understand what we see, yet we interpret what we see. I will discuss all of these themes—the ways in which the different gazes can feature in different transparency settings—in the following chapters.

To conclude, the significance of a gaze is understood in a particular way in governance transparency. On the one hand, it can be reconstructed as a necessary precondition for transparency as an ideal to make sense. On the other hand, although

[43] See, for example, Michael Power, *The Audit Society: Rituals of Verification* (Oxford University Press 1999) 13–14, 122–47.

a gaze may have different effects on its object, as I argued, those effects are not distinguished from each other or theorized in contemporary transparency discourses. In addition, Rousseau's utopia of reciprocal transparency and its logic of a festival has not been adopted in modern transparency practices; instead, the gaze is conceived as unilateral, employing a theatrical logic. This theatrical logic, in turn, has some profound consequences in both our social relations as well as in the arrangement of transparency as a legitimacy strategy. I discuss the fundamentals of theatrical logic in the next chapter.

PART II

THE PROMISE OF TRANSPARENCY

4
Transparency and Social Life

The Positive and Negative Connotations of Transparency

From its inception, transparency as an ideal has been a moral, political, and legal project. In this project, transparency is considered something good, whereas its lack is bad, dangerous, or dubious. Transparency is thus, regardless of its described conceptual limitations (icono-ambivalence, the hand at work), generally considered something desirable: without transparency we cannot see, with transparency we can. Bentham, for example, saw transparency as a tool for moral mechanics and social engineering. With its inspective architectures, transparency could prevent ill motives from emerging and thus guarantee the legitimacy of governance. In the previous chapter, this was referred to as the transforming gaze.

It is not clear, however, why the gaze would have the power to transform. What is the connection between ill motives, human desires, and transparency? To answer that, we need to discuss thoroughly the premises of the assumed connection. In what ways could transparency have the power to control people's behaviour and change it for the better? Building on the logic of 'understanding is seeing' and concomitant metaphors and myths, transparency enjoys large acceptability. As explained, transparency has been able to absorb an array of virtues and aspirations into its meaning. In this process, its connection with human behaviour and its laws has become more apparent.

The connection between social life and transparency is old: in the era of the Enlightenment, when 'publicity' was still preferred in talking about governance, 'transparency' was already in use to refer to people's acts, speeches, intentions, and thoughts.[1] It is not clear, however, why that is the case. What is the value of transparency when referring to human behaviour? What phenomena can transparency make visible in the context of social life? Is it different from the transparency of different objects, for example? In this chapter, I argue that in social life, the assumed empowerment vested in 'understanding is seeing' has another logic to digest: the way in which human behaviour is or can be seen through transparency, and how people consider it.

[1] Sandrine Baume and Yannis Papadopoulos, 'Transparency: From Bentham's Inventory of Virtuous Effects to Contemporary Evidence-based Skepticism' (2018) 21(2) Critical Review of International Social and Political Philosophy 169, 170–71.

The Transparency Paradox. Ida Koivisto, Oxford University Press. © Ida Koivisto 2022.
DOI: 10.1093/oso/9780192855466.003.0004

Besides being a normative concept, transparency is also used both as a descriptive concept and metaphorically. In its descriptive use—perhaps surprisingly—its connotation is negative, if not pejorative. By the pejorative meaning I mean that the term 'transparency' can also refer to undesired or unauthorized exposure. Transparency's negative connotation is systematically unnoticed or overlooked in current transparency debates. In my view, this connotation is, nonetheless, of decisive importance in understanding how transparency works as a socio-legal ideal. I will show that the duality of connotations ultimately makes it possible to argue that the functioning mechanism of transparency is profoundly human.

Therefore, it is important to notice that in social life, seeing and understanding in the form of transparency is not always considered desirable.[2] This is precisely because transparency is not only a virtue but is, under certain circumstances, a sign of failure. This contention has its roots in a linguistic observation, available for anyone to test: 'You are so transparent!' or 'I can see through you!', we might say, when we notice someone's failure comes across in a certain, predetermined way. In that case, the attempt is implausible to the extent that we cannot but see the 'truer truth', or the 'really real' behind that leaking façade, or at least we think we do. Transparency can be a function of the revelatory gaze.

Counterintuitively, we resent this revelation. We prefer to keep hidden motives hidden. If someone is unintentionally transparent, we do not appreciate it; in such cases, transparency means failure and weakness instead of a virtuous demeanour. In fact, unintended transparency is probably one of our worst nightmares: the dream of being naked in the schoolyard is a universal one. It would be even more horrible if someone could read our thoughts.[3] At the same time, in philosophy, transparency is sometimes portrayed as a dream, suddenly rendering visibility to places which in our everyday life would be impossible.[4] Thus, in a curious way, transparency in social life is both a dream and a nightmare.

[2] Jan Teurlings and Markus Stauff, 'Introduction: The Transparency Issue' (2014) 14(1) Cultural Studies ↔ Critical Methodologies 3, 4 (hereafter Teurlings and Stauff, 'The Transparency Issue'): 'The value of transparency is paradoxical: There are some cases in which transparency is very clearly defined as a danger—most people want to keep their private data private. In many more cases, however, the positive value of transparency is simply assumed—transparency even becomes an imperative. It looks as if, depending on different kinds of entities and issues, transparency has to either be complete or completely rejected. There seems to be no in-between.'

[3] It seems that our fear of being transparent is often unwarranted. Thomas Gilovich, Victoria Husted Medvec, and Kenneth Stavisky demonstrate in their study that people often overestimate the extent in which their internal states 'leak out' to others. One conclusion is, thus, that we are better liars than we think. Thomas Gilovich, Victoria Husted Medvec, and Kenneth Stavisky, 'The Illusion of Transparency: Biased Assessments of Others' Ability to Read One's Emotional States' (1998) 75 Journal of Personality and Social Psychology 332, 345. However, along with refining technology, such as brain imaging, the question of mental privacy has emerged. For example, see Amihud Gilead, 'Can Brain Imaging Breach Our Mental Privacy?' (2015) 6(2) Review of Philosophy and Psychology 275; and Sarah D Richmond, Geraint Rees, and Sarah J L Edwards (eds), *I Know What You're Thinking: Brain Imaging and Mental Privacy* (Oxford University Press 2012).

[4] Manfred Schneider, 'The Dream of Transparency: Aquinas, Rousseau, Sartre' in Emmanuel Alloa and Dieter Thomä (eds), *Transparency, Society and Subjectivity: Critical Perspectives* (Palgrave

In this chapter, I expand the conceptual analysis of transparency and discuss it as a metaphor in human relations. Unlike in chapter two, in which I discussed transparency as a medium, here, I discuss the use of transparency as a value judgement. How does the transparency metaphor work in the context of our humanity and in social interaction? What kind of effects can it have on us? To what extent are we transparent to each other and what follows from that? This discussion is important because I argue that the legitimacy-inducing effect that transparency promises in governance contexts builds on the analogy of how it works in social life.[5] What are the social mechanisms that will sometimes lead us to praise transparency, sometimes to treat it with contempt?

This chapter is organized in the following manner. First, I approach the question of how transparency is performed through the intentionality of our social behaviour. I find Erving Goffman's concept of impression management particularly helpful in this analysis. Second, I will look more closely at the theatre imagery that impression management presupposes and examine its connections with transparency. Third, I investigate the motives of keeping certain things hidden in social life: the protection of strategy and the avoidance of shame. Fourth, I ask whether we are transparent to ourselves. Lastly, I summarize the chapter and argue that despite transparency's modern status as the cultural signifier of neutrality, in fact, there is nothing neutral about transparency.

The Performativity of Social Life

The Ethics of Transparency in Interpersonal Relations

As mentioned, the key to understanding how transparency works as an ideal is to look at its pejorative connotation. Namely, unintentional transparency can be highly problematic in social interaction. It makes one appear in a way one does not want to appear, without any control or agency. The reason for this is that socially acceptable behaviour, thoughts, or words could not be filtered from trivial, banal, embarrassing, or downright shameful ones. The problem is that the disclosure of our possible primitive or otherwise socially unacceptable temptations and desires would undermine the credibility of our conscious good intentions and choices of action. The assumption is that individuals should be consistent in their thoughts

Macmillan 2018). See also Manfred Schneider, *Transparenztraum. Literatur, Politik, Medien und das Unmögliche* (Matthes und Seitz Berlin 2013).

[5] Compare Leopold Ringel, 'Boundaries of Visibility in the Age of Transparency: An Integrative Conceptualization' in Leopold Ringel, Petra Hiller, and Charlene Zietsma (eds), *Toward Permeable Boundaries of Organizations? Research in the Sociology of Organizations*, vol 57 (Emerald 2018) 55.

and action, and if their inconsistency is exposed, this is frowned upon. In that case, a person may be considered fake and inauthentic, even untruthful or deceitful.

Sigmund Freud has also recognized the meaning of control in our social behaviour in his classic work on *Civilization and its Discontents* (1929). In it, he contends that our culture, which is supposed to make us happy, is at the same time causing anxiety by defining the ways in which we can pursue happiness. Importantly, our animal instincts need to be suppressed.[6] For civilized social harmony to prevail, much must be left unsaid, undone, and unnoticed. Eviatar Zerubavel, for one, argues that attentional avoidance presupposes certain norms of dis-attention. For example, as a result of various taboos against looking, we typically refrain from staring at people, thereby displaying 'civil inattention' and avoiding 'uncivil attention'.[7] One could even argue that the whole process of socialization is underpinned by this regulative ideal. Under the imaginary condition of total transparency, a universal revelation of all of our temptations and urges would make saving face—our prestige or dignity in social situations[8]—impossible, as there would be no face to be saved.[9] I will come back to this point later in this chapter.

Importantly, however, voluntary or intentional transparency, also conceptualized as honesty, candour, openness, sincerity, etc is not subject to this contempt. On the contrary, it is often celebrated honourably, although it may entail healthy suspicions of the need for that kind of labelling. According to Lionel Trilling, sincerity is a way of characterizing a relationship between words and interior states.[10] The idea of sincerity—I would suggest that this applies also to neighbouring terms such as candour or honesty, and indeed, positively connoting

[6] Sigmund Freud, *Civilization and its Discontents* (WW Norton and Company Inc. 1966). Thomas Nagel also argues that concealment is necessary to our very civilization: 'Concealment includes not only secrecy and deception but also reticence and non-acknowledgment. There is much more going on inside us all the time than we are willing to express, and civilization would be impossible if we could all read each other's minds.' Thomas Nagel, *Concealment and Exposure and Other Essays* (Oxford University Press 2002) 4 (hereafter Nagel, 'Concealment and Exposure'). For instance, Žižek has questioned the basic idea of Freud's book; since Freud, the rules governing acceptable behaviour have become more liberal in Western societies. However, the goal of happiness has been sustained. In addition, what is considered normal is understandable only within that culture. See Slavoj Žižek, 'Nature and its Discontents' (2008) 117(37) SubStance 37.

[7] Eviatar Zerubavel, *Hidden in Plain Sight: The Social Structure of Irrelevance* (Oxford University Press 2015) 60 (hereafter Zerubavel, 'Hidden in Plain Sight'). Interestingly, certain attentional taboos are even prescribed by law. For instance, when screening job applicants, employers are legally required to effectively ignore their age, skin colour, sex, marital status, religion, sexual orientation, etc and to formally exclude those variables from their considerations to ensure equal employment opportunity. Similarly, under the exclusionary rule, unlawfully obtained evidence is to be dismissed by courts, judges, and juries.

[8] Erving Goffman, *Interaction Ritual: Essays in Face-to-Face Behavior* (Pantheon Books 1982) 5: 'The term *face* may be defined as the positive social value a person effectively claims for himself by the line others assume he has taken during a particular contact. Face is an image of self delineated in terms of approved social attributes—albeit an image that others may share, as when a person makes a good showing of his profession or religion by making a good showing for himself.'

[9] This presupposes a split subject, who may have conflicting desires and aspirations. That, of course, goes back to a psychoanalytical interpretation of the human character.

[10] Lionel Trilling, *Sincerity and Authenticity* (Harvard University Press 1972) 26.

transparency—seems to propose a hierarchical relation between these two things, words and thoughts: thoughts seem to come first, and thus determine and impose a limit on the words. Hence, the concept of sincerity is premised on a clear distinction between words and thoughts, as parallel discourses (interior and exterior), which either could or could not match up.[11]

Furthermore, the idea is that the truth of the interiority of a person can be reflected in words, and these words can be considered an authentic representation of the thought: the words thus become a medium, and as such, perhaps, subject to the mentioned chagrin over mediation. Ideally, as Webb Keane argues, if the prior thought and words expressing them would match up, language would become transparent. Nothing significant would remain of the material forms or social origins of the word, allowing the unmediated truth to reveal itself. As a language ideology, the concept of sincerity also seeks the authority of words over thoughts in that matching. To take words as insincere is to cast doubt on them. If praise is considered insincere, that relationship of authority would be flipped around.[12] If words and actions are in contradiction, we tend to believe the latter.

Indeed, seen like this, positively connoting transparency needs to be intentional, as the speaker would make sure that the words would loyally reflect the pre-existing thought, making a 'good copy' of the thought (mimesis1), thus functioning as a transparent medium between them. However, unlike transparency, we do not use the concepts of honesty or sincerity descriptively. As a normative concept, sincerity implies intentionality, and the aptitude to choose this intention, a good or virtuous character. This conscious matching or mediating of thoughts and words is considered desirable: as a rule, we are not indifferent towards it. In Keane's words:

> [s]incerity says something not just about speech, or about speech and thought, but also something about the character of the speaker. That is why one also hears of persons, and not just particular acts of speaking, being described as sincere.[13]

Thus, the speaker's endeavours to use sincere words, or, to speak his mind, as the saying goes, would be considered a token of that virtuous character. Why? Because, following Keane, positively connoting transparency is essentially interactive. By being transparent or sincere, I am not only producing words that loyally reflect my internal states, but I am producing them for *you*. I trust you; therefore, I make a confession. I am making my internal thoughts available to you through external, publicly available expressions, thus ensuring the accurate mimesis of my internal state of mind in words. Positively connoting transparency could thus even be seen

[11] Webb Keane, 'Sincerity, "Modernity," and the Protestants' (2002) 17(1) Cultural Anthropology 65, 74–76 (hereafter Keane, 'Sincerity, "Modernity," and the Protestants').
[12] ibid.
[13] ibid, 75.

as a form of public accountability to others. Thus, transparency could not be, in Keane's words, understood only as ideological, because the interactive dimension presupposes concrete practices.[14] Indeed, in social life, transparency is all about concrete practices and their strategic implications. In other words, it is not enough to live in the condition of transparency. In addition, one must also relate to one's own transparency, and convince others of it.[15]

Largely, sincerity and honesty are virtues associated with transparency, as explained above. Still, honesty or transparency can never be complete. Not all internal states can be translated into accurate verbal expressions because of the mentioned interactivity of transparency and the covert laws that govern it. We do not only attempt to create public accountability with our speeches. We also have other desires, such as maintaining social harmony or gaining social status. On many occasions, these may outweigh the desire to be transparent, sincere, or candid. Additionally, total transparency, even intentional, would mean social suicide. As mentioned, social life requires restraining impulses. By claiming transparency, we metaphorically create a window to our soul, if you will, and by so doing, we indirectly keep other areas in the darkness.

Impression Management

Hence, we can also reformulate the question of intentionality of transparency as a question of performativity. Positively connoting transparency requires conscious exposure and awareness of its potential social consequences; it overlaps with ethics. We can deepen this idea by following Georg Simmel's argument. He claims that one can never really know another because that would require knowing every thought and feeling of that person. To the extent that knowing another person is possible, however, taking a perspective is necessary. It enables looking at that person from a certain vantage point. In consequence, we only see fragments of that other person and indeed, those fragments are largely curated: 'the unity so formed necessarily depends upon that portion of the Other which our standpoint toward him permits us to see'.[16] To translate this idea into the vocabulary of transparency, intentional transparency means allowing others to see us in a certain way, from a certain angle. Obviously, we also see things which are not consciously shown to us (cf the revelatory gaze). However, those things are necessarily omitted from the scope of intentional transparency.

14 ibid, 74–76.

15 Jean Starobinski, *Jean Jacques Rousseau: Transparency and Obstruction* (Arthur Goldhammer tr, University of Chicago Press 1988) (hereafter Starobinski, 'Jean Jacques Rousseau').

16 Georg Simmel, 'The Sociology of Secrecy and Secret Societies' (1906) 11(4) American Journal of Sociology 441, 442 (hereafter Simmel, 'The Sociology of Secrecy').

Erving Goffman discusses the theme of one's appearing to others in his seminal work of social psychology, *The Presentation of Self in Everyday Life* (1959; 1990). Goffman's point of departure is precisely that of a performative self, a person who is in control of her presentation to others. Although Goffman does not discuss transparency in his book, his theory is easy to apply to that theme. Goffman's theory is built around a dramaturgical metaphor of a theatre. He approaches the social self as a performance, as a show addressed to a particular audience.[17] That is to say, every person is an actor of some sort, trying to control the appearance, demeanour, and impression she gives to others and, at the same time, read the current situation to readjust the performance to its requirements.

Everyone is thus both an actor and a spectator. The goal is to induce, consciously or unconsciously, a desired reaction in the audience, to gain the audience's approval, affection, or to otherwise govern their perception.[18] This idea is deep and subversive as it runs counter to the idea of an authentic self that would be blind to a social context, often called for in our contemporary discourses. In today's language, 'Just be yourself', is a frequently heard platitude. In addition, this wish for authenticity was already behind Rousseau's festival as an allegory of desirable social interaction, instead of the logic of the theatre that he despised.[19] Goffman, nonetheless, particularly highlights the meaning of theatricality and the situatedness of the self it requires. We perform ourselves and that performance is largely dictated by the audience and its real or imagined expectations for us (cf the transforming gaze).

A theatre has a stage and a backstage, and of course, an audience. This architectural arrangement is also adopted in Goffman's metaphor. In it, the performance takes place on the 'frontstage' of a theatre, whereas the 'backstage' is not meant for the eyes of the audience.[20] On the backstage, the performance is both prepared and recovered from. The social self as a performance presupposes a time and place for acting as well as not acting. Throughout the book, Goffman emphasizes the importance of an agreed definition upon the situation; both the actor and the audience agree on what is happening.[21] That is logical, because a theatre play is an

[17] Goffman's definition of performance is as follows: '[a]ll the activity of a given participant on a given occasion which serves to influence in any way any of the other participants'. Erving Goffman, *The Presentation of Self in Everyday Life* (Penguin Books Ltd 1990) 26 (hereafter Goffman, 'The Presentation of Self in Everyday Life').

[18] ibid.

[19] Starobinski, 'Jean Jacques Rousseau' (n 15) 95. Rousseau called for the metaphor of a festival instead of that of a theatre. In the latter, dispersed actor-spectator constellations would prevail, and both of the positions would be shared by all: 'The theater is to the festival as opacity is to transparency'.

[20] Goffman argues, that 'we often find a division into back region, where a performance of a routine is prepared, and front region, where the performance is presented. Access to these regions is controlled in order to prevent the audience form seeing backstage and to prevent outsiders form coming into a performance that is not addressed to them'. Goffman, 'The Presentation of Self in Everyday Life' (n 17) 231.

[21] Goffman, 'The Presentation of Self in Everyday Life' (n 17) 15: 'Let us now turn from the others to the point of view of the individual who presents himself before them. He may wish them to think highly of him, or to think that he thinks highly of them, or to perceive how in fact he feels towards them, or to obtain no clear-cut impression; he may wish to ensure sufficient harmony so that the interaction can be sustained, or to defraud, get rid of, confuse, mislead, antagonize, or insult them. Regardless of the

agreement between the performance and the spectators. The performers perform, the audience experiences.

On the one hand, the audience is needed to validate the performance: '[w]hen an individual plays a part he implicitly requests his observers to take seriously the impression that is fostered before them'.[22] Goffman calls this impression management.[23] On the other hand, the performance is also deeply personal.[24] We believe that our personality matches up with our performance. In that sense, we 'are' our performances, although we also are not. We choose how we want to appear and work towards consistency. However, the backstage is an equally 'true' component about us. That also includes the parts which are omitted or suppressed from the performance. Thus, the backstage self is perhaps less consistent and less glamorous but richer in elements.

So, if the social self is essentially performative, are all the performances equally credible? I argue that this is not really the case. This is visible in our metaphoric use of theatre vocabulary. When we blame someone for 'putting on an act' or being pretentious, and in that sense being pejoratively transparent, we actually make an aesthetic judgement on bad acting, or failed impression management.[25] We can see the backstage behind the curtain, and as explained, that is not meant for the eyes of the audience. Therefore, the question is not about whether someone is acting in a social context, but how appropriately, easily, and plausibly that is done.[26] Following Goffman's reasoning it could be argued that everybody acts, but not equally skilfully. Next, I look more closely at the meaning of theatre imagery immanent to the idea of the performative self. I argue that it structures the different connotations of transparency in social life.

particular objective which the individual has in mind, and of his motive for having this objective, it will be in his interests to control the conduct of the others, especially their responsive treatment of him. This control is achieved largely by influencing the definition of the situation which the others come to formulate, and he can influence this definition by expressing himself in such a way as to give them the kind of impression that will lead them to act voluntarily in accordance with his own plan.'

22 Goffman, 'The Presentation of Self in Everyday Life' (n 17) 28.

23 ibid, 203–30.

24 ibid, 28–29, see also 210.

25 Interestingly, theatre language in general tends to be pejorative. See Jonas Barish, who analyses the negative attitudes which theatre is historically subject to in Western thought. As he asks on the very cover of his book, 'Why has theater aroused such passionate antipathy over the centuries? Why has it been attacked not only by straight-laced moralists but by major philosophers—Plato, Saint Augustine, Rousseau, Nietzsche? Does their hostility toward the theater point to a fundamental human failing?' This antipathy is clearly visible in language. Unlike adjectives alluding to other art forms, epithets, terms, and expressions borrowed from the world of theatre seem to be almost systematically belittling: theatrical, melodramatic, stagey, make a scene, putting on an act, putting on a performance, making a spectacle of oneself, etc. None of them evokes positive associations. This effect is not restricted to English. Jonas Barish, *The Anti-Theatrical Prejudice* (University of California Press 1981) 1.

26 In assessing the performance, there is also an interesting aspect of entitlement. Goffman, 'The Presentation of Self in Everyday Life' (n 17) 66: 'Sometimes when we ask whether a fostered impression is true or false we really mean to ask whether or not the performer is authorized to give the performance in question, and are not primarily concerned with the actual performance itself.'

Performativity, Transparency, and the Implications of Theatre Imagery

As described, the idea of the performativity of the self is based on and inspired by an image of the theatre. The implications of this metaphoric conceptualization are worth a closer look beyond its immediate social psychological application. As mentioned, a theatre is a powerful image which entails an entire vocabulary with concomitant functions: there is a stage, a backstage, a curtain, performance, audience, and the credibility, impressiveness, or authenticity of performance. This imagery matters regarding theorizing transparency at least in three, intertwined senses.

First, it seems that the successfulness of our social life depends on our capability of creating and upholding an appropriate persona. Even though 'persona' is not a part of Goffman's vocabulary in a strict sense, the performative self, according to my understanding, means roughly the same thing. It also belongs to theatre vocabulary. According to the Oxford dictionary, persona means '1. The aspect of someone's character that is presented to or perceived by others: her public persona; 1.1. A role or character adopted by an author or an actor'.[27] This duality of meanings is hardly coincidental but analogous. A character does not necessarily need to be performed in a theatre or a film. Neither does a role or a character have any bearing if there are no eyes to see it—regardless of whether those eyes belong to a spectator in a theatre, or to a work colleague, for example.

The origin of the word 'persona' further accentuates this connection. The word comes from Latin. It signifies a theatrical mask, a cover, or a costume. As such, it creates a showable face in rather concrete terms.[28] This idea is also negatively portrayed in the metaphor of 'losing face'; when the mask is removed the person behind it will exposed and the character is lost. The mask is thus a constitutive element of the character. Furthermore, the very term 'person' is part of same etymological root as persona, which makes visible the importance of the social self. According to one explanation—there are others too—' "person" may be related to Latin *personare* "to sound through" (i.e. the mask as something spoken through and perhaps amplifying the voice)',[29] which would make an interesting sensory counterpart for transparency as 'seeing through'.

[27] Lexico, 'Definition of Persona in English' <www.oxforddictionaries.com/us/definition/american_english/persona> accessed 30 June 2021. In psychology, it originates from Jungian thought and may be contrasted to 'anima'. Carl Gustav Jung, *Two Essays on Analytical Psychology* (2nd ed, Princeton University Press 1972) 192: persona is 'a kind of mask, designed on the one hand to make a definite impression upon others, and on the other to conceal the true nature of the individual'. He further associates persona with his idea of a collective psyche.

[28] Interestingly, on the cover of the book *Transparency in International Law* is a picture of a decorative mask. See Ulrich Preuβ, Andrea Bianchi, and Anne Peters, *Transparency in International Law* (Cambridge University Press 2013) 820 (hereafter Preuβ, Bianchi, and Peters, 'Transparency in International Law').

[29] 'Online Etymology Dictionary—person' <www.etymonline.com/index.php?term=person> accessed 30 June 2021. See also Byung-Chul Han, *The Transparency Society* (Stanford University Press

Even if wearing a mask or displaying a persona may sound dishonest, it is crucial for appearing and functioning as a coherent agent in the social world. As Simmel argues, we should not confuse the ethically negative value of lying with the direct positive sociological significance of untruthfulness.[30] As explained, upholding social harmony necessarily requires that we restrict our immediate impulses, and in many cases that requires us not speaking our minds, or, at least, heavily editing what we say and do.

However, the meaning of a persona does not end there. In addition, people may have different personas, different masks for different situations, enabling a flexibly performative identity.[31] In fact, that is necessary. However, the choice and changing of the mask depends on the non-performing or private aspect of the self, whether this is conscious or not.[32] Goffman argues that the self on the metaphorical backstage is the part of a person which is not performative. On the backstage, 'the suppressed facts make an appearance'.[33] Conversely, when a person enters the social realm, she puts a mask on and becomes conscious of the particular audience and its laws; she is exposed to a gaze.[34]

Second, the idea of public and private spheres is an essential part of the theatre imaginary. This goes both for a persona as a showable face, but also for theatre as a space for the performance to take place, including also the audience and the other potential stage personnel. Namely, a constitutive part of a theatre, the curtain, clearly makes the distinction between the public or the performative and the private or the hidden operations of the play. Its function is thus to govern visibilities and enable coherent performance. It also influences the reactions and the expectations of the audience. The non-public-eye-intended operations remain concealed behind the curtain.

2015) 35 (hereafter Han, 'The Transparency Society'). This may hold also institutionally. Watt argues: '[The] mask is the epitome of legal covering. The hand is a powerful medium of social communication but to read a face is to read a mind as directly, probably more directly as a book that the same mind might write. The interposing of an artificial mask between the face the reader, the viewer is therefore an imperious attempt to control the means of communication. It will hardly surprise us then, to discover that our public face, our social personhood and legal personality is a construct conceived in terms of a mask. *Persona* is the Latin word for the type of mask that was used in classical drama going back to the theatre of the Ancient Greeks. The law struggles to hear and to see the nuances of our inner being and so prefers to deal with the abstract superficiality of a legal personality. Even corporations have a legal personality and it is only with reluctance that the courts will occasionally lift the so-called "corporate veil" to reveal the deeper reality of the thing. The mask of legal personality requires the social performance on the law's terms.' Gary Watt, 'Law Suits: Clothing as the Image of Law' in Leif Dahlberg, Klaus Stierstorfer, and Daniela Carpi (eds), *Visualizing Law and Authority: Essays on Legal Aesthetics* (Walter de Gruyter 2012) 38 (hereafter Watt, 'Law Suits').

30 Simmel, 'The Sociology of Secrecy' (n 16) 448.

31 Goffman calls this 'audience segregation'. Goffman, 'The Presentation of Self in Everyday Life' (n 17) 57. If audience segregation fails, it entails impression management problems, see 139.

32 ibid, 63–64.

33 ibid, 114.

34 ibid, 114–40.

In a way, theatre is a place of organized voyeurism, as George Rodosthenous claims. This can be argued, although it is based on a performance, an act of pretence, that is, and in that way it cannot really expose things which would not be intended to be seen. Rodosthenous explains that the voyeur seeks no active engagement with performers but with the spectacle. This voyeurism is intellectual and multi-sensory in nature. Theatre makes voyeurism possible by making it an acceptable form of art in which the audience removes its forbidden attributes through collective viewing. Rodosthenous wonders whether it all starts with the box office: viewers choose where to sit, how close they want to be to the experience of viewing. In that way, the box office functions as the facilitator of the voyeuristic exchange.[35]

Through this voyeuristic aspect, transparency also becomes relevant. Transparency makes theatrical voyeurism adopt a new level. If the curtain was transparent, its very function would be undercut. As it ever is—at least to my knowledge—transparent, here, transparency may become a synonym for exposure. Accordingly, transparency might be seen as an opened curtain, opened either intentionally by the actors or other personnel, exposing the backstage in a controlled manner, or unintentionally, by someone else in an unauthorized way. However, it is important to notice that every spectator in a theatre is aware of the existence of the backstage and the necessary preparatory operations which take place there. It is fair to argue that nobody is under the belief that the performance is all there is to it. Instead, it is commonly understood that a successful performance is underpinned by cautious preparation which is not intended to be seen. This does not cause objection; it is accepted as a structural feature of theatre as an art form.

Third, the opened curtain or a lifted veil entails questions of truth and reality. The concealing function of a curtain, a mask or a veil may cause suspicions of the 'reality' of the performance, and whether there is a 'truer truth' behind the created show. Is exposed reality less relevant or less true than the concealed one, especially when we know that the operations behind the curtain exist and matter? As this is a spontaneously natural way of thinking, the idea of 'truth' about a person or object of another kind, residing on the other side of the curtain, may be too simplistic.

This idea could be interpreted as a lifted veil conception of truth or reality. Jean Starobinski summarizes well the problems of this conception. According to him, the metaphor of a lifted veil is the figurative counterpart of a realist theory of knowledge. That means an image which is employed in a naïvely optimistic fashion, which pretends to see the true visage behind the mask, to capture the 'thing in itself'.[36] In a similar vein, Teuerlings and Stauff argue that transparency is not an act

[35] George Rodosthenous, 'Introduction: Staring at the Forbidden: Legitimizing Voyeurism' in G Rodothenous (ed), *Theatre as Voyeurism: The Pleasures of Watching* (Palgrave Macmillan 2015) 1, 16 (hereafter Rodosthenous, 'Staring at the Forbidden').

[36] Starobinski, 'Jean Jacques Rousseau' (n 15) 74.

of showing or distributing a picture of a certain object. According to them, reality, 'as any more than [a] banal notion of ideology concedes', cannot be exposed by lifting a veil. Namely, the 'reality itself' is intricate and consists also of hidden areas and invisibility. Hence, any kind of mediating entity only adds to the impossibility of full transparency.[37]

Strikingly, it seems that transparency as a normative concept and its metaphorical promise is based exactly on this kind of realist theory of knowledge; it underpins the iconoclastic aspect of transparency. However, transparency necessarily includes the described icono-ambivalent logic, which, however, does not belong to the ideological self-understanding of transparency as an ideal. If we do not subscribe to this understanding, the truth-revealing function of transparency would be questioned.

Therefore, the allure of the idea of a lifted veil or an opened curtain as a method of accessing truth needs to be critically reviewed. Taken too optimistically, it may lead to something that I would call naïve iconoclasm. According to it, façades would always be fake or less real or less true than the veiled reality. However, the social self or the conscious performance need not be any less truthful than the operations 'behind the scenes'; a mask, a veil, or a curtain do not only obstruct or cover but create an alternative appearance, which takes into account the expectations of the viewer, either by adhering to them or deviating from them. Through a mask one has access to more agency. It enables emancipation from the inevitability of the forces out of one's control.

To the extent we can juxtapose the curtain, mask, or a veil with an image, we come back to the idea of iconoclash, the oscillation between belief and suspicion towards an image (cf icono-ambivalence). As argued, all three implications of the theatre metaphor are entangled; they are all united by the same idea of truth, whether is it 'natural' or constructed, or make-believe, designed to be seen or not. As Mersch argues:

> With an emphasis on the 'through,' going through a medium means effectuating an effect in the mode of performativity. It follows that performativity constitutes the condition that both makes things public and precedes and determines rationality. In the end, transparency exists only within economies of making transparent, working through or 'through composing,' which implies that transparency

[37] Teurlings and Stauff, 'The Transparency Issue' (n 2) 5. See also Luc Boltanski, *Mysteries & Conspiracies: Detective Stories, Spy Novels and the Making of Modern Societies* (Polity Press 2014) 13, who approaches the theme of conspiracy from the viewpoint of unveiling: 'A conspiracy is an object that is only perceived as such—as distinguished from ordinary relations—from outside. It is distinguished from ordinary relations only by the operation of *unveiling* that sets an apparent but fictitious reality and a hidden reality side by side, on the same level. This is why the moment when the conspiracy is unmasked has the properties of a *coup de théâtre*, a dramatic turn of events'. (Emphases original). That 'coup de théâtre' can be compared to anagnorisis, discussed in chapter three.

> is neither a state of being nor an attribute, but at best a medially produced operation that is bound up with its own kind of opacity.[38]

In the end, the call for exposure is a call of simplification if not reduction: a totality would be reduced to its constitutive elements, regardless of whether the holistic picture would be lost by this reductive act (cf the projecting gaze). Indeed, as Walter Benjamin states, truth is not a matter of exposure of the secret, but a revelation that does justice to it.[39] How we perceive what we see and how we are supposed to perceive it. In the following, I discuss some of the motives of concealment in social life.

Motivations for Concealment

Protecting Strategy

As explained before, in a social context, positive transparency takes the form of confession. Through confession, on the one hand, the confessor deems someone, or a group of people worthy of knowing the content of her mind. This makes the confession a question of ethics, legitimacy, and trust. On the other hand, however, it is not easy to notice that we do not want everything to be transparent: there are many motives that block transparency in social settings. As I am going to argue, self-control, an ability to deliver a credible performance, or, to manage an impression successfully, becomes a higher-rank value than gaining extensive knowledge about the particular social context.

The preference of the optimal level of transparency is also portrayed in our intrinsic aversion towards 'too much information', or 'oversharing'. It stems from our tacit recognition of the fact that social reality sets implicit boundaries for the appropriate revelation. In the following, I will argue that certain human motivations in particular underpin the avoidance of oversharing—mistaking the extent of the socially acceptable revelation—and more importantly, involuntary transparency. Although many individual reasons for these may exist, for example, protecting someone from knowing a disturbing truth, I claim that there are, however, two

[38] Dieter Mersch, 'Obfuscating Transparency' in Emmanuel Alloa and Dieter Thomä (eds), *Transparency, Society, Subjectivity: Critical Perspectives* (Palgrave Macmillan 2018) 266.

[39] Walter Benjamin, *The Origin of German Tragic Drama* (John Osborne tr, Verso Books 1998) 31. Also, Michael Taussig, *Defacement: Public Secrecy and the Labor of the Negative* (Stanford University Press 1999) 8. Interestingly, Walter Benjamin also conflates the object being veiled with its beauty: 'The beautiful is neither the veil nor the veiled object but rather the object in its veil. Unveiled, however, it would prove to be infinitely inconspicuous [*unscheinbar*] .... For that object, to which in the last instance the veil is essential, is not characterized otherwise. Since only the beautiful and outside is nothing—veiling or being veiled—can be essential, the divine ground of the being of beauty lies in the secret'. Han, 'The Transparency Society' (n 29) 21, citing Walter Benjamin, *Selected Writings: 1913–1926*, vol 1 (Marcus Bullock and Michael W Jennings eds, Harvard University Press 2004) 351.

main negative outcomes of involuntary transparency: the exposing strategy and losing face. Through their analysis, the voluntary nature of transparency as the necessary precondition of a positively charged value becomes even more apparent.

Let us concentrate on the question of strategy first. Here, I approach strategy on a general level. By strategy, I mean a plan of actions towards a goal, which other people also pursue. Why is it important that strategy is not accidently revealed by involuntary transparency? I argue that the logic behind it is competition: winning and losing. Namely, the ability to conceal one's certain, strategic motives is especially essential in zero-sum-game situations, in which the agents—whether individuals, companies, or institutions of another kind—compete instead of cooperating with each other. Simultaneously, the failure to conceal strategy epitomizes the notion that one's gain is the other's loss. Thus, by being involuntarily transparent to the competitor the agent spoils or at least severely jeopardizes her chance of winning.

Gamblers use the term 'tell' to refer to the risk of revealing their cards by subtle facial expressions or body movements. Therefore, poker players, for instance, use sunglasses; they try to hide their expressions. Not 'telling' is, however, difficult. Simmel argues that to anyone with fine psychological perceptions, people betray themselves and their private thoughts and characteristics in numerous ways. Not only in spite of the attempts to do that but often precisely due to that fact. It is the price they pay for trying to anxiously to guard themselves. He writes:

> The greedy spying upon every unguarded word; the boring persistence of inquiry as to the meaning of every slight action, or tone of voice; what may be inferred from such and such expressions; what the blush at the mention of a given name may betray—all this does not overstep the boundary of external discretion; it is entirely the labor of one's own mind and therefore apparently within the unquestionable rights of the agent.[40]

Indeed, our personas are constantly leaking information, although that leaking may be very subtle and hard to detect. In the context of competition, the failure not to tell, to leak information in one way or another, equates to concrete loss of the game and subsequently money. More generally, the so-called game theory employs that rationality. It departs from the idea of asymmetric distribution of information and its effects on strategic behaviour.[41] It is based on the calculations of the other agents' potential moves and their effect on the selection

[40] Simmel, 'The Sociology of Secrecy' (n 16) 456.

[41] Much economic modelling is based on the idea. Subsequently, 'transparency' also belongs to the vocabulary of economics, for instance in the forms of 'market transparency' or 'price transparency'. See, for example, Robert Bloomfield and Maureen O'Hara, 'Market Transparency: Who Wins and Who Loses?' (1999) 2(1) The Review of Financial Studies 5.

of the best possible strategy. Although I am not concentrating on game theory here, it provides a valuable perspective by showing the detriments of involuntary transparency.

Let us take another example. In the context of international relations, states may be considered players of a game. They want to know each other's cards in order to gain international leverage. The desire to know the other players' intentions is where intelligence and espionage come into the picture. Secrecy is both their reason and operational principle.[42] What is publicly known already implies what is not known, an agenda implies a non-agenda, maybe even a hidden agenda. Indeed, this resembles a large-scale card game: every player knows that the others have cards whose content they are not aware of. In a way, that makes the whole game worth playing, and indeed, a game to begin with.

The asymmetry of knowledge constitutes an apparatus of mutual cynicism. The agents in this context want to conceal their own strategy and know the other's strategy, at best so that the other one is not conscious of being revealed. This theme was well dramatized in the film *Imitation Game* (2014). It told the story of British mathematician Alan Turing and his team of cryptographers during the Second World War. Their task was to crack Germany's encrypted communication system Enigma. In the film, a crucial dramatic tension was built around an ethical conundrum: how should the team act after having cracked the code? The team decided to keep the success of their task concealed. This caused some collateral damage, for instance, the death of one team member's brother. However, revealing the de-coding would have been even more detrimental: it would probably have caused Germany to change its encryption technique, prolonging the war and costing more lives.

Thus, involuntary transparency in the context of protecting strategy is an effort to keep the boundaries of the persona, if you will, intact: a secret is safe only so long as its keepers manage to keep it that way. That is the only way that the keepers can really control how to proceed. A strategy in a game or in some political situation, for example, cannot be leaked to those who would take advantage of the leaked information and use it to their own benefit. Transparency, thus, may be misused. At this point, it would be easy to draw the following conclusion: transparency is good when agents are acting *with* and bad when they are acting *against* each other. However, that would be a dangerous simplification. Namely, for transparency to be kept in high regard it needs to be controlled beyond clearly strategic situations, even in the context of cooperation or neutral social interaction. This will be discussed in the following.

[42] Ullrich Preuβ, 'Transparency in International Law' (2014) 12 International Journal of Constitutional Law 820: 'Note that a state's spying on another country is not a wrongful act under international law; it is supposed to be an indispensable instrument of protecting state security.'

Avoiding Shame

I next delve into a second major motive for upholding a persona and avoiding involuntary transparency. I argue that unintentional transparency as signifying a lack of control is avoided, because, in addition to losing a game, as described, it is closely bound to feelings of shame and embarrassment. I argue that it is shame that may follow when we lose control of our self-presentation, and it adopts elements we wish it would not. Shame is a social feeling which undermines the worth and honour of a person in the eyes of a community, stripping her from gained social status. It can be a highly painful experience to an individual and it is often described, as noted, by using the metaphor of losing face.[43] What happens if our persona becomes discredited?

As mentioned, revealed nakedness constitutes the archetypal allegory of the emergence of shame; nakedness is subject to the revelatory gaze.[44] This is also mythically recognized.[45] This, for instance, is interestingly addressed in H C Andersen's famous story of the Emperor's new clothes. In it, a child is in a decisive position. The child alone speaks out that the Emperor is not wearing any clothes, thus breaking the implicit collective agreement of pretending otherwise.[46] The Emperor, in order to save face, continues as if nothing has happened and as if he were not naked. He acts as though he still has control over his self-presentation. What is more, in the story, the shame is triggered specifically by the external eye and its internalization. Something in the concomitant context transforms the innocent, (fallaciously) chosen nakedness into something shameful.

Shame makes a person wanting to hide away from judging or derisive gazes—or gazes in general—disappear. It could also be approached as an injury to the persona. Shame may result from the revelatory gaze, when something unintended is revealed. In a similar vein, Thomas Nagel argues that the conventions of privacy and reticence serve a valuable function. First, they keep us out of each other's faces. Secondly—and more importantly—they give us some control over the face we present to the world. We do not want to reveal ourselves totally to strangers, even when we would not be afraid of their hostility, disgust, or disapproval. Nagel goes even further and maintains that naked exposure itself, regardless of whether it arouses disapproval or not, is disqualifying. The boundary between what we expose and what we do not, and some control over that boundary is one of the core attributes of our humanity.[47]

[43] Erving Goffman, *Interaction Ritual: Essays in Face-to-Face Behavior* (Pantheon Books 1982) 5–45.

[44] Nagel, 'Concealment and Exposure' (n 6) 16: '[h]umans clothe themselves, in one way or another, even if it is only with paint, offering a self-presentation rather than their nakedness to the public gaze'.

[45] Revealed nakedness—in the sense of suddenly understanding its inappropriateness and inherent shamefulness—was also a central consequence of the fall of man in the Bible. Before that, nudity was natural. See Watt, 'Law Suits' (n 29) 25; Han, 'The Transparency Society' (n 29) 23.

[46] This is also an example of attentional socialization; the internalization of the social rules of appropriate attention. Zerubavel, 'Hidden in Plain Sight' (n 7) 63–69.

[47] Nagel, 'Concealment and Exposure' (n 6) 4.

To go deeper into the discussion of the theme, I will mainly follow Moshe Halbertal's theorizing on the covert marriage of transparency and shame: how do these phenomena relate to each other?[48] According to Halbertal, shame can be approached as a two-order phenomenon. To prove that, Halbertal first refers to an example previously used by Jean-Paul Sartre. In it, someone peeks at a naked person through a keyhole, thus transgressing the limits of privacy. When this is happening, another person passes by and witnesses the other person committing the deed.[49] Halbertal then expands on Sartre's story: what if the person in the room opens the door and catches the voyeur watching? This revelation, or, transparency, if you will, creates the two different positions of shame. The person who is naked feels embarrassed as does the person who was caught watching. However, the shame-constituting element differs regarding the two.

First, the person who was caught peeking internalizes the point of view of the catcher. According to Halbertal, in that case, the outside eye does not actually constitute the shame. Instead, it triggers a change in self-perception. That is to say, the one who was watching through the keyhole has been made to perceive himself watching. Thus, one must confront the deed via someone else's perception, which induces shame. In this case, the role of the external eye is important but not decisive: the change of perception might also happen without a catalyzing witness. That would, nevertheless, require self-reflexivity, an ability to watch oneself as though from outside.[50] Here, shame is thus enmeshed with guilt, caused by failure in meeting one's own ethical standards. One is proven worse than one's self-image would readily concede.

Second, the more rudimentary form of shame—the shame of the person who was watched being naked—has a different mechanism of emergence. This is what Halbertal calls primary shame. In it, the shame-inflicting effect of a gaze is more purely constitutive than in the case of secondary shame. Namely, it makes the nudity shameful by exposing it against or notwithstanding the person's will. The constitutive element is stronger, '[s]ince he causes a transformation in the description of the thing exposed, which is not the case in secondary shame. Nudity becomes a concern when it is improperly observed; it is the contact with the eye that makes it shameful.'[51] This comes close to Nagel's idea of naked exposure being disqualifying in itself, regardless of whether it actually causes disapproval or not.

[48] Halbertal's book *Concealment and Revelation: Esotericism in Jewish Thought and Its Philosophical Implications* (Princeton University Press 2007) concentrates mainly, as the title says, on the history of esotericism in Jewish thought. However, the last chapter of the book, chapter 17: 'Taxonomy and Paradoxes of Esotericism: Conceptual Conclusion', discusses the philosophical underpinnings of concealment and revelation, and can, according to the author, be read separately. This is how I use the book here. Moshe Halbertal, *Concealment and Revelation: Esotericism in Jewish Thought and Its Philosophical Implications* (Princeton University Press 2007) (hereafter Halbertal, 'Concealment and Revelation').

[49] Jean-Paul Sartre, *Being and Nothingness. A Phenomenological Essay on Ontology* (Hazel E Barnes tr, Philosophical Library 1956) 261–62; Halbertal, 'Concealment and Revelation' (n 48) 143–44.

[50] Halbertal, 'Concealment and Revelation' (n 48) 143–44.

[51] ibid, 144.

Therefore, in the first case shame is secondary, because it is the shame of inducing shame in another person or the shame of wanting to penetrate wrongfully into the other person's sphere of privacy. In the latter case, it is primary: the eye causes a transformation of a natural, private state of things into a shameful disclosure that is beyond control. As Halbertal argues, this is due to the constitutive role of the observer.[52] Thus, transparency-induced shame may create a hierarchy of positions, causing disparate constellations of emotions. Even though transparency may be contrasted both with strategy and privacy, it seems that violation of either leads, in the end, to shame. In the case of a revealed strategy, it is coloured by exposed weakness or incompetence and guilt, whereas in the case of violated privacy, it is associated with losing face. Still, transparency, in both cases, results in degradation in the eyes of the immediate community, or at least, of one person. Following Halbertal's categorization, it could be argued that the loss of strategy triggers a second-order shame, whereas the loss of privacy causes primary shame.

Moreover, as Halbertal notes, the opposite of shame is not shamelessness but intimacy. It could also be called confidentiality. In an intimate situation, it is possible to reveal more of oneself than otherwise; the fear of humiliation is shut down.[53] As Nagel defines it, 'Intimacy in its various forms is a partial lifting of the usual veil of reticence'.[54] Again, we encounter the metaphor of the lifted veil. Trust and intimacy enable one to approach positive transparency in its confessional mode. However, even in this case, I argue, the call for control remains as the deep structure of positively connoting transparency. Intimacy requires trust, which presumes at least an implicit agreement of further non-disclosure. Thus, the danger of unintentional transparency is minimized; revelation is based on the calculated risk of trusting. In addition, for that reason, intimacy cannot be forced.[55] Through this mechanism, intimacy constitutes a local enlargement of the sphere of the controlled self. In other words, intimacy does not jeopardize one's ability to have a persona.[56]

An example of this kind of situation could be confidential discussions between friends or spouses or a therapist and a patient. Private and institutionally confidential discussions are, however, only partly comparable. Especially in institutionally

[52] ibid, 144–45. Halbertal further argues that secondary shame leads to the loss of self-esteem whereas in primary shame, in the form of forced nakedness, there is no self-esteem to be lost. That is because the subject is deprived of the ability to control when and how to appear to the public eye.

[53] ibid, 146.

[54] Nagel, 'Concealment and Exposure' (n 6) 18.

[55] Halbertal, 'Concealment and Revelation' (n 48) 146. Compare with Han, who detects an ideological shift which he particularly associated with the rise of transparency and normative intimacy: he argues that modern society has stepped out from the idea of theatricality as a metaphor of social life with its public-private distinction and entered into that of normative intimacy to the extent that 'the tyranny of intimacy psychologizes and personalizes everything'. According to him, 'we have entered into the ideology of intimacy in which relations prove more real, genuine, credible, and authentic the more closely they approach the inner psychic needs of individuals. One believes that one attains transparency of the soul by revealing intimate feelings and emotions, by laying the soul bare.' Han, 'The Transparency Society' (n 29) 34–35.

[56] Halbertal, 'Concealment and Revelation' (n 48) 146.

confidential discussions, the possibility of shame prevails. This may become visible in avoiding straight eye-contact. As Halbertal notes, with this in mind, there are institutional arrangements which make straight eye-contact impossible when utterly personal, possibly shame-inducing matters are revealed (a therapist's couch, a priest's confessional).[57] In addition, this makes the inability to control one's representation a historical phenomenon: the shame may be caused by past deeds even though the actual revelation would be intentional.[58] Still, on the therapist's couch or in a priest's confessional nothing is forcefully revealed.

In the institutionally confidential discussions or nonverbal revelations (eg nakedness before a medical doctor), however, shameless revelation becomes possible without mutual intimacy, because the genuine subjectivity of the object of the gaze is bracketed by a particular setup. The person is approached in a certain role, as a patient, for example.[59] The placement into this role keeps the persona otherwise protected from shame. However, again we observe a structural difference between first- and second-order shame: confidential discussions between an attorney and a client would not be subject to avoiding eye-contact. This is probably because these discussions relate more to the choice of the optimal strategy than intimate revelations about privacy.

To conclude, I argue that shame is deeply intertwined with the loss of control.[60] As Freud argued previously, embracing this animality would go counter to our cultural expectations on how to pursue happiness: we need to suppress our animal instincts and act according to the cultural script of socially acceptable behaviour. Indeed, as Vincent Kaufmann puts it:

> Transparency is the way animals do it. Animals are transparent, they don't know modesty or shame, most of the time they are naked anyways and they couldn't care less about their visibility, whatever they do. Animals don't blush, their transparency is not blurred by the stains of modesty or shame.[61]

[57] Or organized voyeurism. For an analysis of the different forms of voyeurism in the theatre, see Rodosthenous, 'Staring at the Forbidden' (n 35) 1–25.

[58] Halbertal, 'Concealment and Revelation' (n 48) 148.

[59] ibid. Shifts in the established roles may cause the shame to return. Halbertal mentions the example of meeting one's therapist at a dinner table.

[60] Luk van der Dries asks an array of important questions: 'What do we see when we look at naked bodies on a theatrical stage? Are we still looking at the representation of the person, or possibly—ultimately—the person himself, who is no longer concealed by a costume? Has a naked actor become more himself—a biographical person—now that he appears to us in the nude? Do the nude actor on stage and the dressed spectator watching him per definition constitute a voyeuristic set-up? Why does the audience always fall tensely silent when an actor disrobes himself? Why do we not encourage him or her like we do at other times, in other settings? Why are we interested at all in nudity in the theatre when it has become so evident, so commonplace?' Luk van der Dries, 'The Pleasure of Looking Behind Curtains: Naked Bodies from Titian to Fabre and LeRoy' in George Rodosthenous (ed), *Theatre as Voyeurism: The Pleasures of Watching* (Palgrave Macmillan 2015).

[61] Vincent Kaufmann, 'Transparency and Subjectivity: Remembering Jennifer Ringley' in Emmanuel Alloa and Dieter Thomä (eds), *Transparency, Society and Subjectivity: Critical Perspectives* (Palgrave Macmillan 2018) 307, 311.

In essence, these cultural expectations of curbing our animality make us recoil from involuntary transparency.

Are We Transparent to Ourselves?

As discussed above, involuntary, off-performance transparency can be detrimental to the persona, to successful impression management, and to upholding a positive self-image. At worst, losing face would mean the very defilement of the persona. According to Halbertal, total transparency would even signify the disappearance of the borderline between self and the surroundings; transparency is not a border-friendly category. Shame, caused by involuntary transparency, is a deep violation of one's consciousness of boundedness; the self cannot be transparent because individuation requires a certain amount of concealment. Moreover, enabled by this concealment, the self operates on the scale of closeness and distance. This happens by revealing different levels of itself as a function of trust, 'though the privileged position he [the self] has to his interiority'.[62]

Indeed, we need a certain amount on concealment to be able to function in society. Yet, the question of the transparency of the self itself remains. Do we know ourselves? It is not easy to notice that the transparency of the self is, in fact, required by the ideal of voluntary transparency. If that was not the case, it simply could not work. To be sincere, so that our thoughts and words match, we need to know what those thoughts are. Because transparency puts much weight on one's privileged position to his interiority, that interiority must be thoroughly examined.

As Keane explains, there seems to be a hierarchy in which the self is the ultimate foundation of sincerity. The accountability based on the alignment between thoughts and words presupposes that the self knows itself. To be intentionally transparent or sincere, for words to match thoughts, those thoughts cannot be more ambiguous, contradictory, or opaque than the words expressing them. Additionally, both thoughts and words must be totally under the control of the speaking self. As Keane points out, it does not seem to make sense, for example, to speak of the sincerity of discussions as such apart from the respective sincerity of each participant separately.[63] Sincerity is ultimately a burden of the individual self.

The demand of fully knowing oneself is a tall order. Even if the performativity of the self can be seen through, can the self itself be the source of that performance?[64] It seems unlikely for a variety of reasons. First, we can question the assumption that

[62] Halbertal, 'Concealment and Revelation' (n 48) 142–43. Also, Han, 'The Transparency Society' (n 29) 3: 'Total illumination [of a human soul] would scorch it and cause a particular kind of spiritual burnout.'

[63] Keane, 'Sincerity, "Modernity," and the Protestants' (n 11) 75–76.

[64] Goffman, 'The Presentation of Self in Everyday Life' (n 17) 28: '[n]o one is in quite as good an observational position to see through the act as the person who puts it on'.

the privileged position we have to our interiority would necessarily signify self-knowledge: We might hold different beliefs than those we are expected to think about or what is socially acceptable to express.[65] This is also the very reason why we desire to filter what we say instead of someone reading our mind. Second, often we do not even know what we think about something. How does one express something if you have no thoughts about it? Or maybe there are thoughts, but they do not succumb to verbal expression. As argued in psychoanalysis, we are often oblivious to what drives us. Third, as Halbertal argues, the self, in order to maintain itself, also needs repression and self-deception.[66] We might need illusions and interpretations that help us to gain and maintain a positive self-image.

Even if we were transparent to ourselves, we would not want to be transparent to others. Otherwise, we would not be able to have a persona; the existence of the self would be jeopardized. It cannot be or become fully transparent. That said, we might be quite blind to ourselves and what drives us to pursue a certain persona. Why this persona and not another? Much of the persona consists of our own construction, the cognitive-hermeneutic narrative of ourselves: who we are, who we want to be, and how we came to be who we are.[67] Possibly, this narrative structure further underpins the performative persona we choose to display in the constant social plays we cannot avoid. Maybe that narrative is a screenplay for the performances.

From a realist or cynical point of view, this also means the crucial self-maintenance mechanism of self-deception, as mentioned. Indeed, the idea of a narrated self and its plausibility is problematic as a complete account of the self. Narrative form is partial at best and is typically based on simplistic causality attributions. Especially when it comes to other people, we perceive things which do not fit the narrated persona. Interestingly, although we cannot falsify other people's autobiographies, we tend to be somewhat suspicious towards them. At the same time, we firmly believe our own.[68]

In the context of this book, it is not necessary to delve into the question of the transparency of the self more deeply. It is enough to say that we can hardly be transparent to ourselves, or to others.[69] More importantly, we might not even desire

[65] Jordi Fernandez, *Transparent Minds: A Study of Self-Knowledge* (Oxford University Press 2013) 19–23.

[66] Halbertal, 'Concealment and Revelation' (n 48) 3–4.

[67] See Anthony Paul Kerby, *Narrative and the Self* (Indiana University Press 1991) 4: 'On a narrative account, the self is to be construed not as a prelinguistic given that merely employs language, much as we might employ a tool, but rather as a product of language—that might be called the implied subject of self-referring utterances. The self, or subject, then becomes a result of discursive praxis rather than either a substantial entity having ontological priority over praxis or a self with epistemological priority, an originator of meaning.'

[68] Timothy D Wilson, *Strangers to Ourselves: Discovering the Adaptive Unconscious* (Harvard University Press 2002).

[69] Han, 'The Transparency Society' (n 29) 3: 'According to Freud, the ego denies precisely what the unconscious affirms and desires without reserve. Therefore, a rift runs through the human psyche and prevents the ego from agreeing even with itself. This fundamental rift renders self-transparency impossible. A rift also gapes between people. For this reason, interpersonal transparency proves impossible

to be that—to ourselves (we might want to keep disturbing thoughts away from our consciousness) or others (to uphold a persona). These two spheres of opacity (opacity to ourselves, opacity to others) need not, and cannot, be identical: some aspects of us may be clear, non-performatively transparent, to others but not to ourselves, and, of course, vice versa. In order to be positive, transparency would need to be intentional.

Summing Up: Not so Neutral Transparency

In this chapter, I have discussed the ways in which transparency vocabulary works in social life, or more accurately, in interpersonal relations. When transparency points to value judgements in social life, it relates to the ways in which we behave in communities, how we want to portray or end up portraying others. This is the main avenue that makes transparency a human-faced ideal. I have shown that transparency dwells in our language in more ways than one—not only regarding its literal and metaphorical meanings, or as an alternative to other similar concepts alluding to accessibility to knowledge (publicity, access to information, openness, etc), but also regarding the value that is attributed to it in human behaviour and social relations.

As David Pozen has put it, transparency is an interpersonal, intersubjective, and relational phenomenon.[70] In social life, transparency no longer serves as a sheer medium, but it becomes a part of the moral vocabulary of authenticity, credibility, and trustworthiness. Rather than a neutral set-up, transparency is often considered a good or a bad thing, depending on the level of intentionality. It is mostly considered good when it is controlled. It can be celebrated as honesty, sincerity, boldness, or generosity. When we declare our actions transparent, we master the exposure, and transparency adopts the rationality of confession, and signifies relative independence of other's possible disapproval. This does not mean, however, that we could choose any level of confession without any repercussions. On the contrary, even if transparency were intentional, there are many social norms that would govern the appropriate revelation. The harmony of social life requires us to turn our gaze away from certain things and not always to speak our minds.

Negatively connoting transparency shows us how detrimental unwanted transparency can be to the person exposed. Involuntary transparency can thus signify failure. This failure, in turn, may lead to unwanted consequences. These can, for

to achieve. It is also not worth trying to do so. The other's very lack of transparency is what keeps the relationship alive.' Also, Judith Butler, *Giving an Account of Oneself* (Fordham University Press 2005).

[70] David Pozen, 'Seeing Transparency More Clearly' (2020) 80(2) Public Administration Review 326, 330.

example, be an exposed strategy in situations in which different actors are competing with one another, thus harming economic interests. Even more fundamentally, it can lead to embarrassment or shame when our persona is discredited. As a rule, we abhor that situation and attempt to avoid shaming ourselves at all costs. Shame strips us from our persona, which is necessary for us to act as coherent and dignified agents in the social world. That said, we still cannot quite understand our own self, it is not often transparent to us.

In light of this, I explained how impression management is an essential concept to describe the successful or unsuccessful social performance: the measuring stick is relational and based on the implicit credibility agreement between the actor and the audience. It helps to form the question, who is believable in his role? It captures the dynamic of how we want to control how we appear to each other. I deepened this analysis by examining theatre imagery and its implications. The duality of transparency's value connotations reveals an important aspect of its general legitimating power. Although we could also arrive at the same idea through different ways, interestingly, the concept itself has the potential to reveal its peculiar functioning logic: performativity, which enables if not mandates the management of visibilities.

We can notice that when pointing to social phenomena, 'the cultural signifier of neutrality' is not that neutral at all. This appearance of neutrality, however, is a practical way of making the best parts of reality seem its entirety. Proliferating normative transparency talk suggests that the more transparency there is, the better. This, however, is an illusion. I have argued that our social life necessarily requires us to restrict our urges to reveal and see things. Indeed, when we blame someone for being transparent, we blame them for being strategically clumsy by unwittingly disclosing a hidden agenda. Transparency—or openness, honestly, or candour—needs to be framed as such in order to be esteemed.

As a result, we encounter a curious paradox: to be appreciated, the visual needs to become performative, which conceptually, is only one subcategory of the visual. It presupposes a conscious agent, which either illuminates or constructs the desired view. Thus, when referring to a value in social life, the everyday meaning of transparency is impoverished from its multitude of connotative meanings and reduced to the performative. Hence, total transparency would be detrimental in non-obvious ways. Under the condition of total transparency, the individuality of people and debatably, even institutions, would vanish. As Simmel argues, if there were such a thing as complete reciprocal transparency, the relationship between human beings would be changed in an unimaginable manner.[71]

[71] Simmel, 'The Sociology of Secrecy' (n 16) 447–48.

5
Transparency and Power

The Promise of Transparency: Legitimacy of Power

In the previous chapter, I demonstrated how unintentional transparency can be problematic in social life by inducing shame or exposing strategy. In addition, in some cases transparency is impossible because it would undermine the endeavour of sustaining borders, erasing the distinction between the internal and the external—it could even demolish its object. This was built on the presumed power of the gaze, discussed in chapter three. In chapter two, I argued that transparency is inherently an icono-ambivalent phenomenon: it cannot be fully captured with the idea of an open curtain or a lifted veil. Transparency is valued when it does not deflate or extinguish its object but when it helps us to understand, and possibly, to accept it (understanding = seeing).

As already pointed out, we seldom speak laudably about people's transparency. Instead, we emphasize the importance of honesty, openness, sincerity, authenticity, candour, etc. In social interaction, 'transparency' seems to refer mostly, if not totally, to its pejorative connotation. Against this backdrop, we can ask, to what kind of intentional phenomena *do* we refer with transparency in a positive sense, because undeniably, that is also done. This very observation on the duality of the connotations of transparency underpins the entire theorizing on transparency.

As I have argued, transparency needs to be intentional to be appreciated. That said, we can ask whether there is a prototypical context in which we specifically use the term transparency in a positive sense. What can we infer from the fact that transparency is clearly a positively connoting metaphor in contemporary legal, governance, or policy contexts? Is there a more general deep structure to be detected? In this chapter, I shall argue that transparency gains a positive connotation when it refers to the exercise of power. The promise of transparency could be summarized as follows: *transparency is good because it makes power visible, and as such, controllable*. In particular, I mean power which is more or less one-sided, vertical or unilateral, and is exercised by the state or otherwise resembles a governor-governed relationship.

Additionally, I will demonstrate how the promise of transparency is inherently flawed or incomplete because it cannot consider the actual ways in which power operates, thus leaving crucial aspects of it in oblivion. Part of this shift is discursive. The elusive nature of power lies not only in calls for increased transparency but also in the decision-makers' claims about transparency: by constantly assuring

The Transparency Paradox. Ida Koivisto, Oxford University Press. © Ida Koivisto 2022.
DOI: 10.1093/oso/9780192855466.003.0005

the public that they operate in the open, they reinforce the notion that secrecy is the baseline.[1] This argument is in harmony with my argument that positively connoting transparency is performative in nature.

It is not clear, however, what power means. No doubt, the meaning of 'power' depends on the definition; it is a complex phenomenon that cannot be easily verbalized or explained. Additionally, many theories of power exist. According to a classic definition, A has power over B if A may make B do something that B would not do without A's contribution. Possibly, this could be called power as domination. Max Weber's definitions are quite apt here: 'the probability that a command with a given specific content will be obeyed by a given group of persons'; and 'the existence of domination turns only on the actual presence of one person successfully issuing orders to others'.[2] In the most rudimentary form of power, when A dictates, B obeys with high probability. A wields power over B. This power could be seen as unilateral or vertical in nature; it emanates from one source and is targeted towards something or someone. Although this illustration articulates our everyday intuition quite well—is all power not vertical?—it is an incomplete account. Many forms of power function in a subtler fashion, as I will show in this chapter.

In line with this argument of the multiple forms of power, the general hypothesis that transparency legitimizes power can easily be made more complex. There are various ways in which this can be done. First, it is not self-evident what exactly we are referring to with transparency's legitimating promise. The hypothesis that 'transparency is a good thing in the framework of power' can be broken down into at least four sub-promises: transparency is good because 1) it produces better decisions and policies; 2) it is perceived as fairer than secrecy; 3) it increases understanding; and 4) it increases the perceived ability to exercise accountability. Each of these sub-promises could be critically reviewed, and to some extent that has already been done.[3] Hence, I will not organize the discussion in this chapter according to these sub-promises.

Second, here too, transparency's multifarious nature makes an appearance. The manifestations of the transparency principle, if you will, are hardly monolithic. For example, transparency can appear in different forms, such as transparency in rationale (justifying decisions), transparency in process (allowing access to witness the decision-making process),[4] or transparency proactively provided or available

[1] Todd Sanders and Harry G West (eds), *Transparency and Conspiracy: Ethnographies of Suspicion in the New World Order* (Duke University Press 2003). See also Jenny de Fine Licht, *Magic Wand or Pandora's Box? How Transparency in Decision Making Affects Public Perceptions of Legitimacy* (University of Gothenburg 2014) 30 (hereafter de Fine Licht, 'Magic Wand or Pandora's Box?').

[2] Max Weber, *Economy and Society* (Guenther Roth and Claus Wittich eds, University of California Press 1978) 53.

[3] De Fine Licht, 'Magic Wand or Pandora's Box?' (n 1) 20–31. De Fine Licht also questions each of these promises and concludes that regardless of their promises, there are also powerful counterarguments against each of them.

[4] This distinction is originally coined by Jane Mansbridge. Jane Mansbridge, 'A "Selection Model" of Political Representation' (2009) 17(4) Journal of Political Philosophy 369, 384–86 (hereafter Mansbridge, 'A "Selection Model" of Political Representation').

by request. In the previous chapters, I have discussed this mechanism in a more fine-grained manner (eg transparency *as* transparency and transparency *as if* transparency; icono-ambivalence). In the next chapter, this theme will be delved into in the context of law.

Third, even if we accept the general rule that transparency is necessary in legitimizing power, this does not tell us how this is perceived by people. Thus, the normative legitimacy hypothesis does not necessarily equate to perceived legitimacy; these two may or may not have a causal relationship. Thus, whether transparency manages to fulfil its legitimating promise is ultimately an empirical question that I discuss only marginally.[5]

Acknowledging these reservations, in this chapter I concentrate on the deep theoretical structure of the legitimacy promise of transparency. How is transparency capable of providing legitimacy when we consider its nature both as a metaphor and a normative concept, as discussed in chapter two? Why is the positive connotation of transparency not subject to more suspicion, given its discussed negative connotation? Why do we not talk about the sincerity or honesty of the state, but about its transparency? In the context of unilateral or otherwise unequal power, transparency may translate into a set of legal or otherwise normative rights and obligations. It may be considered positive in other contexts too—for instance, in consumer relations[6]—but in any case, institutional asymmetry remains as a necessary condition. In dealing with these questions, I will concentrate on the manifold manifestations that power takes.

The chapter is organized as follows. First, I will present some ways in which to approach power. To that purpose, I discuss Steven Lukes's and Michel Foucault's ideas of power. Secondly, I will reconstruct the promise of transparency, the visibility of power. I do this by analysing two different rationalities of transparency, which I call the democratic rationality and the public law rationality. Additionally, I introduce the different mechanisms through which these rationalities operate—I call them transparency's preventive and justificatory mechanism. Thirdly, I will question transparency's promise: can it really make power visible? To answer that, I focus on unpacking the idea of esoteric knowledge. Fourthly, I tackle our assumed desire to see power. Fifthly and finally, I summarize the discussion in the chapter, and argue that power is too complex to be made fully visible simply by means of transparency practices.

[5] This is empirically researched at least by Jenny de Fine Licht in her doctoral dissertation, 'Magic Wand or Pandora's Box?' (n 1). See also Stephan G Grimmelikhuijsen and Albert J Meijer, 'Effects of Transparency on the Perceived Trustworthiness of a Government Organization: Evidence from an Online Experiment' (2014) 24(1) Journal of Public Administration Research and Theory 137–57.

[6] cf Archon Fung, Mary Graham, and David Weil, *Full Disclosure: The Perils and Promise of Transparency* (Cambridge University Press 2007).

The Many Dimensions of Power: Lukes and Foucault

As mentioned, a classical way of conceiving power is looking at it as domination. However, this conception is too simplistic a view to conceptualize power in a modern state. Therefore, a more sophisticated view is needed: a view that considers subtle forms of power. To provide that, I introduce two accounts of multidimensionality of power in the state: those of Steven Lukes and Michel Foucault. How can we see power if it does not provide ceremonious visibilities? How far can iconophilic practices extend?

Social and political theorist Steven Lukes discusses the different dimensions of power in his influential book *Power: A Radical View* (1974; 2005). In this work, Lukes analyses the ways in which power operates in the state. The key goal of the book is to question the idea of 'power as domination'. To that purpose, Lukes creates his own, more multifaceted theory of power, which also considers surreptitious forms of power. Hence, instead of sheer domination, he divides power into three dimensions—decision-making power, agenda-forming power, and ideological power. Every dimension operates according to a different logic.

The first dimension of power, the decision-making power, is the most obvious one. It refers to power which looks like power: it consists of deciding on people's rights and duties.[7] For example, this could mean legislative, administrative, or adjudicative power as it relates to deciding over the scope of freedom of an individual or a group of people. This form of power comes close to the idea of domination, as the power structure is predominantly vertical and asymmetric. Power easily becomes reduced to this aspect, and, importantly, it is the form of power which is typically subject to transparency requirements. In the vocabulary of public law, this is the basic structure how power—public authority—is conceived.

The second dimension, the agenda-forming power, or, the non-decision-making power, does not directly touch upon the decisions on people's rights and duties or the process of how these decisions are made. The second form of power is subtler, but arguably is as important as the first one. It alludes to the power to decide what is decided. It is the power which forms the agenda.[8] In other words, it conceptually precedes the existence of the first dimension. If we look at this form of power from the vantage point of transparency requirements, some signs of transparency's incompleteness can be observed. This dimension of power is not so easily visible, paradoxically because its outcome, the agenda, forms the borders of the discourse. The second dimension of power is also important because it relates to the control of public space. That is to say, the second dimension is in operation when it is decided

[7] Steven Lukes, *Power: A Radical View* (2nd ed, Palgrave Macmillan 2005) 19: 'Thus I conclude that this first, one-dimensional, view of power involves a focus on behaviour in the making of decisions on issues over which there is an observable conflict of (subjective) interests, seen as expressing policy preferences, revealed by political participation.'

[8] ibid, 20, 111.

which voices are allowed to be heard, and which are marginalized or even silenced altogether.

The third dimension of power is hardest to discern, but according to Lukes it is the most important one. He calls it the ideological dimension of power. It refers to power which shapes reality as we perceive it. Its operative logic is, or can be, manipulative. The ideological dimension of power enables the state to influence what its subjects consider a good life. To put it in terms of political and moral philosophy, it affects the conceptions of prudence and the goals and content of rational self-interest. This dimension of power, thus, influences people's attitudes and values. According to Lukes, this may even mean that power makes people approve of values and mindsets which are contrary to their best interests. Lukes uses the example of women endorsing patriarchal structures in a society.[9]

Lukes's categorization is helpful and insightful; not all power looks like power, and the most effective power may in fact be the least ceremonial in nature. Yet, we can argue that the three-dimensional conception of power is still too simple. To enrich the discussion of different forms of power, we can complement Lukes's ideas with those of Michel Foucault. Foucault's main idea is that power is ubiquitous and inherent in our societal practices rather than something that a person or an institution governs. Thus, the way in which power can be understood requires an even wider lens than that suggested by Lukes.

As is well known, Foucault was a notable theorist whose notions of power are famously multifaceted and intricate.[10] It is important to note, however, that Foucault kept on changing his terminology from one theme to another. When referring to power, Foucault uses different concepts such as governmentality, government, the police, political rationalities and technologies, modalities of power, apparatuses of security (*dispositifs*), political sovereignty, discursive practices, biopolitics, bio-power, and so on. It is not always clear how these ideas fit together, whether they form a taxonomy, or are just different perspectives on similar kinds of subject matter.[11] Accordingly, it is difficult, if not impossible, to describe and discuss his thinking without using his idiosyncratic vocabulary.

[9] ibid, 37, 114–24.

[10] Foucault himself, however, did not really attempt to create an overall theory of power: 'If we accept that power is not a substance, fluid or something that derives from a particular source, then this analysis could and would only be at most a beginning of a theory, not of a theory what power is, but simply of power in terms of the set of mechanisms and procedures that have the role or function and theme, even when they are unsuccessful, of securing power. It is a set of procedures, and it is as such, and only as such, that the analysis of mechanisms of power could be understood as the beginning of something like a theory of power.' Michel Foucault, *Security, Territory, Population: Lectures at the Collège de France 1978–1979* (Arnold I Davidson ed, Palgrave Macmillan 2007) 2.

[11] Nikolas Rose also argues that 'Foucault was far from consistent in his own thinking about relations between the different ways in which he analysed power. He certainly cautioned against conceiving of a chronology that went from "sovereignty"—a discontinuous exercise of power through display and spectacle, law as command, sanctions as negative and deductive—to "discipline"—the continuous exercise of power through surveillance, individualization and normalization—to "governmentality" focusing on maximizing the forces of the population collectively and individually. At one point he suggested that one could identify a "triangle" of sovereignty, discipline and governmentality. Elsewhere he argued

Why do we need to discuss Foucault, then? First, the most important addition of Foucault to this discussion is the idea of the productive effect of power. Foucault emphasizes that the effects of power do not always need to be portrayed in negative terms, although suppression is easy to associate with it. Instead, power is also productive, it can make things appear, manifest, and bring into existence. As Foucault puts it, 'We must cease once and for all to describe the effects of power in negative terms: it "excludes", it "represses", it "censors", it "abstracts", it "masks", it "conceals". In fact, power produces; it produces reality; it produces domains of objects and rituals of truth. The individual and the knowledge that may be gained of him belong to this production.'[12] Hence, Foucault's conceptions of power are wide, fine-grained, and original.

Second, an important aspect in Foucault's conceptions of power is considering their historical preconditions. For example, his concept of governmentality (*gouvernementalité*) is important in this respect. Linguistically, it includes the words 'governing' and 'mentality', which give a clue to its meaning. It can, according to my interpretation, be used both analytically—to diagnose the nature of governing mentalities—and historically, referring to actual transitions of governmental ideologies and practices in time and place. Partially, this is because Foucault was not systematic in using the term himself and had different definitions for it, such as 'the art of government', or 'the conduct of conduct'. At the most general level, governmentality can be seen to refer to different historical mindsets or mentalities explaining and justifying the use of governmental power, its philosophical and teleological underpinnings, which however extend to material practices.[13]

that it was simplistic to see the societies of normalization of the nineteenth century as disciplinary: rather, in such societies, life was taken in charge by the interplay between the technologies of discipline focused on the individual body and the technologies of bio-politics, which acted on those bodies *en masse* intervening in the making of life, the manner of living, in how to live.' Nikolas Rose, *Powers of Freedom: Reframing Political Thought* (Cambridge University Press 1999) 23.

12 Michel Foucault, *Discipline and Punish* (Penguin Books 1991) 194.

13 Michel Foucault, *The Government of Self and Others: Lectures at the Collège de France 1982–1983* (Arnold I Davidson and Graham Burchell eds, Palgrave Macmillan 2010) 2 (hereafter Foucault, 'The Government of Self and Others'): 'So "government" in a strict sense, but also "art", "art of governing" in the strict sense, since by "art of government" I did not mean the way in which governors really governed. I have not studied and do not want to study the development of real governmental practice by determining the particular situations it deals with, the problems raised, the tactics chosen, the instruments employed, forged or remodelled, and so forth. I wanted to study the art of governing, that is to say, the reasoned way of governing best and, at the same time, reflection on the best possible way of governing. That is to say, I have tried to grasp the level of reflection in the practice of government and on the practice of government. In a sense, I wanted to study government's consciousness of itself, if you like, although I don't like the term "self-awareness" (*conscience de soi*) and will not use it, because I would rather say that I have tried, and would like to try to determine the way in which the domain of the practice of government, with its different objects, general rules, and overall objectives, was established so as to govern in the best possible ways. In short, we could call this the study of the rationalization of governmental practice in the exercise of political sovereignty.' See also Mitchell Dean, *Governmentality: Power and Rule in Modern Society* (SAGE Publications 2010).

Interestingly, Lukes's ideas—in particular the third dimension of power—come close to Foucault's conceptions of power. The second edition of Lukes's book from 2005 even includes an epilogue in which he discusses Foucault's effect on his thinking. To give an example of the structural similarity between these thinkers, let us look at the case of how power affects how we talk about things. Both Lukes and Foucault would agree that power can be retraced to some agent's capacity to decide the vocabulary and modality by which certain things are talked about—if they are talked about at all.

In Lukes's vocabulary, the theme of who decides on what will be decided would come close to the second dimension of power, as discussed above. Following Foucault, this can be called *discursive power*, whose connection to individual views is more indirect. Discursive power relates to the use of words and the power implications in that use. Discursive power is, however, structurally pre-linguistic: its manifestations, discourses (a mode of speech or text), are made of signs, but the power configurations that enable them reside in societal structures. What is more, this kind of power can affect the problematization of things, meaning that some subject matters are brought into discourse, into the realm of the manifest, whereas some things may remain (intentionally) unverbalized and thus left to oblivion.[14] Discursive power can make or break objects of discussion.

Concerning Lukes's third dimension of power, however, the theorists' conceptions are more divergent. Whereas Lukes thinks that ideological power may cause people to endorse ideas which contradict their own immediate interests, Foucault would maintain that the subject herself, whether endorsing or adopting a certain mindset or not, is a product of power. She cannot escape the condition of power as she is a corollary of it. Thus, Foucault goes even further in his ideas on the ubiquitous and surreptitious nature of power: people do not only choose what they believe, their entire social make-up is deeply intertwined with the power embedded in society. That said, power can be recognized from the possibility of resistance.

In the context of this chapter, many Foucauldian questions could be posed. However, applying Foucauldian concepts and ideas to contemporary social, political, or legal phenomena is challenging. On the one hand, they offer a matrix for innovative thinking, allowing inspiration for novel kinds of questions. On the other hand, one remains painfully conscious of the threat of twisting these notions into an unrecognizable form. I have already referred to Foucault in chapter three (the panoptic modality of power) and will do so in this chapter (the preventive function of power; the question whether we want to see power) as well as in chapter seven (discursification).

[14] Michel Foucault, *The Archaeology of Knowledge* (Pantheon Books 1969).

The Promise Unpacked: The Democratic and Public Law Rationalities of Transparency

At this point, I have discussed some ways in which to approach governmental power. I have questioned the exclusivity of the power-as-domination model by referring to Lukes and to Foucault. I am aware that this could all be seen as straw man argumentation of a kind—does anyone today actually believe in such a simplistic conception of power as I am attempting to question? Have we not all read our Foucault by now? Although these concerns are understandable, I will nevertheless argue that this reminder of the multifaceted nature of power is still warranted. It is so because much of how law conceptualizes power is based on unilaterality and the clear detectability of power. This relates also, as I argue, to how transparency can, as normative narratives go, legitimate such power.

For transparency to provide legitimation, a certain unilateral, hierarchical, or vertical structure needs to be presupposed, regardless of whether power actually operates in that way or not. In a way, we need to act as if Lukes's first dimension of power was all there was to it. This, of course, does not exclude other forms and mechanisms of power; it only excludes them from the ways in which governmental power or public authority is typically understood in the state. For the sake of clarity, I shall call this kind of agent 'the governor' which uses power over 'the governed'. In this context, I am interested in this unilateral form of power, or, more importantly, that it appears unilateral and what follows from that appearance. In the following, it is assumed that transparency is capable of accessing the 'truth' about governing and is also at the same time able to provide legitimacy. However, later in the book, I will show that this premise is debatable.

Transparency seems to have become a policy virtue when there is a governing agent (the governor) who wields power over some group of governed or subjected (the governed), even though this exercising of power may happen in an individualized form. In the most general terms, transparency is required when decisions that concern the governed are being made (cf Lukes's first dimension of power). However, concerning this point, we need to separate two different positions of the governed. Depending on the point of view, the governed may be approached as the principals of power or the subjects of it. Furthermore, this positioning affects how transparency can legitimize power. The answer is different whether we follow *democratic rationality* or *public law rationality*. In the following, I will break down the overall legitimating narrative of transparency and reconstruct its two main sub-rationalities.

As mentioned previously, transparency is typically considered an ideal of a democratic society, in fact, one of its very cornerstones. Correspondingly, it makes sense to talk about *the democratic rationality of transparency*. By that I mean seeing the governed as the ultimate wielders of political power (principals), which is further subject to transparency requirements.[15] Fundamentally, it concerns the existential legitimation of governmental power. From that point of view, the governor would use his power only insofar as the governed would allow it, his mandate would depend on the acceptance of the constituents. The agent would thus represent the principals and act instead of them. In other words, the agent, the governor, would be using the power of the principals, in the name of principal, the governed. From that it follows that the governor is also accountable to the governed for his use of power over the governed.[16]

In that way, the accountability structure that democratic rationality attempts to create is based on a social contract style of legitimation. In the simplest terms this would mean that the governed would give up part of their natural power to the governor, because it is in their interest. Only under the reign of that instituted governor could the peace and protection of individuals be sufficiently and predictably provided. Those would not be available in the state of nature, in which, in the gloomiest, Hobbesian scenario, everyone would be at war with each other. Founded on this existential logic, transparency would serve a key function. The social contract needs a system of checks whereby the governed would have the ability and the machinery to make sure that the contract is working. Transparency would allow the principal, the governed, to know how the agent, the governor, is faring in using the vested power. Democratic rationality is often manifested as the demands of accountability.[17]

What is accountability and why is it so often associated with transparency? There are many ways of defining accountability. That said, to give a simple answer, we need to look more closely at the principal-agent model that underpins the

[15] Jeffrey Edward Green connects the idea of candour with gaze in the context of democracy: 'Candor is a political value that is unusual in the sense that it rests on the People's capacity for sight, not voice. It is, accordingly, a critical ideal responsive to the citizen-being-ruled, who is a spectator of politics rather than a decision maker and who, unlike the more familiar figure of the citizen-governor, is in fact representative of the ordinary political experience of everyday citizens in contemporary mass democracy.' Jeffrey Edward Green, *The Eyes of the People: Democracy in the Age of Spectatorship* (Oxford University Press 2010) 178. He also sees a connection between transparency and candour, but also a crucial difference on p. 181: 'The difference is this: transparency is *impersonal*, referring to facts, information, knowledge—the things about which a decision maker would like to know. If a person is described as "being transparent," it is only in connection with a specific public issue or problem. A political event is not itself something that is transparent. Candor, however, especially when defined institutionally, refers to the extent to which the conditions of a leader's public appearance are outside the control of the leader him- or herself. With candor, the personal element is key—since it is precisely the individual's relation to his or her publicity that determines the degree of candor. Thus, whereas transparency seeks truth, candor seeks spontaneity and eventfulness, which are related to the pursuit of truth but still irreducible to it.'

[16] cf Sandrine Baume, 'Publicity and Transparency: The Itinerary of a Subtle Distinction' in Emmanuel Alloa and Dieter Thomä (eds), *Transparency, Society, Subjectivity: Critical Perspectives* (Palgrave Macmillan 2018) 210, 221; on the historical genealogy of this conjunction, see 214–16.

[17] This is visible in current discourses. For example, Google Scholar gives over 1,5 million hits with the search words 'transparency' and 'accountability'. See also Christopher Hood, 'Accountability and Transparency: Siamese Twins, Matching Parts, Awkward Couple?' (2010) 33(5) West European Politics 989.

democratic rationality of transparency. The most basic idea of accountability could be described like this: A, the principal, has power or assignment which he delegates to B, the agent. In return, B is accountable to A for how B chooses to exercise or to execute that power. B needs to give an account, a report, an explanation: this and that was done with the vested power. Does A accept B's account? Ideally, the vested power should be used to enhance the common good, not for some personal interests. Indeed, in addition *to whom* the agent is accountable, the agent is accountable *for* something. For example, the government may be accountable to the people for its expenditure. Thus, accountability includes at least two constitutive elements: a task or a mission defined by A, and B working on behalf of A, and accountable to A.

Based on the acquired information provided by transparency practices, the governed could either sustain the governor, suggest changes, or overthrow the governor. In that way, transparency would provide a tool for ensuring that the governor would sustain his authority to govern.[18] Thus, the legitimacy structure in democratic rationality is based on the following narrative: I can see how the vested power that ultimately emanates from me, and my fellow governed (principals), is used by the governor (agent). This enables me to constantly assess his performance. Therefore, I accept it, unless I consider it, based on what I can see, illegitimate. In that case, I can overthrow it.[19] This is, of course, an idealization, because, in reality, people may well choose to remain 'rational ignorants' and thus be ill-equipped for such informed overthrowing.[20] Namely, as Baume and Papadopoulos argue, the informational asymmetry between the principals and the agent does not necessarily result from subterfuge on the part of the agents but rather from indifference on the part of the principals. The expression of grievances of the performance of the governor is constrained by cognitive restrictions or people's choices.[21]

The public law rationality of transparency, for one, is based on a functional rather than an existential point of view. It concerns the questions on the ways in which the governor uses his power over the governed, and how this can be considered legitimate. Public law rationality probably also represents better our everyday experience of governmental power than democratic rationality; we can hardly overthrow power as soon as we consider it unjustified. We live in a world dominated by deeply rooted social constructions and practices rather than uninhibited freedom or the circumstances assumed in social contract theories. This is to say, it does not suffice

[18] See Sandrine Baume and Yannis Papadopoulos, 'Transparency: From Bentham's Inventory of Virtuous Effects to Contemporary Evidence-based Scepticism' (2018) 21(2) Critical Review of International Social and Political Philosophy 169, 182–84 (hereafter Baume and Papadopoulos, 'Transparency: From Bentham's Inventory').

[19] cf Deirdre Curtin and Albert Meijer, 'Does Transparency Strengthen Legitimacy? A Critical Analysis of European Union Policy Documents' (2006) 11 Information Polity 109, 111: 'According to political theory, giving citizens the possibility of monitoring policymaking and scrutinizing its results will enhance the legitimacy of the institutional structures.'

[20] cf Joanne Roberts, 'Organizational Ignorance: Towards a Managerial Perspective on the Unknown' (2012) 44(3) Management Learning 215.

[21] Baume and Papadopoulos, 'Transparency: From Bentham's Inventory' (n 18) 183.

that the governor is in place, however legitimated. Namely, in modern liberal democracies, a governor cannot operate however he chooses, unless we commit to a Hobbesian idea of a social contract. If it did, it would, as presented, be subject to the measures enabled by the democratic rationality of transparency. Instead, the governor exercises the assigned power over the governed, fulfilling his mission, realizing rights, regulating behaviour, because he is legally and politically authorized to do so.

This authorization cannot be based only on existential legitimation, it needs additional procedural guarantees. Adherence to these procedural guarantees enables the governed to know whether the governor has done his job; it provides a matrix for criticism. This is where public law enters the picture. In liberal democracies, governmental power needs constitutional guarantees and legal safeguards against the misuse of power. This means different principles and procedural conditions guiding the use of power. Transparency practices are quintessential in this regard. They function as a tool for providing information on the use of that power—not only in general, but also in individualized cases, in administrative and judicial decision-making.

This is premised on the idea that when the subject is made aware of how and why the power is being used over her, this knowledge further results in legitimacy. In other words, the legitimacy structure in public law rationality is based on the following narrative: 'I was informed on why and how power is exercised upon me, and based on this information, I understand how this use of power was not arbitrary but motivated by law and reason, therefore I accept it. If it is not, however, the case, I can question it.' In this rationale, transparency comes close to the idea of giving reasons.

The separation or these two rationalities enables us to see the question of transparency's promise as parts of two, partially distinct, albeit overlapping legitimacy narratives; they are intertwined, but they still follow a somewhat different logic. In democratic rationality, transparency provides a tool for assessing the fundamental legitimacy of governmental power, whereas in public law rationality, transparency provides a tool for assessing its correct intensity and quality in individual cases.[22]

It is important to point out, however, that these questions on democracy and legitimacy are highly debated within political, constitutional, and legal theory.[23] I am aware of this and am not primarily attempting to join these debates. Instead, I am separating the two rationalities mainly for heuristic and analytical purposes,

[22] Similarly, Abazi and Tauschinsky divide the functions of transparency into control and trust approaches. Vigjilenca Abazi and Eljalill Tauschinsky, 'Reasons of Control and Trust: Grounding the Public Need for Transparency in the European Union' (2015) 11(2) Utrecht Law Review 78.

[23] For example, on the meaning of 'people' from the metatheoretical vantage point in constitutional theory, see Zoran Oklopcic, *Beyond the People: Social Imaginary and Constituent Imagination* (Oxford University Press 2018).

to tease out some nuances of the legitimating promise of transparency. This may happen at the price of oversimplification, and objections are easy to find. In particular, from the governmentality point of view, it is possible to argue that we are specifically constituted as free by governmental practices, and we use this freedom, among other things, to reproduce those governmental practices. Thus, a strict separation is ultimately unsustainable.

Transparency, thus, is connected to the understandability of power. This understandability is further a necessary precondition for legitimacy (cf understanding is seeing). Legitimacy is premised on the potential dangerousness, illegitimacy, and incomprehensibility of power, otherwise the concerns of legitimacy and comprehensibility would not make sense, as we remember from the discussion in the first chapter. As hinted above, this is where transparency's legitimacy narrative comes into play; transparency is seen as a tool for combatting those dangers. In Mark Fenster's words: 'Citizens are ignorant of state action; their ignorance impedes their ability to participate rationally in the democratic process; the disclosure of state information enables citizens to act collectively as a polis that is capable of deliberative, reasoned action; this action in turn will hold the state responsible for its actions; and thus transparency insures that the state is truly representative of the public's beliefs, preferences, and interests. The state that is made visible proves to be more truly democratic, as well as more accountable and efficient. Transparency enables—and, indeed, forces—this virtuous chain of events.'[24]

The Preventive and Justificatory Mechanisms of Transparency

I have now reconstructed two ways in which transparency promises legitimacy of power: democratic rationality and public law rationality. The functioning logic is somewhat different in these two, as explained. To complete the picture of transparency's promise, we also need to take a closer look at the mechanisms in which transparency can fulfil it. In the following, I suggest that positively connoting transparency mainly uses two different mechanisms: the preventive mechanism and the justificatory mechanism. The first mechanism is more peculiar to democratic rationality, whereas the second one is more associated with public law rationality, although the distinction is not absolute.

The first mechanism through which transparency can legitimize power can be called *the preventive mechanism of transparency*. It presupposes that power corrupts its wielders. This corruption is further assumed to take place in secrecy. For this reason, secrecy is considered a dangerous condition for power, and consequently,

[24] Mark Fenster, 'Transparency in Search of a Theory' (2015) 18 European Journal of Social Theory 150, 151. Also, Mark Fenster, *The Transparency Fix: Secrets, Leaks, and Uncontrollable Government Information* (Stanford University Press 2017) 5.

it needs to be diminished or abolished, and transparency established. This is to enable the continuous and active monitoring of power. Transparency would do that by creating an arrangement in which hiding would be impossible. This was also one of the effects of transparency that Bentham referred to: it functions as a deterrent.

As Baume and Papadopoulos argue, according to Bentham, public judgements are feared because if they are negative, they diminish the happiness of the governor. This is further based on the fear of dishonour, which may destroy a political career (cf the emergence of shame). This fear, in turn, can have a constraining or rectifying effect on behaviour, because the governor can be assumed to avoid such shame. In addition, the mission of public opinion, according to Bentham, is to prevent rulers from pursuing 'sinister interests' and to keep government actions within the utilitarian principle, that is 'the greatest happiness of the greatest number'.[25] Hence, the preventive mechanism could also be called the classic 'sunlight is the best disinfectant' logic. According to this logic, transparency would promise unimpeded controllability of power whereby no sinister interest could flourish. I discussed this previously in relation to Foucault's panoptic modality of power and the idea of the transforming gaze in chapter three.

Thus, the preventive mechanism of transparency has its roots in the fear of undesired or unauthorized exposure, as discussed in the previous chapter. However, when it comes to the context of power, the idea of underpinning becomes more particular. The one who would be exposed would not be any person in a haphazard social context, but the governor, using power over the governed. For this reason, the governor is subject to certain kinds of impression requirements. He is expected to perform a certain role, and to fulfil those expectations that come with it. He is thus not free to choose, even if controlled, any performance. Instead, the audience, the governed, would expect the governor to favour an impression that would make him seem worthy of being a governor: law-abiding, just, and meeting the legitimate expectations of the governed. As presented, according to the democratic rationality of transparency, the failure to meet the reasoned expectations of the governed would jeopardize the legitimacy of the governor to govern.

This preventive mechanism of transparency would thus assume that the governor would not want his potential 'sinister interests' to be a visible part of his managed impression, and they would instead be omitted from it. The preventive mechanism would, however, go further: it is particularly premised on the corruptive effect of power. It is biased in the way that it rather assumes the existence or the emergence of the sinister interests of the governor. The governor cannot be trusted

[25] Baume and Papadopoulos, 'Transparency: From Bentham's Inventory' (n 18) 177 citing Jeremy Bentham, 'Of Publicity' in Michael James, Cyprian Blamires, and Catherine Pease-Watkin (eds), *The Collected Works of Jeremy Bentham: Political Tactics* (Clarendon Press 1999) 37: 'It is objected against the régime of publicity, that it is a system of distrust? This is true; and every good political institution is founded upon this base. Whom ought we to distrust, if not those to whom is committed great authority, with great temptations to abuse it?'

to tell the truth about his intentions. For that reason, the preventive mechanism would aspire to prevent those interests from emerging altogether. This would be done by allowing no refuge from the public eye. It would make the self-controlled disclosure—the prerequisite of transparency to be valuable in social life—futile or impossible. Everything would be immediately visible.

If we consider this in connection with the aforementioned icono-ambivalence of transparency, we can argue that the preventive mechanism would mean an arrangement of constant iconoclasm. It would be impossible to exit the frontstage, if you will. Seen like this, transparency becomes a pre-emptive tool (understanding = seeing = good), and a synonym for surveillance. It follows *ex ante* logic, namely it attempts to prevent the misuse of power by making it compatible with the rational self-interest of not being publicly humiliated. The preventive mechanism of transparency is also transforming; it makes the surveilled adjust his behaviour so that he is aware of that monitoring and changes his behaviour accordingly (chapter three).

The preventive mechanism, however, does not completely explain why transparency is supposed to create legitimacy, other than it is assumed to prevent the governor's sinister interest from emerging. As discussed, in addition to law-making and policy-making, the governor uses his power over the governed in an individualized form, making decisions over his rights and duties (cf Lukes's first dimension of power). This form of power is subject to transparency requirements too (the public law rationality of transparency). That is to say, the governor need not only operate under the public eye, but also needs to explain and justify himself when it uses power over individuals. I call this *the justificatory mechanism of transparency.*

The justificatory mechanism of transparency also seeks to function as a legitimating tool, but from a somewhat different angle than in the preventive mechanism. If the preventive mechanism is concerned about creating a condition whereby the misuse of power would be as little tempting as possible, the justificatory mechanism is concerned about arguing why the object of power should accept the power used particularly on him. Unlike in the case of the preventive mechanism, the justificatory mechanism follows *ex post* logic. It comes close to Mansbridge's idea of transparency in rationale (justifying decisions).[26] This is further based on the assumption that following certain procedures that are generally considered legitimate influences how people accept the outcome of that use of power. That outcome can be, for example, a decision on an individual's rights or benefits. This is often referred to as procedural justice.

In liberal democratic societies, the justificatory mechanism is closely tied to the rule of law and its adherence. This especially concerns administration and adjudication; in legislation, democratic rationality and preventive mechanism arguably

[26] Mansbridge, 'A "Selection Model" of Political Representation' (n 4) 384–86.

play a greater role. I will come back to the theme of law and transparency in more detail in the next chapter. However, it is useful to mention now that the justificatory mechanism often takes the form of legal argumentation. This is to say, the governor would struggle to argue that the objects should accept his decisions were they not legally justified.[27] What I mean by that is the basic formula of legal argumentation: there is a norm premise (a paragraph, for example), a fact premise (a description of a particular situation), and an inference in which these two premises are brought together (what does law require in that particular situation?). Indeed, law does not do anything in the abstract, but it needs to be applied to fit the concrete situations of the lifeworld.

Why would we, then, talk about transparency in this context, and not, for example, simply talk about legal argumentation or reason-giving? These would be feasible alternatives too, but I would still maintain that talking about transparency is also useful in this context. Namely, as already mentioned, one of the key elements of that justification is understandability. This means a performance of a peculiar kind. It means making visible the applicable legal grounds, and importantly, the way in which they have been applied in a certain context. This gradual approach—the logic of justification, if you will—is to demonstrate the good will of the governor. The aim is to convince the governed that the governor uses his powers only for the purposes he is assigned to, and not, again, to furthering some sinister interest.

Thus, the justificatory mechanism is also concerned about the misuse of power, but, in the context of public law rationality, the specific concern is the standing of an individual (or a legal person), and her rights and duties. It is important to notice that how the governor has actually come to a decision is irrelevant. In other words, the so-called logic of discovery—how the heuristic of the decision actually took place in the brain of the governor—does not really matter; it matters only insofar as it can be plausibly translated into the logic of justification.

The goal is to create a legally plausible narrative of the power used. Moreover, the justification needs to be such that it enables its object to understand why the use of power in a certain way was correct. The legal scaffolding of the decision is thus made transparent for the object to review and, if she thinks that her rights have not been met, to appeal. Then, the justificatory mechanism is also iconophilic; the justification does not just 'emerge' from the power used, but it needs to be consciously created. The justificatory mechanism cannot be subject to a direct gaze as it lacks a physical appearance. It needs the hand at work.

[27] This presupposes approaching the legitimacy of governing that builds on legal-rational authority: the authority to govern stems from its rational and legal organization and functioning. According to Max Weber's classical categorization of authority, the alternatives for this would be traditional authority and charismatic authority. See Max Weber, *Economy and Society: An Outline of Interpretive Sociology* (G Roth and C Wittich eds, University of California Press 1978). See also Hubert Treiber, *Reading Max Weber's Sociology of Law* (Matthew Philpotts tr, Oxford University Press 2020).

The justificatory mechanism may also become entangled with the preventive mechanism. This stems from transparency's fundamental characteristic: as explained, it constantly oscillates between its literal and metaphorical meaning; it both is, and needs to be, created ('mediated immediacy'). For this reason, being subject to the transforming gaze or constant monitoring may also be symbolic. One can thus be *as if* a subject to a transforming gaze, *as if* a subject to constant monitoring. This means that also different ways of self-reporting—explaining how the governor has used and continues to use his vested power—may serve as the preventive mechanism. They enable discussion on how the governor is faring in his governing. In this case, the preventive mechanism adopts the functioning logic of the justificatory mechanism: it requires verbalization. Being subject to constant surveillance would thus be transformed into providing explanations, the iconoclastic exposure of the gaze would be transformed into the iconophilic creation of appearances, into self-reporting.

When we approach the preventive mechanism symbolically, we encounter the iconoclastic ideology of transparency, the bias towards immediacy over mediatedness. Ideally, what would there be to self-report if the entire reality that would form the raw material for that reporting were available for the external reviewer to witness immediately? Would we not, again, encounter the truer truth this way, without obfuscating impression management? Favouring immediacy over mediatedness acknowledges the intrinsic flaws of controlled disclosure; self-reporting always consists of a selected array of information, and it enables the hiding of potential sinister interests.[28] We encounter the chagrin over mediation. At least in theory, the preventive mechanism would make this selection of the reported reality—in other words, the omission and/or distortion of certain things—retraceable. This kind of transparency aspires to impede the emergence of misuse-enabling opacity.

Can Transparency Make Power Visible?

The Forms of Esoteric Knowledge

I have now reconstructed the premises on which the legitimacy promise of transparency is based. As said, this required approaching power as a unilateral condition, regardless of whether it in fact operates like that. However, things became more complicated when we discussed the multidimensionality of power. As presented, even if we need to hypothesize the unilaterality of power to reconstruct the promise of transparency, power cannot be reduced to its most obvious forms

[28] Compare Mansbridge, 'A "Selection Model" of Political Representation' (n 4) 370. She talks about *narrative accountability*.

of violence, physical coercion, or simple arrangements of command and control. These elements were already touched upon when discussing Lukes's and Foucault's notions on power. Can such an abstract, multifaceted, and contextual thing as power be made visible as the transparency narrative suggests?[29] This question deserves to be taken under closer scrutiny.

Many theorists argue that power and transparency are not necessarily a good match. Canetti, for example, argues that 'secrecy lies at the very core of power'.[30] Similarly, Han contends that transparency and power do not get on well together; power tends to cloak itself in secrecy.[31] Halbertal puts even more weight on the visibility of power, but from the opposite point of view. He insists on the visibility of power: '[p]ower, in order to exist, has to be made visible'.[32] By saying so, Halbertal couples the very existence of power with its visibility. Hence, ontology would paradoxically follow epistemology; in order for something to be *made* visible it first needs to exist.

Although no consensus can be argued to exist whether power needs to be visible or hidden to operate, we can say at least that the visibility of power has deeper layers to it than one might expect. Visibility does not only show how power operates but it may also question or even alter it. Although too much weight should not be given to the quotations provided in the previous paragraph, it seems possible that the visibility of power relates even to its very existence.

Let us approach the question of the visibility of power from a different angle than previously discussed: I argue that scrutinizing the realms of concealed or otherwise inaccessible knowledge may help us to understand the limitations of the visible-making effect of transparency. To that purpose, power must be approached as a form of knowledge or information. This aligns with the Foucauldian idea that power and knowledge imply each other and are not therefore independent categories. We also need to dismantle the overall group of 'the governed' and the monolithic nature of 'the governor'; both entities consist of groups of people with different rights, duties, and privileges. This is because not all information is equally accessible or discernible to everyone, as I will argue in the following. In other words, the democratization of knowledge that transparency presupposes has its limits.

[29] Fenster argues that the state is too bureaucratic and intricate to be seen. See Mark Fenster, 'Transparency in Search of a Theory' (2015) 18(2) European Journal of Social Theory 150. If that holds for an abstraction such as a state, what does it mean in regard to the even more abstract concept of power?

[30] Andrea Mubi Brighenti, *Visibility in Social Theory and Social Research* (Palgrave Macmillan 2010) 48 (hereafter Brighenti, 'Visibility in Social Theory and Social Research'); Elias Canetti, *Masse und Macht* (first published 1960, Seabury Press 1973) 290.

[31] Byung-Chul Han, *The Transparency Society* (Stanford University Press 2015) 47 (hereafter Han, 'The Transparency Society'): 'The praxis of arcana is one technique that power employs.'

[32] Moshe Halbertal, *Concealment and Revelation: Esotericism in Jewish Thought and Its Philosophical Implications* (Princeton University Press 2007) 149 (hereafter Halbertal, 'Concealment and Revelation').

Here again, Moshe Halbertal's analysis is helpful. His theorizing on transparency and the philosophical underpinnings of esoteric knowledge is highly useful here. The term 'esoteric' may sound at least exotic, if not downright inappropriate. In this context, I use it to label and analyse knowledge with limited, impeded, or impossible access.[33] It contrasts with exoteric knowledge, which is commonsensical in nature and accessible to a large audience. Partially, it can be seen as an account of different reasons for keeping secrets, which was already touched upon in the previous chapter. However, it is not restricted to that because not all esoteric knowledge has a keeper or keepers, as I will show.

Esoteric knowledge may mean many things and that is why it is not useful to approach it as a monolithic category. Halbertal distinguishes three different groups of esoteric knowledge, each of which is based on different assumptions of the effects of revelation. They are *instrumentally*, *internally*, and *essentially esoteric knowledge*. In particular, these categories differ in regard to presupposed agency: is certain information deliberately kept from sight or is it simply unfit to be presented? Let us look at each of these categories more closely.

Instrumentally esoteric knowledge refers to a type of knowledge which is deliberately concealed, because its disclosure could cause severe harm to some private or public interest. That is to say the possible benefits of the revelation would be considered less than its costs. Revelation would be generally detrimental. Let us take an example. In 2015, *The New York Times* wrote about a new police gadget, StingRay, which would make it possible for police officers to track mobile phones. The police departments adopting this powerful surveillance tool across the USA needed to meet an unusual requirement: to purchase it, law enforcement officials had to sign a non-disclosure agreement that would prevent them from saying almost anything about the technology. The FBI argued that any disclosure about the technology of StingRay could allow criminals and terrorists to circumvent it, which is why this concealment was warranted.[34]

[33] Esoteric knowledge has a long history in Jewish tradition, which is Halbertal's primary topic. However, as mentioned, the philosophical part of his book does not require commitment to that tradition. Therefore, I am not introducing any mystical or magical components into the concept of esoteric here, although it is typically associated with the occult. Instead, I approach it as a conceptual avenue to address the limits of accessibility of power as knowledge. Thus, the esoteric is approached here from the structural rather than from the genealogical point of view. Its function is first and foremost heuristic. However, suspicion towards transparency on the basis of occult worldviews is also a possible view. On this, see Todd Sanders and Harry G West (eds), *Transparency and Conspiracy: Ethnographies of Suspicion in the New World Order* (Duke University Press 2003).

[34] For example, Matt Richter, 'A Police Gadget Tracks Phones? Shhh! It's Secret' *New York Times* (New York, 15 March 2015) <www.nytimes.com/2015/03/16/business/a-police-gadget-tracks-phones-shhh-its-secret.html> accessed 2 July 2021: 'A powerful new surveillance tool being adopted by police departments across the country comes with an unusual requirement: To buy it, law enforcement officials must sign a nondisclosure agreement preventing them from saying almost anything about the technology. *Any disclosure about the technology, which tracks cellphones and is often called StingRay, could allow criminals and terrorists to circumvent* it, the F.B.I. has said in an affidavit. But the tool is adopted in such secrecy that communities are not always sure what they are buying or whether the technology could raise serious privacy concerns' (emphasis added).

The case of StingRay illustrates well the nature of instrumentally esoteric knowledge. We can notice that when instrumentally esoteric knowledge is at hand, someone needs to make the cost-benefit analysis—whether to make a certain piece of knowledge public or not—and act accordingly. It thus presupposes a keeper or a group of trusted keepers. That is to say, the information is not considered dangerous to the extent that it would need to be forbidden or demolished once and for all, but it is dangerous in the wrong hands. Similarly, Leonardo da Vinci refused to publish the exact design of his early submarine: 'I do not publish nor divulge these, by reason of the evil nature of men, who would use them for assassinations at the bottom of the sea'.[35] In this sense the knowledge is indeed esoteric, as it is accessible only to a selected individual or to a group of people who are considered fit for keeping that secret safe or used only for legitimate purposes.

Here, the esoteric nature does not thus stem from the knowledge itself but from its anticipated effects. If we look at the functioning logic of instrumentally esoteric knowledge more closely, we can observe that the motivation of the concealment is consequentialist (revelation leads to harm) and speculative (a certain harm needs to be anticipated as well as the causality between the revelation and the harm). In a way, it is covertly based on the biblical idea of good and bad knowledge. Indeed, powerful knowledge in the wrong hands needs to be prevented and that motive functions as a motivation for keeping it secret.

Internally esoteric knowledge, for one, is founded on an equally consequentialist (the connection between revelation and harm is presupposed) but more substantial motivation for concealment. Internally esoteric knowledge means that its revelation would somehow lessen its value. Unlike in the case of instrumentally esoteric knowledge, the revelation of internally esoteric knowledge does not need to be detrimental to externalities as for example to some private or public interest. Instead, the subject of the harm would be the knowledge itself, because the very value of that knowledge is intertwined with its restricted accessibility. Its rarity makes its valuable. For example, confidential discussions between a therapist and a patient could be seen as internally esoteric knowledge; their value lies in their confidentiality, their exclusion of unfit or uninterested parties.

Internally esoteric knowledge may also extend to the idea of authenticity, as discussed in chapters three and four. As Halbertal notes, referring to Walter Benjamin, reproduction may banalize internally esoteric knowledge. An illustrative example would be replicas made of great works of art: the production of cheap souvenirs waters down their uniqueness. These replicas make the original seem unworthy of higher appreciation; the banalization easily leads to the diminishing value of the original.[36] Availability to everyone, in a banalized form, may mean diminished

[35] Leonardo Da Vinci, *The Notebooks of Leonardo da Vinci*, vol 1, Part 1 (compiled and edited from the original manuscripts by Jean-Paul Richter, London 1883) 11.

[36] Halbertal, 'Concealment and Revelation' (n 32) 147.

or inexistent value to the original beneficiaries. Again, this feature presupposes a keeper or a group of keepers, someone who is accountable for the knowledge to stay pure and intact. Moreover, the keeper or keepers need to consider whom to initiate into their circle.

If we compare instrumentally esoteric knowledge with internally esoteric knowledge, the crucial difference between the two is the beneficiaries of the concealment: in the case of the instrumentally esoteric knowledge, the beneficiaries would be the majority of people being protected from harm, whereas in the case of internally esoteric knowledge, they would be the keepers of the secret themselves, those who are considered fit, justified, or privileged to enjoy it. It could be argued that the motivations for the concealment of instrumentally esoteric knowledge often translates into the language of safety and security, whereas in the case of internally esoteric knowledge that would be the language of confidentiality or privacy.

The most radical form of esoteric knowledge is, nevertheless, that of *essentially esoteric knowledge*. It means that the object of knowledge is such that it cannot be revealed or captured by any direct mode of verbalization. It may be ineffable. In the field of religion and spiritual practices, essentially esoteric knowledge refers to mystical experience.[37] In that sense, it is debatable whether it is knowledge to begin with, or does it instead articulate the borders of the knowable or the explicable? Essentially esoteric knowledge poses epistemological questions: how can we know what is knowable? Anthropomorphically expressed, does the knowledge reveal itself, when, whom, and how it chooses? The previously discussed acheiropoietic representations, which allegedly emerge without human contribution, would be an example of essentially esoteric knowledge expressing itself.

Essentially esoteric knowledge thus lacks keepers: rather than a secret it could be approached as a mystery. This was recognized by Wittgenstein, who famously said that what cannot be talked about, must be left in silence. By saying so he did not actually argue that ineffable knowledge would not exist. Instead, he called for clear use of language, outside of which essentially esoteric knowledge fell. It is neither evident to whom this knowledge is or can be accessible. As Halbertal puts it, when it comes to essentially esoteric knowledge, 'transparency is essentially blocked; we can only intimate the truth by way of symbols and hints'.[38] Thus, the knowledge itself may even be public, but understanding its 'true' or deeper meaning remains esoteric. That is to say that access to information as signs and understanding its

[37] ibid, 157. cf Cathryn Vasseleu, 'Simulated Translucency' in S Cubitt, D Palmer, and N Tkacz (eds), *Digital Light* (Open Humanities Press 2015) 168: 'In the stained glass windows of Gothic cathedrals, translucency was used to create the impression of the unveiling of veiled truths.'

[38] Halbertal, 'Concealment and Revelation' (n 32) 157. Halbertal also argues that allegory is the medium of instrumental esoteric, whereas a symbol is the medium of essential esoteric. See also Han, 'The Transparency Society' (n 31) 22: '[F]or Kant ... an object is sublime when it exceeds representation, any effort to picture it. The sublime exceeds the imagination [*Einbildungskraft*].'

meaning, the 'real' signified, diverge.[39] Essentially esoteric knowledge may not be understandable to most people.

Esoteric Knowledge and the Transparency of Power

What do the structures of esoteric knowledge mean in the context of transparency and the visibility of power? What kind of added value can they offer? I argue that they enable us to combine the idea of power and its many forms with the questions of the knowability of society through transparency and its preconditions. As discussed previously, the first dimension of power in Lukes's categorization is the one that is mostly, if not solely, subject to transparency requirements. The assumption is that we want to know how we are being governed. In the name of transparency, we encounter the calls for access to documents, access to proceedings, and effective communication. We are constructed as subjects who want to know what is decided for us and over us. If we are not happy with the way in which this is done, we can either try to get rid of the power as citizens (democratic rationality) or, if that power is exercised on us in particular, contest it as its subjects (public law rationality). To those ends, transparency attempts either to pre-empt the misuse of power from occurring (preventive mechanism), or it can attempt to persuade us to accept the power used (justificatory mechanism).

However, these rationalities and mechanisms do not automatically mean a lack of concealment. In the previous chapter, I discussed this issue in the context of social life, arguing that the main motives of concealment are the protection of strategy and the avoidance of shame. In the context of power, transparency neither allows us an unlimited access to documents, for example, nor does sunlight always function as a disinfectant. Quite the contrary: there are many reasons why some things are considered better to be kept secret from most of the governed than be freely available. The hand is, again, at work. This is where power as a form of instrumentally and internally esoteric knowledge comes into play. As explained, there are forms of esoteric knowledge that can also include different positions for keeping secrets. As argued, some knowledge may be detrimental in the wrong hands, which is why it is available to only a few. Additionally, some knowledge may lessen in value if made public and that is why its accessibility is restricted.

That said, in order to answer the question posed in this section—can transparency make power visible?—we still need to address specifically the connection between power and essentially esoteric knowledge. As argued, we need to notice that surreptitious forms of power can be so subtle or elusive that they lack a representable form. How can we make governmentality visible, for instance, when

[39] Alexander Galloway, 'Are Some Things Unrepresentable?' (2011) 28(7–8) Theory, Culture and Society 85, 91.

its constitutive feature is that we think that we are merely following our free will? The structural characteristics of essentially esoteric, non-democratized, and non-democratizable knowledge pose ontological, epistemological, and phenomenological questions to transparency's potency. Ideologically, transparency favours presentable over unpresentable, and by so doing unpresentable power may go unnoticed.[40] To be detected, surreptitious forms of power require laborious reconstruction to say the least; immediate visibility is not available (cf iconophily). Are some forms of power essentially esoteric? If the answer is positive, transparency is, indeed, blocked.

Radical transparency scepticism may, however, be equally problematic. If transparency's visible-making effect cannot be trusted at all, we could easily succumb to a conspiratorial worldview in which no appearance whatsoever can be trusted.[41] Conspiracy theories do, however, require an even more elaborate construction of assumptions of how the world works than just naïvely trusting in the illuminating potency of transparency. Such theories tend to assume that there is a bigger plan behind the deceitfully apparent. This requires us to assume two things. First, we need to believe that an invisible hand organizes the apparent transparency to fool us. Secondly, this invisible force would organize seemingly haphazard events into an esoteric totality behind the transparency façade.

If we accept the presumption of control as the functional prerequisite of transparency as a socio-legal ideal, capable of creating legitimacy through planned self-presentation, we can interpret certain societal practices through that lens. In the context of governance, esoteric knowledge translates into practices which pursue the protection of certain values, such as claims of privacy, trade secrecy (internally esoteric), and safety and security (instrumentally esoteric). Furthermore, these practices follow a legal script, as I will argue in the next chapter. Essentially esoteric power, however, cannot be reached through any obvious transparency practices.

To sum up, not all knowledge is accessible through transparency. That also means, as explained, that not all forms of power can be made visible through transparency practices. This is because some forms of information may be harmful to the knowledge itself, to other people, or simply be too complex to be verbalized, visualized, or delivered. In the cases of the instrumentally, internally, and essentially esoteric knowledge described above, transparency's intrinsic inadequacy to live up to its promise becomes apparent. To the extent that power can be seen as knowledge, transparency cannot make it all visible and as such controllable. Therefore, the sphere of the public or the transparent does not only contrast with privacy, it also contrasts with the epistemic or ethical impediments of revelation or

[40] Michael Schudson, *The Rise of the Right to Know: Politics and the Culture of Transparency, 1945–1975* (The Belknap Press of Harvard University Press 2015) 21.

[41] Brighenti, 'Visibility in Social Theory and Social Research' (n 30) 63.

even with the construction of certain information. The problem is, as Halbertal observes, the ultimate non-transparency of transparency.[42]

Do We Want to See Power?

I have now established that transparency and power are a difficult match for several reasons. Transparency can make only certain aspects of power visible and additionally, some aspects may be kept deliberately out of sight. These factors make transparency's potency partial, at best. The assessment of transparency's promise does not end there, however. Thus far, the eyes to look at power have been taken as a self-evident starting point. This is natural, because transparency as an ocularcentric ideal would have no bearing without eyes to look through that transparency. This was discussed in chapter three. As discussed, transparency promises visibility of power which further makes its control possible. This is its basic structure for providing legitimacy.

Hence, the idea of the controllability of power presupposes someone who has not only the ability but also the desire to control. This assumption, too, needs to be addressed critically. In other words, even if we could agree on the definition of power, and all power could be made visible through transparency practices, notwithstanding any restrictions of icono-ambivalence, impression management or esoteric knowledge, it remains unclear whether we *want* to see power. This is what de Fine Licht has called the 'sausage argument', referring to a famous quote from Otto von Bismarck: 'We might want to know how laws are made as little as we would want to know how sausages are produced.'[43] We might not always want to know how power is exercised whether or not it ends up as laws.

As argued, during the last couple of decades, transparency talk has proliferated at an unprecedented rate. Against such a backdrop it is interesting to note that historically, governmental power has become less and less visible. That development forms an overarching idea in Foucault's oeuvre. In *Discipline and Punish*, he argued how spectacular power, such as public punishments and executions—common up until the mid-eighteenth century—eventually lost their meaning, being superseded by prison as the main form of punishment.[44] This followed from a change in governmentality, if you will: the juridic rationality of power, based on the logic of prohibition and repression, began to be substituted by disciplinary power, with the panopticon as its symbol. The idea was to reduce deviance rather than to function as a deterrent, which is what public executions were intended to do.

[42] Halbertal, 'Concealment and Revelation' (n 32) 165.
[43] De Fine Licht, 'Magic Wand or Pandora's Box?' (n 1) 38–39, 111–34.
[44] The context is mainly the changes in the penal system in France. However, more extensive arguments based on that analysis can be, and have been, made.

In liberal rationality of power, discussed in particular in Foucault's *The Birth of Biopolitics*, the goal became to guarantee people as much freedom as possible and to prevent different societal risks from occurring. Governing becomes even less ceremonial and rather managerial in style, using statistics and economics as a tool for governing rather than discipline or retribution.[45] Obviously, this development was not linear, and many details would need to be omitted to argue for the existence of this kind of grand narrative. It would, however, be dangerous to assume that the less spectacular power became, the less it existed. Quite the contrary: according to the liberal rationality of governing, power lies first and foremost in conducting people's use of freedom. This power, as argued, does not necessarily look like power and it does not readily adopt a visible form. In some ways, it can even be essentially esoteric.

What we can infer from this is that the freer we are constructed as individuals, the less visible power becomes. Furthermore, we need to assume that our self-conception as free individuals is based on the assumption that the way in which our freedom is restricted is—ideally transparent—decision-making. Put differently, it may be an anathema for us to think that the very freedom we may use for controlling power is, in fact, a corollary of that power.

If we go back to the idea of shame, discussed in the previous chapter, the question is the following. Can we tolerate seeing power? Are we ashamed of being governed badly, governed in general, or otherwise subordinate to power? The visibility of being subject to power would not necessarily fit well with our attempts to govern ourselves and as a salient part of that, control our self-presentation. This relates to the questions of to what extent can we freely choose how we portray ourselves to others, what choices can we make, how do we lead our lives, and what kind of political action, if any, do we engage with? When we think about subtle technologies of governmentality, do we really want to know how, in Foucault's words, our conduct is being conducted? Or would we prefer to think that all we do is exercise our free will, even though we would acknowledge that it is a useful fiction?

It could be proposed that what defines us—even if it is at least partially a product of governmental power—needs to stay out of sight. Thomas Docherty analyses this aptly in his book *Confessions: The Philosophy of Transparency* (2014), through the ideas of 'office' and 'official'. He argues that our current prevailing modes of critical thought or our identities are not autonomously determined. Instead, they are typically given to us. Their primary function is to officially delimit and to regulate our possible behaviours. Our identity is 'official' in the sense of a matter of office, which further defines how we are allowed to be. Consequently, any genuinely historical act that we would commit would be inevitably clandestine, as it would break with the conformity expectations of our office. In other words, according to

[45] Foucault, 'The Government of Self and Others' (n 13) 291–316.

Docherty, we are being denied the possibility of acting as autonomous historical agents exactly by being ascribed an 'official identity'.[46]

Docherty's ideas go well together with the governmentality approach. We can assume that governmental power also operates by putting the governed into different official boxes, and in this way different identities and different outlets for expressing those identities are created. We might think of these boxes as a matter of a natural state of affairs, or our own choice. For that reason, it is difficult to identify to what extent our behaviour is subject to conduct ('conduct of conduct') in what ways we are given social and political identities and agency, and what follows from that. Correspondingly, our own power, so to speak, eludes our attention most of the time. We do not necessarily know when we have power, when we are using it, or even when we are subject to it. Brighenti suggests that it is precisely the covert or unseen that seems to make us unfree,[47] although, as argued, it may simultaneously define us. The invisible elements in us make it difficult to understand who we are and what we can do.

Therefore, if we think of governmental power, which transparency practices are to make at least partially visible, how does that affect us? What do we want to see? How would this seeing make us feel or act? Does it cause acceptance, resistance, aggravation, immediate action, powerless resignation, apathy, enthusiasm, or a desire to know or to change things? Does the emotional colouration matter? Importantly, transparency practices do not only make certain information accessible or create a certain image of governance, they also create subjects who are defined by their assumed need and desire to know in a particular way. It makes us see governing in the way in which it is designed to be seen. It makes us citizens whose right it is to know the information, and only that information, which that right defines. This comes close to Flyverbom's observation: 'While transparency can certainly be considered and researched as an administrative, organizational and political norm, it can also be viewed as a form of governance in itself.'[48]

We are thus portrayed as the users of transparency, we are assumed to want to see power, in particular in its decision-making aspect. Transparency as an ocularcentric ideal is thus capable of hiding power by intimating that power can be made visible, and beyond that visibility there is no power or that power is less important. Furthermore, the assumption is that we as the governed—either as the principals of power (democratic rationality) or subjects to it (public law rationality) are willing and able to react to it if we do not like it. Visibility of power is thus not

[46] Thomas Docherty, *Confessions: The Philosophy of Transparency* (Bloomsbury Publishing 2014) 23.

[47] Brighenti, 'Visibility in Social Theory and Social Research' (n 30) 67.

[48] Mikkel Flyverbom, 'Sunlight in Cyberspace? On Transparency as a Form of Ordering' (2015) 18 European Journal of Social Theory 168, 169. Similarly, Etzioni argues that it is easy to miss the fact that transparency is itself a form of regulation. Amitai Etzioni, 'The Limits of Transparency' in Emmanuel Alloa and Dieter Thomä (eds), *Transparency, Society and Subjectivity: Critical Perspectives* (Palgrave Macmillan 2018) 179, 189–90.

only about showing how things are (iconoclasm) or about creating representations (iconophily), but also a tool of power itself. It enables us to create certain kinds of realms of knowledge which, by definition, are limited. They are limited depending on how we are created as subjects.

Summing Up: Assessing the Credibility of Transparency's Promise

In this chapter I have examined the relationship between power and transparency from different angles. Let us summarize the discussion. I argued that in governmental—and perhaps vertical power relations in general—we typically talk about transparency as a positive thing. We consider transparency to be a guarantee of the legitimacy of power by making that power visible and controllable. Power is, however, a manifold thing, as I have explained, referring to Lukes's and Foucault's theories. But regardless of this, when we talk about the triangle of transparency, legitimacy, and power, we need to act as if power could be reduced primarily to its decision-making aspect.

I argued that the transparency-legitimacy nexus functions through two main avenues. I referred to them as the democratic rationality and the public law rationality of transparency. Depending on the position in question, the way in which transparency promises legitimacy differs. In democratic rationality, the legitimacy is based on the idea that the governed are the principals of power, and as such, they need to be kept informed on how the governor as an agent is faring. The governor is therefore accountable for his constituents. In public law rationality, in turn, the legitimacy promise of transparency stems from a different source. In it, instead of the principal of power, the governed is in the position of its subject. When that power is transparent, it is so in the sense of understandability. Ideally, one accepts being a subject to power because it is based on the governor's legitimate authority, which the subject can see and thus, understand and accept.

Furthermore, I argued that the way in which these legitimacy promises of transparency operate could be broken down into two mechanisms. The preventive mechanism is in operation when such circumstances are created that ideally, the governor cannot escape the controlling gaze of the governed. This gaze is intended to make the governor behave a way that can endure that gaze (compare with the panoptic modality of power, the transforming gaze). In Goffman's vocabulary, there would be no backstage to prepare a credible performance. Thus, transparency so created would not reveal anything *per se*, as it would attempt to prevent the sinister interests of the governor from emerging in the first place. Democratic rationality typically utilizes the preventive mechanism.

The justificatory mechanism, for one, serves the purpose of justifying the power used, after it has been used. It does so by giving reasons: this means going through the rules and norms which authorize the power used and the way in which it has been applied in the case in question. It makes the power used visible and justified by showing the applied logic and making it ideally understandable to the governed.

In the rest of the chapter, I argued that these promises of transparency are flawed because they are based on a simplified conception of power. To prove that I discussed the structures of esoteric knowledge that are only available for a certain group of people. I used Moshe Halbertal's categorization of instrumentally, internally, and essentially esoteric knowledge. Instrumentally esoteric knowledge refers to knowledge which is kept secret because its revelation would likely lead to harm. In the case of internally esoteric knowledge, the object of protection would be the knowledge itself, as its meaning would lessen were it made public. Essentially esoteric knowledge would be the most enigmatic, since it would not have interested keepers, unlike in the other two groups. Essentially esoteric knowledge would not have any clear way of presentation, but it would emerge only indirectly, if at all.

Consequently, I argued that transparency is necessarily blocked due to the impediments posed by esoteric knowledge. Power can be seen as knowledge, which is at least partially esoteric. Some forms of it are kept from the eyes of the governed, whereas some forms of power, such as some delicate modes of governmentality, may even be essentially esoteric, unfit for visual, and possibly even verbal presentation.

Lastly, I questioned whether we really want to see power, as the transparency narrative inevitably assumes. I discussed how that power has become less visible when we have been moving from power as a deterrent, or even as a means of discipline, towards a liberal way of governing. It seems that transparency discourse and requirements have proliferated simultaneously with the diminishing ceremoniality of power. Our desire to see power intertwines with our self-knowledge or the lack thereof. We are often strangers to ourselves. We are not only free to control power, but our different identities as the governed are also products of power. We are constituted into subjects which have a desire to control power through transparency practices.

In this chapter, I have attempted to construct a simple argument through the mélange of theories I discussed. It can be summed up thus: transparency is generally considered a good thing especially in the context of power. However, power is a complex phenomenon: it is debatable to what extent it can be made visible through transparency practices. Neither is it clear whether we want to see power, even if we could. Thus, even when transparency is generally seen as a value in the context of power, its potency to live up to its promise as well as our desire for transparency is more complicated than normative transparency narratives typically suggest. In other words, the fulfilment of transparency's promise is far from obvious. Thus, less obviously, transparency is not only about attempting to make power visible it is also about contributing to the make-up of society more generally. This is done by creating a socio-political subject onto whom a certain kind of desire to know is projected.

6
Transparency and Law

Law Creating Transparency

I have now established that as a socio-legal ideal, transparency is essentially intertwined with asymmetrical power and its legitimatized use that is characteristic of the state and other forms of public authority. In examining the functioning mechanisms of transparency, I have moved from the general towards the specific. So far, I have not directly talked about the legal arrangement of these ideas. As argued, transparency is closely related to democracy and rule-governed administration, and those are quintessentially legally organized. Thus, law matters, even though it cannot colonize the entirety of transparency discourse.

Mark Fenster argues that:

> A transparent state removes the obstructions that keep the government hidden and the public imperfectly informed. This solution does not occur naturally because the state will not reveal itself willingly. The public needs a powerful external mechanism to force the state bureaucracy to make itself visible. Commonly, such instruments are administrative laws, enacted by legislative bodies and enforced by the judiciary, and constitutional protections against excessive secrecy developed and enforced by courts, which impose obligations upon government entities and officials to make their work more visible.[1]

In this quotation, law appears to be something opposite to the state, a counterweight to its natural predilection for keeping itself hidden (view 1). This is not the only viable way of interpreting the role of law in transparency practices. Alternatively, it could also be seen as an integral part of the state, instead of something external to it (view 2).

Both views are, nevertheless, possible; the first can be seen as an application of the iconoclastic idea (removing impediments to visibility; the preventive mechanism of transparency), whereas the second and alternative view can be seen as iconophilic (constructing elements of appearance; the legal production of visibility). When we talk about the ways in which government makes itself known, these two approaches are not as far from each other as it may seem. In law,

[1] Mark Fenster, *The Transparency Fix: Secrets, Leaks, and Uncontrollable Government Information* (Stanford University Press 2017) 4 (hereafter Fenster, 'The Transparency Fix').

The Transparency Paradox. Ida Koivisto, Oxford University Press. © Ida Koivisto 2022.
DOI: 10.1093/oso/9780192855466.003.0006

transparency often translates into practices of access to documents—or, to put it more modernly—access to information, which relies on the iconophilic aspect of transparency, as I will explain. Whether the concealment of these documents is broken, is, for one, an iconoclastic question. Furthermore, in any case, the scope of transparency is planned and typically, legally regulated.

However, the way in which this duality of views works is not necessarily easy to decipher. Our choice of concepts may reflect our deeper understanding of how law is or should be, and in what way government should make itself known. Perhaps culture and fiction further inform that understanding, or as van De Port put it, inform the cultural production of the really real. As Cornelia Vismann states in her insightful book *Files: Law and Media Technology* (2008), literary fictions that deal with administration highlight media and the realities of law, which non-fictional, scholarly self-presentations of the law and history tend to suppress and overlook. Thus, Vismann claims, Franz Kafka's chancery fantasies can be used to write a genealogy of law, or Herman Melville's 'Bartleby, the Scrivener' and his refusal to write mirrors the facts of recording.[2] Indeed, sometimes, we may need to turn to fiction to gain a clue of this dynamic of administration, namely to decipher the cultural-legal production of the real.

Before proceeding to transparency's relationship with law, a reminder of the concepts used and the approach adopted to these concepts is needed. As I have argued, there can be at least two points of departure in approaching the meaning of transparency: the cognitive analogy approach and the contingent signifier approach. The former departs from the idea that 'transparency' as a signifier is based on the cognitive metaphor according to which access to unmediated reality is possible. That is why it is appealing to us: it makes intuitive sense. As presented, there are also historical reasons for backing up this idea.[3] The latter is based on the opposite point of departure. According to it, it does not really matter what we call the issue, it is in any case contingent. As Shakespeare put it, 'a rose by any other name would smell as sweet'. If we call transparency 'transparency' and not something else, it is simply because it is customary to do so.

It is useful at this stage to provide a reminder about the goals of this book. In order to answer the question on 'transparency in law' fully and in a detailed manner, one could take a look at transparency formulations in different legal systems and legal cultures. After that, some comparative remarks could be made, and

[2] Cornelia Vismann, *Files: Law and Media Technology* (Stanford University Press 2008) xiii (hereafter Vismann, 'Files: Law and Media Technology'). See also Daniel Solove, *The Digital Person: Technology and Privacy in the Information Age* (New York University Press 2004) 27–55.

[3] Emmanuel Alloa, 'Transparency: A Magic Concept of Modernity' in Emmanuel Alloa and Dieter Thomä (eds), *Transparency, Society and Subjectivity: Critical Perspectives* (Palgrave Macmillan 2018) 23–29; Vincent August and Fran Osrecki, *Der Transparenz-Imperativ: Normen—Praktiken—Strukturen* (Springer 2019).

conclusions drawn. This would be a viable approach, and it could provide some interesting insights. However, that approach is not adopted here, as the focus of this book is not on comparative law. Instead, the emphasis is on the question of how can law manifest and channel the paradoxical nature of transparency? To that end, I theoretically analyse the ways law can make power visible or hide it following those rationalities and mechanisms of transparency that were discussed in the previous chapter.

In this chapter, I discuss the ways in which transparency constitutes a legal concept in the state. How does law—a set of rules, principles, and concepts—manage to manifest something as intangible as transparency? What kind of transparency practices does law create? Using Mark Fenster's vocabulary, I argue that transparency is interpreted as specific technocratic translations in law. These translations further reflect the conceptual characteristics of transparency, explained in the previous chapters—icono-ambivalence, the hand at work, performativity, and democratic and public law rationality.

The chapter is organized in the following way. I first discuss the closer meaning of the metaphor of transparency in law. Second, I analyse documents, documentation, and information as manifestations of legally informed iconophilic practices. Third, I discuss the different ways in which law can create matrixes for transparency. What are the technocratic translations of the transparency metaphor? Three of them are forms of intentional transparency, and thus are subject to controlled impression management logics: the access to documents, the attendance of the public, and the forms of proactive communication. Fourth, I discuss how the negative connotation of transparency can be understood in law: it takes the forms of information leaking and whistleblowing. Finally, I summarize the chapter and argue that transparency is not reducible to its technocratic translations even in law. Transparency can be seen as a condition which law either underpins, overlooks, or denies.

The Metaphor of Transparency in Legal Vocabulary

Let us start by looking more closely at how the metaphor of transparency, which was discussed in general in chapter two, is considered in legal vocabulary. What does it imply when power is being used in a legally expressed way? The intellectual history of the concept of transparency was already briefly discussed in the introduction. However, particularly in the context of law, more recent changes in the vocabulary may be worth noticing. Schudson, for example, explains how transparency as a concept is a newcomer; before that, the term 'disclosure' was preferred. Indeed, legislation and concomitant administrative practices may be called 'access to information', 'open government', 'the principle of openness', 'the right to know', 'publicity', 'freedom of information', or even 'sunshine acts'. However, it is 'transparency' that has become the preferred term over the last couple of decades.[4]

In the following, I concentrate on two accounts, one from the viewpoint of the state (Mark Fenster), and the other from that of international law (Andrea Bianchi). However, this discussion by no means attempts to be a comprehensive mapping of all the uses of the metaphor in legal language. Instead, it serves as an illustration of possible ways in which the metaphor of transparency may be relevant in the field of law.

In his article 'Seeing the State: Transparency as Metaphor' (2010), Mark Fenster examines the metaphor of transparency as part of the vocabulary of public law and policy. He discusses the concept and its implications in particular in the USA. As already mentioned, Fenster approaches the state as the object of transparency, rather than as a primary source of transparency. He argues that transparency entails two main dimensions: the metaphorical, populist, promise ('the democratic wish') and its technocratic translation.[5] Correspondingly, Fenster argues, transparency in a state operates in two ways: first, it constitutes a technical concept, which can, at least in theory, be implemented in legislation. Second, however, the metaphorical promise indirectly portrays a state as a corrupt and secretive unit that needs to be exposed and made visible.[6] Seen in this way, transparency encompasses the twin ideals of access to the state and revealing potential mismanagement. It seems that this paradox stems from a single conceptual precondition: the assumed distance and borderline between the governor and the governed.[7]

The role of transparency as a 'democratic wish' or 'aspirational goal', as Fenster calls it, makes transparency a metonym for democratic government. This wish covertly suggests that more transparency or openness automatically leads to less distance between the governor and the governed.[8] This reduction of distance may, however, be too ambitious a goal. As Fenster argues, a state is territorially too big and bureaucratically too intricate to be made wholly visible:[9] 'The democratic wish for transparency may (or may not) lead to a more visible state, but it will certainly produce more of the state to be visible.'[10] That is to say, the metaphorical utopia of

[4] Michael Schudson, *The Rise of the Right to Know: Politics and the Culture of Transparency, 1945–1975* (The Belknap Press of Harvard University Press 2015); Sandrine Baume, 'Publicity and Transparency: The Itinerary of a Subtle Distinction' in Emmanuel Alloa and Dieter Thomä (eds), *Transparency, Society, Subjectivity: Critical Perspectives* (Palgrave Macmillan 2018) 204–05.

[5] In an earlier article Fenster argues that 'As both an instrumentalist project to achieve open government and, more broadly, a descriptive concept claimed to be at the core of democracy, transparency fails to consider the tensions it conceals.' Mark Fenster, 'The Opacity of Transparency' (2006) 91 Iowa Law Review 885, 892.

[6] Mark Fenster, 'Seeing the State: Transparency as Metaphor' (2010) 62 Administrative Law Review 617, 628 (hereafter Fenster, 'Seeing the State').

[7] David Heald, 'The Varieties of Transparency' in C Hood and D Heald (eds), *Transparency: The Key to Better Governance?* (Oxford University Press 2006) 27.

[8] Fenster, 'Seeing the State' (n 6) 628–32.

[9] ibid, 671.

[10] ibid, 632; also Mark Fenster, 'Transparency in Search of a Theory' (2015) 18 European Journal of Social Theory 150.

transparency undergoes a substantial transformation along with its technocratic translation into rules and norms. The technocratic reading of the concept produces more texts, more law, more state bureaucracy, and arguably, more mediated bureaucracy.[11] Although Fenster's analysis largely concentrates on the American legal realm, due to the general nature of the analysis, it can be assumed that a similar rationale buttresses most Freedom of Information Acts (FOIAs) in states.

In order to widen the institutional landscape, let us move to the other account, that of Andrea Bianchi. Like Fenster, Bianchi also analyses the metaphor of transparency as part of legal language. Bianchi's context is, however, that of international law in which transparency discourse is a more recent phenomenon than in the state. His essay 'On Power and Illusion: The Concept of Transparency in International Law' is the opening chapter of the edited volume *Transparency in International Law* (2013). Bianchi analyses the new rise as well as the pitfalls of the concept of transparency and its implications in international law. Interestingly, he is open about his well-founded confusion concerning the concept; it is obvious that its definition is difficult and no consensus about it exists. As in this book, he approaches transparency as a concept which is a magnet for many different, possibly contradicting, connotations.

Bianchi argues that transparency constitutes a normative concept, which however has little bearing in traditional sources on the doctrine of international law. Its legal standing is vague: it is ceremoniously talked about and yet its binding character and concrete ramifications remain unclear. It seems to be 'emerging' and 'developing', in *statu nascendi*, a work in progress.[12] Bianchi discusses the different ways in which transparency could be categorized: is it a 'principle'[13] or a so-called 'interstitial concept'—roughly, a concept which is used for filling in gaps in the law when more elaborate rules or concepts are lacking? Is it a general cultural demand, which is in the process of finding its legal avatar?

In international law, transparency's increasing desirability is, however, beyond doubt. There seems to be a transition in general attitudes from favouring secrecy to favouring openness. This enables transparency also to have subtle and therefore surreptitious ways of functioning: it may work as a discursive strategy that power-wielding bodies use in order to control the access and production of knowledge. As Bianchi notes, information does not speak for itself but needs an agent. This

[11] Compare Amitai Etzioni, 'The Limits of Transparency' in Emmanuel Alloa and Dieter Thomä (eds), *Transparency, Society and Subjectivity: Critical Perspectives* (Palgrave Macmillan 2018) 179, 189–90 (hereafter Etzioni, 'The Limits of Transparency').

[12] Andrea Bianchi, 'On Power and Illusion: The Concept of Transparency in International Law' in Andrea Bianchi and Anne Peters (eds), *Transparency in International Law* (Cambridge University Press 2013) 1, 5 (hereafter Bianchi, 'On Power and Illusion').

[13] It has its most articulate legal anchor in the Statute of the International Court of Justice (San Francisco Conference 26 June 1945). According to its article 38(1) (c), transparency can be considered a 'principle'. ('38 (1) The Court, whose function is to decide in accordance with international law such disputes as are submitted to it, shall apply: ... c) the general principles of law recognized by civilized nations').

reliance enables the instrumental use of information. Indeed, making information available is not synonymous with transparency.[14]

On the basis of the two accounts, transparency as a metaphor in law builds on an uncanny combination of cynicism and naïveté. It is cynical in the way in which Fenster describes it: it posits a state in need of discipline and control. As an abstract agent, it needs to be made accountable to the principal, the people (compare this with the democratic rationality of transparency). Therefore, it assumes the state to be a potential nest where power is abused. On the other hand, the governed, the users of transparency that is, are assumed to be benevolent and constructive. The information which transparency potentially offers is assumed to strengthen the democratic accountability of government. However, there is nothing, conceptually or practically, that could hinder the governed from using the acquired information for something generally destructive.

We can notice that transparency as a metaphor can be approached somewhat differently in the context of public law and the state, and in international law. In a state, its promise is established, although suspicions towards its functionality remain well founded for the reasons explained above. The conjunction between the state and transparency is deeply rooted, as was already discussed in the previous chapter. The metaphor and its connection to the state date back all the way to Bentham, as mentioned. The people should be able to see the state, and that 'democratic wish' may have its technocratic translations in law.

In international law, transparency has a much shorter history, and potentially, it could be considered a legal transplant. This might be due to strategy exposure avoidance, which was previously discussed together with concealment motives in chapter four. Nonetheless, in the doctrine of international law, transparency has been moving from the margin towards the centre. Previous perils and dangers attributed to transparency seem to be losing significance, whereas its moral authority is becoming unquestionable.

Potentially, this shift can be traced back to transparency's nature as a magic concept, discussed in chapter one. It seems that magic concepts can be so strong that even traditional doctrines in law may be powerless before them. That is to say, these doctrines may absorb magic concepts, regardless of the actual practices they may encompass.[15] The inherent legitimacy attributed to transparency may thus be utilized by law. I will delve into the globalizing and discursifying nature of transparency more closely in the next chapter.

[14] Bianchi, 'On Power and Illusion' (n 12) 14.

[15] In a similar way, 'good governance' and 'good administration'. See Ida Koivisto, 'From Moral Rules to Individual Rights—and Beyond? The Institutionalization of Good Administration in Finland and in Europe' (2018) 1 Förvaltningsrättslig tidskrift 71.

Documentation, Documents, and Information

Following Fenster, transparency as a metaphor in legal language is two-fold. On the one hand, its metaphorical authority constitutes a solemn promise of legitimizing power and law; it entails a 'democratic wish', as it were. On the other hand, this promise trickles down to more concrete practices and rules, to different dos and don'ts, and to margins of deliberation. This general idea was referred to as 'technocratic translation'. Through technocratic translations, the metaphor of transparency becomes practices.

The actual chronological trajectory between the promise and the rules concretizing it, does not, of course, necessarily move in that direction; rules may come first and from them, the promise can be inferred or reconstructed. In this chapter, however, these technocratic translations are treated as manifestations of the theoretical promise with its already described functional characteristics, in other words, as a reconstruction. I depart from the assumption that public access to government-held information makes the most important technocratic translation of the promise of transparency. That information is traditionally conserved in documents—however, this may be changing, as I will argue.

Before going on to the question of access, a few words about documents, documentation, and information are in order. What is a document and why does it play such a huge role in legal transparency practices? The idea of a document is more multifaceted than one could imagine. As argued, in many instances, government has no way of creating a physical appearance without different constructs (iconophily); without these constructs, in most cases there is nothing to see through transparency practices. Although these constructs can be of various kinds—memoranda, judgements, decisions, plans, maps, images, statistics, correspondence, e-mails, computer files, etc—most prototypically they all fall into the category of 'documents'. Documents can thus also be electronic, and thus not pieces of paper, as is increasingly the case.

The idea of documents and transparency as access to them is essentially iconophilic. It relies on the concept of a document as a messenger of the inner workings of governmental power as well as its external affairs. Documents can be either produced by government or delivered to it. These documents are, in a way, little singular representations of governmental power. Moreover, they are products of *documentation*, a meticulous mimicry of reality, which takes place sometimes in visual and mostly in verbal form. As legal anthropologist Annelise Riles has argued, the practice of documentation includes a utopian vision of information and transparency in its ability to record all human activity everywhere.[16] Indeed,

16 Fenster, 'The Transparency Fix' (n 1) 108; Annelise Riles, 'Introduction: In Response' in Annelise Riles (ed), *Documents: Artifacts of Modern Knowledge* (University of Michigan Press 2006) 1, 5–6.

documentation is decisive to the extent that it forms the very watershed between pre-history and history.

Documentation thus ensures the existence of a past event. If there is no document, there is no proof of the events it would refer to. As Hansen argues, 'Much of our knowledge does not come from our own direct experience of being co-present, but from material objects and social processes that translate what is distant into knowledge that can be deployed and mobilized in another context.'[17] For example, if there is no official, documented administrative decision, would its content still exist in our minds? If yes, for how long—a day, a week, five years, a hundred years? How accurate would the details be? What about an unrecorded phone call between high-level bureaucrats on a politically contested matter? Did it ever take place when there are no documents of it? Without carefully documented and stored information—documents—the iconophilic variant of governance transparency could not work. Access to documents is meaningless without documents and documentation.

What is a document, then? According to media historian Lisa Gitelman, a 'document' comes from a Latin root 'docer', to teach or to show. This suggests that a document exists so as to document, to teach, or show how things were. In that way, documents are 'epistemic objects' that serve as the 'recognizable sites and subjects of interpretation across the disciplines and beyond, evidential structures in the long human history of clues.'[18] Hence, as Fenster notes, documents exist to reflect and represent knowledge. This knowledge resides in the very act of communicating it. Namely, documents both exhibit and communicate knowledge, thus they function as evidence that can constitute something official when held or produced by the state.[19]

One could even suggest that government has traditionally been dependent on documentation and the documents it produces. This reliance on—if not fetishizing of—documents, is premised on the unexpressed assumption that those documents are indeed capable of representing the 'thing in itself', or at least that they are reliable messengers of it. In their piecemeal way, documents make 'the thing for us' to witness. They tell us no less than what government is and what it does—with, however, the important reservation of documentation. What is not documented, does not formally exist, or ceases to exist in a short time. In that way, documentation is the gatekeeper of the iconophilic aspect of transparency; it could, perhaps, be seen as legally motivated icono-genesis. Although documents necessarily imply the pre-documented existence of the things documented, they become independent of those events, becoming avenues of legal production of reality.

[17] Hans Krause Hansen, 'Numerical Operations, Transparency Illusions and the Datafication of Governance' (2015) 18(2) European Journal of Social Theory 203, 208.

[18] Lisa Gitelman, *Paper Knowledge: Toward a Media History of Documents* (Duke University Press 2014) 1 (hereafter Gitelman, 'Paper Knowledge'); Fenster, 'The Transparency Fix' (n 1) 110.

[19] Fenster, 'The Transparency Fix' (n 1) 114.

Once produced by documentation, documents have a life of their own. A document may communicate many things, which stems from their nature as epistemic objects, as it were. Fenster discusses this in detail. He poses some important questions: 'Do the (...) documents speak to a particular purpose that a reader can isolate? Does the information that the documents purport to know and show, constitute a knowable truth?'[20] The existence of documents is, thus, one thing, and the information they contain, another. In one object, they are simultaneously sites or containers of knowledge, as well as the contained knowledge itself. The distinction is important both theoretically and practically; it is not hair-splitting. For example, when we talk about access to documents, some piece of information in a document may be public, whereas the rest of the document may not. The publicness of the container in all its contained information, and the pieces of those contained information selves, may thus bifurcate. The question of access pushes towards that distinction.

Vismann, too, has an interesting approach to the significance of documents and documentation. Although she discusses 'files' instead of 'documents'—though files can be seen as a collection of documents—her words can be seen as an answer to Fenster's questions: 'files are the basis of legal work. Their validity resides in their truth value and their everyday operations.... It is only when records are removed from the self-referential, administrative context—for instance, when they are introduced as evidence before courts or parliamentary inquiries—that their own status becomes an object of scrutiny.'[21] Informed by this, we can argue that the 'knowable truth' is radically contextual; it changes along its point of reference. A document refers both to itself, as a site of knowledge, and outside itself, to particular pieces of information, as was argued, through 'knowing-showing', as Gitelman puts it.[22] Following Vismann, in turn, the context defines which of the points of reference is more important on a given moment.

However, here the focus is not on documents in general, but their meaning in making government known, their significance in the iconophilic aspect of transparency. Those documents are thus in the possession of the government, which makes it a repository of government information.[23] Simultaneously, this possession makes the government the controller of the subsequent informational asymmetry that this possession of the documents constitutes and on which government is based on. This is visible in the assumptions that, according to Fenster, both transparency advocates and secrecy advocates share: '1. Government constitutes a producer and repository of information, and it can be made to control that information. 2. Government information constitutes a message that can be isolated and

20 ibid.

21 Vismann, 'Files: Law and Media Technology' (n 2) 11.

22 Gitelman, 'Paper Knowledge' (n 18) 2.

23 This idea—the spatial understanding of the files and their organization—stems from the Romans. Vismann, 'Files: Law and Media Technology' (n 2) 57–61.

revealed, 3. A receiver of the message awaits disclosure of government information and is ready, willing and able to act in predictable, informed ways in response to the disclosure of government information.'[24]

It is important to note that in the era of digitalization and datafication, it is no longer clear whether the concept of a document is always optimal when we talk about access to information—information that makes up huge repositories held by the government. Should documents as the site of knowledge lose their legally privileged position? It is important to note that if a document builds on particular assumptions of being an information repository, information, too has its theoretical underpinnings. As Tsoukas explains, in an information society, it is possible to view everything as information—in particular digitized information—as an object that can be processed, stored, sent, and retrieved. Indeed, in a society obsessed by information, communication tends to be conceived in terms of the 'conduit metaphor': ideas are thought to be like objects that can be sent through a channel of distribution (a conduit) to a recipient, who in turn, recovers them in their original form.[25]

Indeed, along with the digitalization and datafication of our societies and governance, this fetishizing of information may intensify at the same time as the materiality of documents as a site for information decreases. The production of knowledge may in future rely less on documentation as a mimicry of reality than it used to. Instead, due to recent technological developments, there are signs of information emerging from the data itself, from data that we all produce. This data may also be gathered and processed without conscious human documentation. This may be done through data analytics, computer programs, automated decision-making, perhaps even artificial intelligence (AI)—products of human intelligence that when in operation are not reliant on humans.

That said, recent technological developments have led to a situation in which government information is increasingly independent of documents and even documentation that precedes that information. To the extent that governance is becoming digital and data-driven, the mindset behind the traditional technocratic translations of transparency may need reimagining. If the gathering, processing, and storing of data are increasingly automatized, we need to analyse the way in which that affects the iconophilic side of the transparency of governance. As Adams argues, 'information laws work to exclude and delimit other realities, and particularly other forms of governance that are not centralised and bureaucratic, and other forms of knowledge or information that cannot be contained within a disclosable record'.[26]

[24] Fenster, 'The Transparency Fix' (n 1) 77.

[25] Haridimos Tsoukas, 'The Tyranny of Light: The Temptations and the Paradoxes of the Information Society' (1997) 29(9) Futures 827, 829–30.

[26] Rachel Adams, *Transparency: New Trajectories in Law* (Routledge 2020) 38.

This is to say, it is possible that the state is moving from the controller of documents to an increasingly digitalized repository of information. How it governs that repository is a form of silent power, and it is increasingly conceptualized using the vocabulary of data protection and data management. The knowable truths are moving from the realm of knowledge to that of information and data. The governor would thus control the information if not the data, the raw material of information we all give out quite willingly.[27] This may enable new forms of governance when the amount of data we all produce proliferates in an unprecedented way. I will return to this topic in chapter eight. Next, however, let us look at the different technocratic translations of transparency more closely.

Access to Documents

In the realm of law, the FOIA provides the principal script for external gatekeeping practices of government information. It regulates the identity of documents and the information they encompass. In this way, government attempts to keep the governed sufficiently informed of its operations. In the form of the FOIA, a legal way of governing the visibility of governance is instituted. This assumption is prevalent to the extent that in many instances, transparency is seen as the very synonym for access to documents. At least in some contexts, it may also be seen as the oldest stratum of government transparency.[28] Hence, calling the access to documents 'transparency' not only abbreviates language but also gives those practices a positive connotation, as was suggested in the thought experiment in the first chapter.

The access to documents is the business of the FOIA *par excellence*. Unless transparency is considered something external to law, how law guarantees transparency means mostly the way in which the FOIAs do it. Although the regulation on access to documents is indeed usually given a positively connoting name (see above: the Freedom of Information Act; the Sunshine Act, etc) these acts, paradoxically, mostly govern the secrecy of those documents and the information in them. They define how and to what extent government-held documents are available to the public and on what conditions. If that were not the case, no particular regulation would be needed: every document would be accessible, or inaccessible. As is well known, this is not however the case, and hardly is it desirable, either. There are many well-founded reasons for concealment in order to protect esoteric knowledge, as discussed earlier.

[27] See, however, Lisa Gitelman (ed), *'Raw Data' Is an Oxymoron* (MIT Press 2013).

[28] cf Deirdre Curtin and Albert Meijer, 'Does Transparency Strengthen Legitimacy? A Critical Analysis of European Union Policy Documents' (2006) 11 Information Polity 109 (hereafter Curtin and Meijer, 'Does Transparency Strengthen Legitimacy?').

Nevertheless, which specific documents are available, to whom, and under what conditions, depends crucially on the context: the legal system, the details of the relevant legislation, the interpretation of that law, the piece of information requested, the right of that particular person to have that particular piece of information, and so on. This leads us to ask whether there is any point in discussing access to documents out of context—history, political landscape, and legal culture—in other words, as a general phenomenon? Although it would be easy to argue otherwise, I claim that a general logic underpins most regulation governing access to documents. In the following, I discuss briefly two examples, Finland and the European Union (EU). They are hardly universally representative but hopefully will otherwise be illustrative.

Let us first take the example of Finland. Like other Nordic countries, Finland has a reputation for being a country of high transparency and with a long historical tradition of open government. From a comparative point of view, this reputation may indeed be warranted.[29] Unlike many European countries, for example, Finland's legal culture is transparency optimistic; the principle of publicity, as it is called, forms a default condition in governance.[30] Exemptions from it need to be laid down by law and should only be made for 'necessary reasons'. Public access to documents is a fundamental right laid down in the Finnish Constitution (section 12), which gives it a strong status in the legal system. In theory, the legal architecture governing access to documents is simple: the fundamental right to access government-held documents is concretized by parliamentary acts, primarily by the FOIA (*Laki viranomaisten toiminnan julkisuudesta*, 1999), which further defines the mentioned 'necessary reasons'.

Despite this optimism, in Finland, too, the FOIA is a tool for regulating accessibility instead of purely creating or allowing it. It is the main forum of concretization of the mentioned fundamental right, which is why access to government-held documents is a strong legal principle and a point of departure. However, the Finnish FOIA is notoriously convoluted and hard to interpret; the mentioned simplicity of the legal architecture is indeed only theoretical. There are various reasons for this complexity.

To start with, there is a long list of cases under which derogation from the default principle of accessibility is allowed: privacy, trade secrets, and national security, etc—thirty-five different grounds. There are also many cases in which the publicity of a particular document is less clear-cut. This means the existence of so-called publicity assumptions and secrecy assumptions. In these cases, it needs to be assessed whether the release of the document in question would cause harm or not, or whether a strong public interest would favour its release. Relatedly, a part of

29 On Nordic transparency and its evolution, see Tero Erkkilä, *Government Transparency: Impacts and Unintended Consequences* (Palgrave Macmillan 2012) 45–104.

30 For an overview, see Olli Mäenpää, *Julkisuusperiaate* (TalentumPro 2020).

a document may be public, and part of it may be subject to concealment. The public parts need to be released by request, whereas the concealed parts need to be left out, making the document subject to piecemeal deliberation and assessment of the potential consequences of the release.

Additionally, a 'document' ('*asiakirja*' in Finnish) may include all sorts of tangible or electronic products and different pieces of information in them, as was discussed more generally above. That said, the use of this term 'document' differs from our everyday understanding of it—let alone, as argued, the entire idea of a document being theoretically rich and potentially also somewhat dated. In many cases, the term 'information' would be better suited than a document (cf a document as a site of information). Indeed, also more generally, the vocabulary adopted in the act is partially counter-intuitive and hard to decipher. For example, a document may 'become public' and yet be subject to a concealment clause.

Lastly, the scope of the act may be regarded as obsolete, because it does not sufficiently take into consideration the recent trends of privatization of administration, digitalization, and developments in data protection regulation.[31] In many cases, it is difficult to say whether some individual document or information in it is actually accessible to the public or not. In the last instance that will be decided in an administrative court through an appeal process.

The courts should interpret the act in the way that favours publicity rather than restricts it. This stems from the fundamental rights-friendly interpretation method, peculiar to the Finnish constitutional doctrine. Case law is not, however, consistent in the interpretation of the scope of publicity. As mentioned, the intricate character of the act makes it subject to many possible interpretations. In particular, this is the case in situations whereby the FOIA should be applied by a private body performing a public duty enabled by the Finnish Constitution (section 124). In such situations, it has been difficult to pin down where the borders of appropriate release of government-held documents lie, namely which documents and what information in fact fall into the scope of the FOIA.[32]

If we move to our next example, the EU, the business of accessing documents is even less straightforward. In principle, access to documents is an important right, guaranteed in the Treaty of the Functioning of the European Union (TFEU) (article 15) as well as the Charter of Fundamental Rights (article 42). The regulation governing the documents held by EU institutions has existed since 2001 (Regulation (EC) No 1049/2001 of the European Parliament and of the Council of 30 May 2001 regarding public access to European Parliament, Council, and Commission

[31] For that reason, the Ministry of Justice of Finland established a committee to reform the act for the period 2021–23. See Ministry of Justice of Finland, 'Julkisuuslain Ajantasaistaminen' (Public Release 9 February 2021) <https://oikeusministerio.fi/julkisuuslain-ajantasaistaminen> accessed 24 June 2021.

[32] See, for example, the Supreme Administrative Court of Finland, KHO 2018:164, ECLI:FI:KHO:2018:164.

documents), before which access was regulated with Treaty provisions and the Council's and Commission's own codes.

The legitimacy-inducing narrative of transparency can found in the Treaties as well as in the case law of the Court of Justice of the European Union (CJEU).[33] It is also summarized in the preamble of the Regulation 1049/2001 (recital 2): 'Openness enables citizens to participate more closely in the decision-making process and guarantees that the administration enjoys greater legitimacy and is more effective and more accountable to the citizen in a democratic system. Openness contributes to strengthening the principles of democracy and respect for fundamental rights as laid down in Article 6 of the EU Treaty and in the Charter of Fundamental Rights of the European Union.'

Despite the solemn goals attributed to 'openness',[34] Regulation 1049/2001, too, is based on the management of secrecy. The regulation requires assessing the extent to which documents held by the Parliament, the Commission, or the Council could be given to the public. Although its purpose is to grant access to documents to all EU citizens (Article 1), it is by no means absolute. For example, its Article 4 lays down a whole array of exceptions to that main rule. The article also allows refusal of access in certain cases, unless an 'overriding public interest' in disclosure is at hand.[35]

In addition, the world has changed after the adoption of Regulation 1049/2001. For example, there have been Treaty changes, new international commitments, a growing body of case law from both the CJEU but also from the European Court of Human Rights (ECtHR), and a considerable amount of adopted new legislation—among it, the General Data Protection Regulation. New technologies of document creation and processing have also changed the landscape of the ideas of documents and documentation, as presented. None of these developments shows in the text of the regulation.[36] In consequence, like the Finnish FOIA, Regulation No 1049/2001 is hardly up to date.

Transparency has also been proven to vary according to the institution. In the member states, the FOIA does not typically extend to legislative matters but concentrates rather on public administration. In the EU, legislative transparency is also

[33] See the Consolidated Version of the Treaty on the Functioning of the European Union [2012] C326/47 Art 15; Consolidated Version of the Treaty on the European Union [2012] OJ C326/01 Art 10(3); and in particular *Kingdom of Sweden and Maurizio Turco v Council of the European Union* [2008] ECR I-04723 (hereafter, *Sweden and Turco v Council*).

[34] It can be also argued that 'openness' and 'transparency' have a different normative content in the EU legal order. See Alberto Alemanno, 'Unpacking the Principle of Openness in EU Law: Transparency, Participation and Democracy' (2014) 39 European Law Review 72 (hereafter Alemanno, 'Unpacking the Principle of Openness in EU Law').

[35] Critically, Daniel Wyatt, 'The Anaemic Existence of the Overriding Public Interest in Disclosure in the EU's Access to Documents Regime' (2020) 21(4) German Law Journal 686.

[36] Päivi Leino, 'Disruptive Democracy: Keeping EU Citizens in a Box' in Inge Govaere, Sacha Garben, and Paul Nemitz (eds), *Critical Reflections on Constitutional Democracy in the European Union* (Hart Publishing 2019), 295, 297–98 (hereafter Leino, 'Disruptive Democracy').

of legal concern, in particular due to the recent case law of the EU Court (CJEU). Although the EU has been struggling with the accessibility of all kinds of documents, legislative transparency, especially, has been lagging behind: documents have been subject to excessive concealment. Most notably the Council has been reluctant to make its decision-making more transparent and release its documents, acting as a diplomatic assembly (compare with how transparency is traditionally conceived in international law) rather than a legislative body. This runs counter to the Court's particular emphasis on the importance of legislative transparency.

The ethos seems to be that transparency—although potentially increasing democratic accountability—would however lead to the decreasing efficiency of decision-making, thus forming a problematic trade-off. This is understandable from the point of view that usually public access rules do not deal with legislative matters but focus on public administration. Päivi Leino has even argued that this aversion towards formally demanded citizen participation is in practice seen as a distraction in some EU institutions.[37] Of course, not all access to document rules and requests deal with the legislative process, for administration, adjudication, and external relations are also concerned. The legislative process is mainly discussed here in order to show how democratically motivated requests for access to documents may even translate into some kind of hindrance to democracy.

As is well known, EU law crucially develops through the case law of the CJEU. Recently, the CJEU has pushed EU institutions towards more transparency, although they have remained reluctant.[38] The CJEU jurisprudence has thus adopted nearly the opposite approach to that of other institutions: it turns Regulation 1049/2001 into a quasi-constitutional document whose main function is to defend the EU's democratic credentials. Since Regulation 1049/2001 is, however, vague on legislative transparency, the CJEU relies heavily on Treaty provisions and its own jurisprudence.[39] As the CJEU says in Case T-540/15 *Emilio de Capitani*: 'The Principles of publicity and transparency are therefore inherent to the EU legislative process.'[40] Transparency is, thus, in theory, an important regulative ideal in the EU, but in practice, it has encountered much suspicion. According to the CJEU, it is, however, no less than 'inherent' to the EU legislative process.

Hence, it seems that regulation has not quite fulfilled its goals. Over the last couple of decades, there has been an aspiration to increase the transparency of EU governance. The main reason for this has been the infamous democratic deficit in

[37] Leino, 'Disruptive Democracy' (n 36) 315; see also Deirdre Curtin and Päivi Leino, 'In Search of Transparency for EU Law-making: Trilogues on the Cusp of Dawn' (2017) 54 Common Market Law Review 1673.

[38] *Sweden and Turco v Council* (n 33); *Council of the European Union v Access Info Europe* [2013] ECLI:EU:C:2013:671; *Emilio de Capitani v European Parliament* [2018] ECLI:EU:T:2018:167 (hereafter *Capitani v EP*); *ClientEarth v European Commission* [2018] ECLI:EU:C:2018:660 (hereafter *ClientEarth v Commission*). It is important to note, however, that the CJEU's own documents are not public.

[39] Leino, 'Disruptive Democracy' (n 36) 298–99.

[40] *Capitani v EP* (n 38); *ClientEarth v Commission* (n 38).

the EU. To alleviate that, the EU has attempted to make itself more legitimate in the eyes of its citizens. In Curtin's and Meijer's words, 'A central ailment is its [the EU's] limited legitimacy, and greater transparency has been propagated as a means to boost the legitimacy of the European Union.'[41] Alemanno goes even further and states that 'openness, through its participation component, is no longer conceived exclusively as instrumental to the improvement of the quality of the decision-making process and outcome, but it appears to carry an autonomous, self-standing normative value'.[42]

What should we learn from these two examples? First of all, we can notice that access to documents is far from self-evident or even binary. Much grey area, subject to the deliberation of potential harms and benefits, exists. As argued, in Finland, transparency through law is, as a rule, a strong point of departure. How that transparency is administered is, nonetheless, less strong. Access to documents is subject to consequence evaluation, made particularly difficult by intricate legislation. Whether a single document or piece of information in it is accessible or not, is thus hard to say in the abstract. If the agency in question refuses to release a document, the courts—the supreme administrative court in the last instance—are to decide.

Secondly, in the EU, a similar basic logic is in place, namely main rules, exceptions to them, and harm-benefit assessments. However, the attitude towards access to documents seems to be somewhat schizophrenic. In theory, it is increasingly called for, but in practice, some reluctance to release documents has been witnessed. It may even be conceived as a disturbance, having a negative influence on effective decision-making, thus countering the inherent promise of transparency in its democratic rationality. In the end, much of the actual access to documents depends on the courts whether they push the agencies and institutions in question towards it or not.

Too much weight should not be put on these examples, especially because they are discussed neither in detail nor in a fully commensurable way. Nor should one settle for too structural an analysis: not all jurisdictions create an equally wide or narrow access to documents, and differences do exist. Nonetheless, it is important to note that even when an FOIA is in place, it does not mean that all government-held documents and information would be available for everyone. Neither does governmental power—legislative, executive, adjudicative—manifest itself to the viewer transparently as it is, but in some curated form. Access to documents is always about access to some documents, possibly some parts of some documents, or some particular piece of information in that document.

In summation, we can notice that the FOIA defines the legal borders of the discourse of access to documents. It defines how the state sees its own appropriate visibility to the governed. The FOIA outlines the ways in which a certain document

[41] Curtin and Meijer, 'Does Transparency Strengthen Legitimacy?' (n 28) 110.
[42] Alemanno, 'Unpacking the Principle of Openness in EU Law' (n 34) 89–90.

or piece of information in it can be released, or alternatively, a request for it declined. When we talk about access to documents, 'transparency' as a metaphor does not only govern the extent of the release of documents and information. It also becomes a technocratic synonym for assessing the potential benefits and harm of giving out information, as the publicity of a singular document is subject to legal deliberation on the effects of the release.

In this sense, by the release of exoteric information, the government, in fact, simultaneously defines and governs esoteric information and access to it. This governing follows a legal script of the FOIA and further by civil servants' and judges' interpretation of that script. The grounds for secrecy as well as the margin of appreciation left for relevant civil servants to decide are legally conceptualized ways to govern this information. This applies both to instrumental esoteric knowledge and internally esoteric knowledge. By defining the scope of access to government-held information, the governor manages no less than its iconophilic appearing to the governed.

The Attendance of the Public

In addition to access to documents, transparency can make a more immediate technocratic translation of transparency in law, allowing the public to attend different operations of the governor. Instead of accessing the information in documents, people would be allowed to witness the pre- or extra-documented existence of governmental power. In practice, that may mean the openness of administrative or legislative or judicial procedure, in person or with the aid of some technological arrangement, such as TV broadcasting or online streaming.

The idea is to show, (seemingly) without mediation, how the governor is operating, how its inner workings, later sedimented into documents, are taking place. In this way, the governor and the governed ideally encounter each other eye to eye in a structurally asymmetric setting: the governed can see how power is being exercised in real time. The mediating hand at work would not obfuscate the representation of governance, but people could see 'really real' power in action, and its spectacular aspect. However, through the recoding of those meetings or events—documentation, that is—the live streamed or broadcast material may also come to form a document. As such, they may later be subject to the FOIA and access to documents.

We could call this technocratic translation of transparency the attendance of the public. It, too, is typically governed by legislation: the attendance of the public is not spontaneous or without limitations.[43] It comes close to the mentioned idea of

[43] Fenster, 'The Transparency Fix' (n 1) 97–99.

transparency in process, which means transparency as allowing access to witness how decisions are being made.[44] Like access to documents, allowing the attendance of the public is subject to consequence evaluation: are the costs or benefits of public attendance greater? Would allowing people's presence enhance the legitimacy of the used power, or would it jeopardize the protection of esoteric knowledge? Should people be allowed to follow, for example, a court case, or a meeting of a legislative body? Again, national and other contextual differences exist; the level of physical accessibility of governance depends greatly on the legal system and legal culture in question. That said, this does not mean that we could not examine this aspect of transparency on a theoretical level. This will be done in the following.

It is worth noticing that, in principle, all aspects of governmental power, legislation, adjudication, and administration may be subject to requirements of public attendance. It is clear that each of these branches operates according to a different mechanism and serves a different societal function in governmental power; we could talk about legislative, adjudicative, and administrative transparency separately.[45] If we take the example of Finland again, the attendance in court proceedings is regulated by two acts, one concerning the publicity of trials in general courts, one the publicity in administrative courts. When it comes to the publicity of administrative procedure, the publicity is regulated in the Administrative Procedure Act. The publicity of the parliament is, in turn, laid down specifically in the Constitution, accentuating the democratic rationality of transparency, if you will.

Here, however, I am not primarily interested in the particularities of making different processes accessible to the public and the legislation it follows. Instead, the main point is to argue that when transparency is about allowing people directly to witness the operations of the governor, the way in which transparency operates as an ideal differs from that of access to documents. When access to documents is based on iconophilic, 'as if' transparency—relying on different constructs and the management of exoteric and esoteric knowledge—the attendance of the public represents the opposite, iconoclastic ideal. The attendance of the public attempts to embody transparency in its connotation of immediate visibility. Even if this immediacy were only a useful fiction, it nonetheless forms a regulative ideal for this technocratic translation of transparency.

The governor's power is in most immediate play when the attendance of the public takes place. Ideally, no mediation would take place: we would receive an acheiropoietic image of the governance in action. However, the object of this iconoclastic transparency is necessarily social, and as such, performative. As

[44] Jane Mansbridge, 'A "Selection Model" of Political Representation' (2009) 17(4) Journal of Political Philosophy 369, 384–86.

[45] cf Robert G Vaughn, 'The Associations of Judicial Transparency with Administrative Transparency' in Padideh Ala'i and Robert G Vaughn (eds), *Research Handbook of Transparency* (Edgar Elgar 2014).

presented in chapter four, in social life, transparency needs to be framed as such to be considered morally valuable. Unintentional transparency, in turn, is often subject to contempt. The same general logic is at play in instances when legal performances are subject to the public eye. They, too, are subject to the mentioned value judgements—was that performance perhaps particularly framed as transparent (good), or was it revealed as such (bad), regardless of the attempts to make it look like something else?

However, when we talk about the attendance of the public as a technocratic translation of transparency, transparency approaches the idea of a public space or sphere. The preventive function partially builds on this kind of spatial understanding of transparency (cf Fenster and the assumed distance between the state and its citizens). In line with this, the attendance of the public presupposes performativity from the object of the gaze, in this context, primarily the representatives of the governor. As described in chapter five, the operating mechanism of the preventive mechanism is based on the following assumption: it prevents 'sinister interests' from emerging. By so doing, it aligns the self-interest of the subject of a gaze with the perceived—or assumed—expectations of the one gazing. Indeed, the point of departure is that the subject of the gaze wants to appear in a favourable light, that she is interested in the way she appears, and is thus not indifferent towards appearing in this way.

It is ultimately an empirical question whether the presence of the public actually would prevent the 'sinister interests' from emerging, and whether legitimacy and trust would increase like that.[46] If a trial, for example, were held behind closed doors, would there be a greater danger of the misuse of power? This is hard to say. How does one verify something as invisible and intangible as an individual interest? We can only witness words and behaviour. Based on that behaviour, we might have an intimation of the motivations behind it, but we cannot be sure. It needs to be stressed that the immediacy of the attendance of the public does not mean access to the naked 'truth', although the promise of transparency suggests otherwise. There is no revelation. Given the nature of the attendance of the public, we are dealing with the most immediate application of the theatrical nature of transparency.

As mentioned, the legislative and administrative adjudicative processes that are made accessible for the public to attend can be seen as plays of a kind. The scripted behaviour of the members of parliament, civil servants, attorneys, judges, and other legal professionals, as well as private citizens making their case, becomes the object of transparency. A theatre defined by law emerges, although the play itself is necessarily somewhat improvised. Even though the attendance of the public is ideologically based on the iconoclastic side of transparency, what we are allowed

[46] Compare Stephan G Grimmelikhuijsen and Albert J Meijer, 'Effects of Transparency on the Perceived Trustworthiness of a Government Organization—Evidence from an Online Experiment' (2014) 24(1) Journal of Public Administration Research and Theory 137.

to see as the public is inherently performative and cannot but be otherwise. That means people do not see the backstage of these procedures, but only the performance designed to be seen. This is also recognized, for example, in the praxis of the ECtHR: 'Justice must not only be done; it must also be seen to be done.'[47]

That said, the scripted plays of governance, if you will, are not only, possibly not even primarily, performed to the public for the sake of information and legitimacy, with the public exercising its monitoring in the spirit of the democratic rationality of transparency. In addition, there are other audiences, internal to the plays themselves: there are colleagues, there are interested parties, there are possibly judges or civil servants. In the form of professional performance, the performer's credibility, expertise, reputation, and professionalism are at stake.[48]

Consequently, it is hardly a coincidence that many of our most popular television dramas take place in the world of law. The most exciting moments happen in the court room, in which attorneys, judges, witnesses, and juries play their designated roles. Who has the most compelling arguments? Who will win the case? This professional performativity may further obscure the way in which the external, democratic gaze works. The interesting thing is that although these plays follow a strict script, they are also essentially unpredictable. Like in a football game, for example, all that can possibly happen is in theory already known by reading the rules of the game, but how the actual game plays out in a particular context is still a matter of suspense and surprise.

However, the presence of the public as a form of transparency complicates matters when there is no performance to be witnessed. Many judicial and administrative processes are partially written, and some are completely written, and as such do not form much of a performance to be looked at. The attendance of the public is blocked, and the immediate preventive mechanism along with it. This goes in particular for administrative procedure. In addition, in some jurisdictions, such as in Finland, court trials in administrative matters are also principally written processes, and oral hearings are rather rare. How can these kinds of procedures be made transparent in the sense of the attendance of the public? What is there to see when someone is typing a document or pondering a savvy legal argument? In this case, thus, the iconoclastic aspect of transparency would be impossible, because it would only show the visually rather unimpressive icono-genesis, if you will.

An interesting approach to these questions can be found in Bruno Latour's book *The Making of Law* (2010).[49] In it, he describes his observations in the Conseil d'État, the supreme administrative court in France. Following his ethnographic approach, he explains how a day in the court proceeds, how different documents

[47] *Delcourt v Belgium*, App no 2689/65, 17 January 1970, para 31.

[48] David Kennedy, *A World of Struggle: How Power, Law and Expertise Shape Global Political Economy* (Princeton University Press 2016) 160.

[49] Bruno Latour, *The Making of Law: An Ethnography of the Conseil d'État* (Polity Press 2010).

are moved from desk to desk, making law a play of travelling documents. It is a 'description of the law compatible with the practice of judges', in a way that provides a material description of how decisions are reached, recorded, and put into circulation.[50] Latour is thus less interested in what these documents contain, say, or signify, but instead takes a radically external, and importantly, radically material point of view.[51]

If we build on that materiality, and consequently a radically visual approach to transparency, this kind of show of travelling documents would make an equally justifiable performance of transparency. However, because it would not make much sense to the public, it would hardly communicate anything meaningful to it, either. As mentioned earlier, to the extent this procedure becomes digitalized, this uneventfulness may shift its shape. Indeed, transparency as the attendance of the public is not only about visibility but also about communicability. All visibility is not equally valuable.

The attendance of the public it thus structurally closest to the value judgement side of transparency, it can be considered a metonym for all transparency practices. It departs from the idea of the direct see-ability of governmental power. Ideally, the impediments blocking the visibility of power are removed and immediacy is instigated in it (iconoclasm). This is, however, partially an illusion. Namely, as argued, the public is allowed to see the performance but not the backstage, and the performance needs to be something else than documents travelling from one desk to another. This allowing is an effect of the hand at work, although it may look like the opposite. In the end, it can be asked whether the attendance of the public can reveal anything unintended, although it definitely makes visible the application of the legal procedure. Revelation in the sense of the revelatory gaze may only take place if the performers mistake the stage as the backstage, and accidently take their masks off. Otherwise, transparency as the attendance of the public is also in the realm of curated visibility.

Communication

As argued, the access to documents may be considered the most important, most institutionalized technocratic translation of transparency in law. This access typically requires a preceding request: a document or piece of information in it is given to the public, if someone has particularly asked for it, typically following a certain legally defined procedure. In the case of the attendance of the public, people can, as the ideal suggests, follow how pre-documented power is being used in

[50] ibid, 195.

[51] See also David Saunders, 'The Making of Law: An Ethnography of the Conseil d'État' (2012) 5(1) Journal of Cultural Economy 125.

real time. Both of these technocratic translations of transparency are, however, typically available by request. The power is there—embedded in documents, in procedures—and seeing it requires active interest from the governed.

These technocratic translations are not always considered enough to keep the governed informed. The state should not only answer when it is asked a question, so to speak. Instead, it and its agencies are increasingly also required to inform others about their activities proactively. I call this technocratic translation of transparency simply 'communication'.[52] The idea is that information on how democratically legitimated governmental power is exercised, should not be only a matter of haphazard individual interest; it should be readily available to all in order for the democratic rationality of transparency to work. The ideological starting point is thus that the governor should educate and enlighten the governed of its inner workings. The metaphoric promise of transparency, 'understanding is seeing' needs to be actively made possible.

In the era of the internet, this function has become more important than ever: the easy accessibility of information in general creates pressures for governments to keep on a par with that general condition. Let us again take the example of the European Union. The EU has stated in its policy documents that the internet should increase its transparency by providing more information to citizens. Curtin and Meijer argue that the meaning of this kind of proactive transparency has increased in the 2000s, that a transition from access-to-documents-based, or 'thin' transparency towards more politically motivated 'thick' transparency can be detected.[53]

Today, internet pages have become the primary source of acquiring information on the government and its different institutions. Indeed, it is difficult to imagine a government institution without internet coverage. The more digitalized our world becomes, the more is required from the webpages: their informativeness, usability, comprehensiveness, and their user interface. At best, proactive communication may help people to realize their rights. For example, a website may provide information on how to start proceedings in an administrative matter. The grounds of due process, information on how to appeal and on what grounds is easier to find online than from a dusty law book. Simultaneously, this increased information may create legitimate expectations towards the government.

The significance of communication cannot, however, be reduced to information being available to the public. In addition, it has crucial impression management implications. This is because the governor is in charge of what it releases and what kind of online presence it creates. How some piece of information is presented may be of surprisingly significant importance; the medium is (also) the message, as

[52] cf Onora O'Neill, 'Transparency and the Ethics of Communication' in Christopher Hood and David Heald (eds), *Transparency: The Key to Better Governance?* (Oxford University Press 2006).

[53] Curtin and Meijer, 'Does Transparency Strengthen Legitimacy?' (n 28) 109.

argued previously. Hence, the question is not only about the quantity of the available information being important, it is also about its quality. How much does the public understand of what it is informed? Is understanding really seeing? These questions need to be addressed, for not all information produced or received by the government is either relevant to the public for democratic control, or concerns the individual interest of legal protection. Even if this information were relevant, it would not be understandable to most people.

In this sense, much of the communicated information may be too esoteric for the average citizen. For example, complicated financial, legal, or technical information, possibly highly relevant to the public at large, may be too complex for most people to grasp. These questions have recently become topical particularly in the context of the increasing use of automated decision-making and algorithmic governance. Even if a decision-making algorithm were disclosed in the name of transparency, it might be so esoteric that even highly educated experts could not understand it.[54] What would be the legitimacy implication of that? I will come back to this theme in more detail in chapter eight.

Indeed, people's cognitive capacities have their limits, nor do people always act rationally in trying to make the most of the provided information.[55] If the provided information does not consider its average receiver, disappointment may follow: overly convoluted information for an average citizen may affect the desire to stay informed (see chapter five: Do we want to see power?). Consequently, if participation requires too much expertise, it may exclude many people from its scope and thus undermine the democratic rationality of transparency in general. As Joanne Roberts puts it, 'managing the unknown is limited by our ability to recognize ignorance'.[56] Often, as Fenster argues, the government fails to meet its citizens' expectations of acting in a way that would make it visible, accessible, and above all, communicative.

Although people are constructed as democratic citizens, willing and able to monitor the government's use of power, not all are capable of doing that. People may appear incapable of acting like the democratic public that transparency assumes.[57] Much of this may stem from the capacities that such democratic monitoring presupposes. In Finland, for example, there is lobbying in favour of more government information being available in simplified language, so that it could also reach people who have difficulties in understanding bureaucratic language: immigrants, people with reading or learning difficulties, and so on.

[54] See Mike Ananny and Kate Crawford, 'Seeing without Knowing: Limitations of the Transparency Ideal and its Application to Algorithmic Accountability' (2018) 20 New Media and Society 973.

[55] Etzioni, 'The Limits of Transparency' (n 11) 191–94.

[56] Joanne Roberts, 'Organizational Ignorance: Towards a Managerial Perspective on the Unknown' (2012) 44(3) Management Learning 215, 217 (hereafter Roberts, 'Organizational Ignorance').

[57] Fenster, 'The Transparency Fix' (n 1) 11.

This leads us to ask to what extent should the authorities be in charge of screening relevant information from irrelevant, and of further simplifying the relevant information into an easily understandable form? Most probably, this kind of simplification would enhance the public law rationality of transparency, as its legitimating promise is individualized to begin with. However, things are less clear when we talk about the democratic rationality of transparency. Would such screening and simplification benefit or be of detriment to the premised democratic monitoring? To what extent would such attempts to create understandability also favour impression management purposes?

If no screening is required, the darker side of communication becomes visible. That is to say, the authorities could, in theory, drown people in information. Overflow of data may be seen as a strategy of obfuscation.[58] Indeed, even if all the information produced or received by an agency were not bound by concealment grounds laid down by the FOIA, navigation in the vast pool of information would require expertise in order to be successful. Crucial information may be hidden in plain sight. Highlighting what is important can thus paradoxically serve dual purposes: it may help the democratic rationality of transparency to work and simultaneously, help the institution in question to display its inner workings or the institution itself in a favourable light.

Simultaneously, proactive communication implies omission. It inevitably obscures what is not on the website, what is not open to the public. This omission may also be embedded in the overflow of information. So much is available, how can I know what is not? Proactive communication can be an indirect method for keeping deep secrets. Deep secrets are secrets whose existence we are not even aware of. Sometimes, they are also referred to as ignorance about knowledge, or in Donald Rumsfeld's famous words, the 'unknown-unknowns'.[59] In contrast, a shallow secret is a known-unknown; we know that we do not know a certain thing. That is to say, the public knows that a certain piece of information is denied it.[60] The paradox of a deep secret is that as soon as we can articulate it, it is transformed into a shallow secret. As Fenster argues, this creates information *about* secrecy, as well as speculation on the content of those secrets.[61] That said, trying to find meaningful deep secrets would be like searching for a needle in a haystack.

The structures of knowns, unknowns, and knowability, and their different combinations underpin the questions of proactive communication as a technocratic translation of transparency. As explained, these structures also entangle with impression management logic. That said, proactive communication is an increasingly

[58] Emmanuel Alloa and Dieter Thomä, 'Transparency: Thinking Through an Opaque Concept' in Emmanuel Alloa and Dieter Thomä (eds), *Transparency, Society and Subjectivity: Critical Perspectives* (Palgrave Macmillan 2018) 2.
[59] Roberts, 'Organizational Ignorance' (n 56) 220–22.
[60] David Pozen, 'Deep Secrecy' (2010) 62(2) Stanford Law Review 257.
[61] Fenster, 'The Transparency Fix' (n 1) 122.

important avenue for government to make itself known. This is especially due to the internet and technological development in general, as well as the increasing complexity of relevant information that requires 'translation' to deliver a message to the average citizen. Because communication often follows the logic of shame avoidance, it makes transparency through proactive communication the most suitable tool for impression management.

Uncontrolled Transparency: Leaking and Whistleblowing

So far I have discussed transparency as a legal concept based on the underlying assumption that the governor itself is in charge of the information release, whether that takes place in the form of allowing access to documents or information, the attendance of the public, or proactive communication. At best, all these forms are aspects of intentional and legally defined transparency, which is needed for legitimacy to follow. Thus, when we are talking about transparency in the sphere of law, it is seen as a positive and desirable thing. The negative connotation is absent. Government and its different operations should be *made* transparent, they are not *revealed* as such. Hence, we could argue that there is no point in talking about the negative connotation of transparency in the context of law.

That said, it is important to notice that the very same logic of unauthorized exposure can also be argued to have a kind of technocratic translation in the realm of governance and law. Government agencies also attempt to manage their impression, as already mentioned. Max Weber has argued that 'bureaucratic administration always tends to exclude the public, to hide its knowledge and action from criticism as well as it can'.[62] In a similar way, Amitai Etzioni claims that 'Government agencies are not prone to allow the public to learn about their failures, cost over-runs, and illegal actions unless such disclosure is required'.[63] Conversely, as David N Gibbs argues, 'The underlying principle in law, psychology and historical research is the same: When people make declarations that go against their interest, such declarations have high credibility'.[64] All of these quotes point in the same direction: impression management logic, peculiar to social life, also characterizes states and governments.

Thus, we can notice that uncontrolled or coerced transparency is not entirely external to law, as law is an important gatekeeper of the availability of information. Courts or supervisory authorities may order a governmental institution to release a document; or the disclosure of certain documents may indeed be legally

[62] Max Weber, *Economy and Society*, vol 2 (Guenther Roth and Claus Wittich eds, University of California Press 1978) 992.

[63] Etzioni, 'The Limits of Transparency' (n 11) 189.

[64] David N Gibbs, 'Sigmund Freud as a Theorist of Government Secrecy' (2011) 19 Research in Social Problems and Public Policy 5, 15.

required. Different kinds of inspections and auditions may result in reluctant disclosure of potentially compromising documents or states of affair. This kind of externally coerced transparency can be seen as a democratic rationality of transparency by proxy: not only do the principals control the agents, but they may also control agents who monitor the agents proper, exercising power through democratic representation.

That does not mean, however, that we would necessarily agree with the way in which law regulates transparency. Although the FOIA would be democratically legislated, and it would govern information release in a detailed manner, it is still premised on a certain conception of appropriate release—and further, certain conceptions of esoteric knowledge—and not some other conception. *Should* law allow larger or narrower access to information than it does is another question. In other words, the limits of appropriate release of information may be subject to ethical, legal, and political contestation.[65] What should the public be allowed to see?

Law is not designed to constitute ways of breaching it. That is why transparency as unauthorized exposure is not a normative legal concept *per se*. Nevertheless, there are ways in which governmental, esoteric information is not released intentionally or through the official channels, but yet it manages to escape its keepers. In consequence, although concealed on legal grounds, some information may become accessible to a wider audience than is legally intended. If this happens through conscious activity, we can talk about radical or illicit transparency, or transparency vigilance. In practice, the terms 'information leaking' and 'whistleblowing' are often used.[66]

What is an information leak or leaking? According to David Pozen, there is no settled definition of a leak in the academic literature or in journalistic usage. Some commonly used criteria exist, however. A leak can be considered a) a targeted disclosure b) by a government insider (civil servant, employee, former employee, contractor) c) to a member of the media d) of confidential information whose exposure is generally proscribed by law, policy, of convention e) outside any formal process f) with an expectation of anonymity. In addition, some commentators further argue that the exposure should be 'unauthorized'.[67]

Thus, a leak is motivated by attempts to obtain more information about governance than would be possible through conventional legal avenues. On the one hand, leaking, albeit illicit, may also be seen as a form of civil disobedience where the breach of law is considered necessary in order to achieve a higher ethical or

[65] Fenster, 'The Transparency Fix' (n 1) 42–43.

[66] ibid, 42–55. Mark Fenster calls this 'the vigilante fix' of transparency, as opposed to the administrative and institutional, and technological fixes he discusses in his book.

[67] David Pozen, 'Leaky Leviathan: Why the Government Condemns and Condones Unlawful Disclosure of Information (2013) 127 Harvard Law Review 512, 521 (hereafter Pozen, 'Leaky Leviathan'). Pozen argues that revelations made in a signed memoir, speech, etc do not count, because there is no mystery as to their source.

political goal. As for the most famous example, WikiLeaks sees its role that way, invoking the Universal Declaration of Human Rights (UDHR). In particular, it endeavours to take Article 19, calling for freedom of expression, seriously. By its leaking activity, WikiLeaks enforces this right by allowing readers to evaluate the truth and objectivity of a news story by creating access to the original documents on which the story was based. As Julian Assange, the founder of WikiLeaks, has argued, in that way 'you can judge for yourself: Is the story true? Did the journalist report it accurately?'[68] In this way, Assange's words make a good example of the iconoclash and the chagrin over mediation: the suspicion towards mediation—in this case, reporting—and the hand at work.

On the other hand, leaking can involve an agenda, and also serve other motives than 'more truth to the people'. This may mean gaining personal benefit, leverage, fame, etc. Alternatively, it can imply an entire ideology of a better world. For example, WikiLeaks, Fenster argues, cares less about the content of any disclosure and its effects on the democratic polis. Instead, it is mainly concerned about the disruptive effect that the threat of mass disclosure will have in the operations and abilities to suppress dissent. WikiLeaks's goal is, rather, to instigate a more radical form of popular sovereignty, be it via legal or illegal ways. Its technological capabilities could thus serve a collective political uprising.[69] Hence, the 'more truth to the people' idea, seemingly just questioning the extent and quality the state sees disclosure appropriate, may also include assumptions or fantasies about what people should or could do with that more accurate understanding on what the state does.

Whistleblowing, for one, is otherwise similar, but it is narrower in scope. In my view, it could be considered a subcategory of leaking. In the EU's so-called whistleblower directive proposal, it is defined like this: 'Whistleblowers, i.e. persons who report (within the organisation concerned or to an outside authority) or disclose (to the public) information on a wrongdoing obtained in a work-related context . . . .'[70] Thus, whistleblowing has an inherent moral component to it, which leaking does not necessarily contain: the idea is to reveal some kind of act of mismanagement, illegality, or other defect in government in order to make it subject to public debate. The same logic applies to other powerful actors, such as multinational companies. This kind of revelation will not create legitimacy; on the contrary, it jeopardizes the successful impression management of the institution revealed.

[68] Fenster, 'The Transparency Fix' (n 1) 51; Julian Assange, 'Don't shoot messenger for revealing uncomfortable truths' *The Australian* (7 December 2010) <https://www.theaustralian.com.au/in-depth/wikileaks/dont-shoot-messenger-for-revealing-uncomfortable-truths/news-story/43b912ca277c90355fab12cc83cd4e69story/43b912ca277c90355fab12cc83cd4e69> accessed 7 July 2021.

[69] Fenster, 'The Transparency Fix' (n 1) 53.

[70] Commission, 'Proposal for a Directive of the European Parliament and of the Council on the protection of persons reporting on breaches of Union law' COM (2018) 218 final, 1.

A famous and hugely influential example of whistleblowing is Edward Snowden and his revelations of the National Security Agency (NSA) spying on American citizens. It can even be argued that the continuously strengthening paradigm of protection of data and privacy are indirect consequences of those very revelations.[71] Leaking may happen for the same reason, though it need not necessarily entail a similar truth-telling-for-greater-good goal. As mentioned, it may also serve the personal interest of the leaker, too. The distinction is not clear, however: for example, sometimes WikiLeaks is referred to as a whistleblower. Here, for the sake of clarity, simplification is in any case useful.

Less obviously, leaking may be an indirect form of impression management too. This depends on how strategically information is being leaked. Strategy implies control, in which form impression management logic is in place. For example, in the EU, the material of a legislative process may be strategically leaked before it has become accessible to the public through conventional procedures.[72] In this way, leaked material may form a laboratory of approval so that a new policy might potentially be adopted by a wider audience. At the same time, the institution in question that allowed the leak may still uphold its official policies of information release. Indeed, as Samuel Stolton points out, 'With the "art of the leak," the executive has a greater sway over the public narrative than it would have had otherwise, remaining as it was a passive subject to media reports without much authority in the stories that would manifest, and subsequently [have] little influence in the public perception of the European Union.'[73]

That said, as already hinted, the legitimacy of whistleblowing has been increasingly recognized in law. In Sweden, for example, there is an unusually strong, constitutionally protected right to tell secret information to the mass media, a journalist, or a writer under the '*meddelarfrihet*' (the right to report). This right extends even to civil servants in some cases.[74] In the USA, whistleblower protection law has been in place for decades.[75] In the EU, in turn, a directive has recently been given to improve the position of those 'telling the truth', even at the expense of their own immediate interest.[76] In addition, there are other legal ways of protecting those

[71] cf Jockum Hildén, 'The Politics of Datafication: The Influence of Lobbyists on the EU's Data Protection Reform and its Consequences for the Legitimacy of the General Data Protection Regulation' (DPhil, University of Helsinki 2019).

[72] This happened, for example, with the EU's AI Act proposal in spring 2021. See, for example, Melissa Heikkilä, 'Europe Eyes Strict Rules for Artificial Intelligence' *Politico* (14 April 2021) <www.politico.eu/article/europe-strict-rules-artificial-intelligence/> accessed 7 July 2021.

[73] Samuel Stolton, 'Leaky Commission' *Brussels Times* (9 February 2020) <www.brusselstimes.com/brussels-behind-the-scenes/94244/a-leaky-commission/> accessed 7 July 2021.

[74] Svensk Tryckfrihetsförordningen (1949:105) section 7; Svensk Yttrandefrihetsgrundlagen (1991:1469) section 10.

[75] For example, see Pozen, 'Leaky Leviathan' (n 67) 522–27.

[76] Council Directive 2019/1937 on the protection of persons who report breaches of Union law [2019] OJ L305/17; see more, Vigjilenca Abazi, 'New EU Directive on Whistleblower Protection' (23 April 2019) <http://eulawanalysis.blogspot.com/2019/04/new-eu-directive-on-whistleblower.html?m=1> accessed 7 July 2021.

disclosing unpleasant truths. For example, source protection in journalism is considered an important part of the freedom of expression in many jurisdictions; it can even be considered a human right. Legally protected anonymity is a guarantee of transparency vigilance and has a direct bearing in journalism.

Whistleblowing is clearly a matter of courage. Unless there is effective whistleblower protection in place, reporting wrongdoing entails a considerable personal risk. For example, a recent United Nations (UN) survey points out that many employees are afraid of whistleblowing because of the revenge that might follow.[77] Tellingly, the retaliation—lawful or unlawful—towards famous whistleblowers, such as Chelsea Manning or Edward Snowden, has reached the proportions of a global witch-hunt. This is not to say that there might be laws breached and potentially also self-serving motives, but the magnitude of the repercussions is symptomatic in comparison to other breaches of law.

Leaking and whistleblowing may thus be considered an individual's or a group's attempt to question the appropriate distance between the state and the public, the underlying idea that Fenster argued to be the basic assumption of government transparency. In other words, the legitimacy of the official way of assessing the importance of a particular document or a piece of information is thus questioned; the impression management implicit in the logic of official transparency practices is recognized, and the esoteric nature of certain information is denied. Following this thinking, people should know the 'truth' about government that it attempts to hide, and also enhance their knowledge about secrecy.

It still remains unclear what that truth is. We re-encounter the question of whether the backstage is 'truer' than the frontstage. Slavoj Žižek's words about WikiLeaks are noteworthy: 'You are not just simply telling the truth. You are telling the truth in a very precise way of confronting explicit lines of justification and rationalization—the public discourse with its implicit presuppositions. It's not just about telling the truth.'[78] Although unauthorized revelation does not have an immediate legitimizing effect on the leaking institution, it may lead to questions about the meaning of the revelation.[79]

However, truth gained through questioning the limits of legally defined revelation does not necessarily lead to objective truth. Instead, it leads to a truth which

[77] Sophie Edwards, 'Leaked UN Staff Survey Shows Fears over Whistleblowing, Ethical Accountability' *Devex* (1 March 2018) <www.devex.com/news/leaked-un-staff-survey-shows-fears-over-whistleblowing-ethical-accountability-92234> accessed 7 July 2021; United Nations Chief Executive Board, 'United Nation Staff Engagement Survey: UN Secretariat Survey Results' (February 2018) <https://pages.devex.com/rs/685-KBL-765/images/UN-Secretariat-Survey-Results-February-2018.pdf> accessed 7 July 2021.

[78] Benedetta Brevini, Arne Hintz, and Patrick McCurdy, 'Amy Goodman in Conversation with Julian Assange and Slavoj Žižek' in Benedetta Brevini, Arne Hintz, and Patrick McCurdy (eds), *Beyond WikiLeaks: Implications for the Future of Communications, Journalism and Society* (Palgrave Macmillan 2013) 265.

[79] Umberto Eco, 'Not Such Wicked Leaks' in Emmanuel Alloa and Dieter Thomä (eds), *Transparency, Society and Subjectivity: Critical Perspectives* (Palgrave Macmillan 2018) 15–18.

the leakers consider worth revealing, and which is, by law, intended to be concealed. In that sense, it is reactive to concealment, as Žižek noted. This may lead to a very specific kind of truth, which is biased towards revealing mismanagement; as A J Brown et al argue, it is more likely that evidence of organizational wrongdoing gains public attention than evidence of organizational performance and integrity.[80]

Here, the point was to show how in law and governance, information leaking and whistleblowing are functionally equivalent to the involuntary transparency characteristic of social life. In this way, leaking and whistleblowing demonstrate that different forms of transparency vigilance question the transparency-legitimacy nexus in the legal discourse on transparency. As whistleblower protection has been increasingly recognized in law, it might have lost some of its vigilant character. That said, the basic structure of informational asymmetry between the governor and the governed is sustained. To the extent that law forms the script of releasing government information, intentional transparency falls outside law and the legitimacy it, in many cases, provides.

Summing Up: Technocratic Translations of Icono-ambivalence

In this chapter, I have discussed the metaphor of transparency in legal vocabulary. I looked at the ways in which governance transparency greatly relies on documents and documentation, and the assumptions they are based on and the ramifications they entail. I also named different technocratic translations, or legal variants, of transparency—access to documents, the attendance of the public, communication, and information leaking and whistleblowing—and analysed their meaning with the conceptual tools that I have adopted in this book, primarily icono-ambivalence and impression management.

I argued that those technocratic translations represent both the iconoclastic and the iconophilic side of government transparency. As argued previously, sometimes transparency refers to the attempts to expose government in its essence by removing obstacles that block its visibility (iconoclasm). Often, however, that is not possible. Government is, in the end, an abstraction, and in many instances it lacks immediate physical appearance. Therefore, transparency also needs different constructs (iconophily), and transparency may mean controlling access to and the use of those constructs.

In the field of law, those constructs are mostly referred to as documents. Documentation, which is a necessary precondition of documents, can be considered a tangible manifestation of the legal production of reality; with no

[80] A J Brown, Wim Vandekerckhove, and Suelette Dreyfus, 'The Relationship Between Transparency, Whistleblowing, and Public Trust' in Padideh Ala'i and Robert G Vaughn (eds), *Research Handbook of Transparency* (Edgar Elgar 2014) 30, 34.

documentation, documents, and appropriate registers, governance cannot withstand the test of time. Access to the resulting documents is thus perhaps the most important technocratic translation of transparency in law. It allows people to access those singular representations of governmental power. In the wake of digitalization, however, it is unclear to what extent the meaning of documents and documentation is decreasing. This raises an important question: Is the construction of a document increasingly replaced with information management on the one hand, and data protection on the other?

As for the other technocratic translations of transparency, the attendance of the public, in particular, represents an iconoclastic variant of transparency. It allows the public to witness the pre-documented and legally scripted use of governmental power. It is, however, subject to mediation, although that mediation may be hard to detect; there, too, we can find the hand at work. That is to say, the allowed visibility is subject to mediated practices, and it cannot allow access to the 'backstage' of governmental performances. Vice versa, due to its inherent performativity, transparency can hardly show the non-curated reality of government, although the performances surely carry a truth function of their own.

Communication, in turn, is the way in which the governor can make itself known proactively. This makes it the most obvious tool for impression management. So long as the governor itself decides what it communicates externally, and how, the attempt to obtain positive self-presentation is assumed. In consequence, in this technocratic translation, the hand at work is most evident: in addition to the impression management purposes of the government, it also serves the understandability and accessibility purposes for the public. To that end, transparency practices need to become interactive as they attempt to inform different groups of people for different purposes. Transparency becomes customized.

Lastly, I argued that transparency's negative variant—unauthorized disclosure—also makes an appearance in legal discourse, although admittedly, not from a normative point of view. I explained how information leaking and whistleblowing make a structural equivalent of that negative variant. They expose confidential governmental (or private) material to the media and to the larger public, and thus question the appropriate extent of available government information. Motivations for those vigilant practices may vary. In any case, the legal understanding of appropriate transparency is questioned, and information is released in an unauthorized manner.

These technocratic translations can be argued to be the principal way in which the ideal of transparency is conceived in law. Nevertheless, I am not arguing that it would or could be reduced only to those translations. This idea of transparency not being reduced to those translations underpins the entire study. As argued, not only is transparency a language-abbreviating term for its technocratic translations (the contingent signifier approach), it is also a legitimating idea in its own right (the cognitive analogy approach). If that were not the case, transparency could not function as a magic concept, as it undoubtedly does. Through this mechanism, transparency as a concept has the potential to legitimize the concrete practices that are supposed to concretize it, as I demonstrated with the thought experiment in the first chapter. I will discuss this more in the next chapter.

In this chapter, I argued that the promise of transparency—making unilateral or otherwise unequal power visible and as such, controllable—functions through different legal mechanisms. At the most general level, this promise translates into a demand of accountability. Transparency should guarantee accountability, in other words that those in power, the agents, should be accountable to the principals, to those from whom their power emanates. Thus, controllability through transparency is a way of making sure that those who are supposed to be accountable also want to be accountable. As argued, the idea manifests a form of mechanistic morality whereby the self-interest of the agents overlaps with the socio-legal expectations of the principals.

PART III
THE REALITY OF TRANSPARENCY

7

The Discursification of Transparency

Transparency Escaping its Natural Habitat

In the previous chapter, I argued that the ideal of transparency is a concept of law, trickling down to various technocratic translations. Although legitimacy is a contested notion, it is exactly legitimacy that is the expected result of normative transparency, at least indirectly. On the one hand, transparency as a metaphorical ideal has evolved along with the democratic civil society; it has deep intellectual roots in democratic theory and traditional manifestations in law. The way in which this legitimacy promise works was discussed in chapters five and six. On the other hand, transparency functions as a contemporary technocratic concept: it is considered an institution worth keeping, cultivating—and spreading. This aspect will be discussed in this chapter.

Despite the tight conjunction between the state and transparency, transparency has spread to new institutional habitats. Although transparency is something we typically associate with the state and popular sovereignty, it is not restricted to it. Something has happened to the 'economics' of transparency—its supply and demand—over the last couple of decades.[1] Governments, corporate entities, and other institutions are increasingly implementing transparency standards and releasing transparency reports.[2] As a norm, transparency is decreasingly restricted to law, the Freedom of Information Acts (FOIAs) and state governance. Instead, it has also become a term to talk about legitimacy outside of these institutional structures. This point of departure has, of course, been present already in the earlier chapters.

Over the last few decades, transparency has become immensely popular, to the point that the 'transparency turn' has been referred to.[3] In public discourses,

[1] For example, Micah L Sifry describes the emergence of the 'global transparency movement' in his book: Micah L Sifry, *WikiLeaks and the Age of Transparency* (OR Books 2011) ch 5.

[2] Emmanuel Alloa, 'Transparency: A Magic Concept of Modernity' in Emmanuel Alloa and Dieter Thomä (eds), *Transparency, Society and Subjectivity: Critical Perspectives* (Palgrave Macmillan 2018) 24 (hereafter Alloa, 'Magic Concept of Modernity').

[3] cf Aarti Gupta, 'Transparency Under Scrutiny: Information Disclosure in Global Environmental Governance' (2008) 8 Global Environmental Politics 1 (hereafter Gupta, 'Transparency Under Scrutiny'); Anne Peters, 'Towards Transparency as a Global Norm' in Anne Peters and Andrea Bianchi (eds), *Transparency in International Law* (Cambridge University Press 2013) (hereafter Peters, 'Towards Transparency as a Global Norm'); Ida Koivisto, 'The IMF and the "Transparency Turn"' (2016) 25 Minnesota Journal of International Law 381 (hereafter Koivisto, 'The IMF and the "Transparency Turn"').

The Transparency Paradox. Ida Koivisto, Oxford University Press. © Ida Koivisto 2022.
DOI: 10.1093/oso/9780192855466.003.0007

it has travelled from the margins to the centre, making it a modern marker for legitimacy. Does this mean that the world is becoming a better place now that transparency is widely taken into the discourses of legitimation? Not necessarily: this new popularity has also diluted its meaning. If almost anything can be argued to represent transparency, does it really mean anything at all? In Alloa's words, 'The lucidity promised by the concept is inversely proportional to its semantic clarity'.[4]

In this chapter, I discuss how and why transparency has become an increasingly fuzzy concept that is used liberally and strategically outside law. I call this process *the discursification of transparency*. In the following, I discuss discursification theoretically—what it is in general, and how it relates to transparency—and then in two contexts in particular: global governance institutions and multinational technology companies. These contexts are telling for two, overlapping reasons. First, today global governance institutions and tech companies use power that resembles public authority. In some important respects, these institutions and companies resemble states. However, as they often lack legally defined accountability mechanisms, they are accused of an 'accountability deficit'. Transparency is one of the most popular solutions to tackle this problem. Therefore, how global governance institutions and technology companies conceive of transparency is important. Second, by investigating the role of transparency in these contexts, the extent to which the concept can be stretched may become more visible. Are there in fact any limits to the spreading of transparency discourse?

This chapter is organized in the following way. First, I discuss the notion of discursification theoretically and then in the context of transparency. Second, I move on to analysing the discursification of transparency in the two mentioned contexts: in global governance and in multinational technology companies. The aim is to show the lure of transparency and to argue that transparency no longer necessitates the state as its institutional habitat but can also justify power outside of the state. Third, I connect the discursification of transparency to another megatrend: the relativization of legal thought (the discursification of public law). Finally, I conclude the chapter by arguing that the main collateral damage of this process is the democratic rationality of transparency. It seems that along with discursification, the justification of transparency has become circular: transparency is needed for the sake of transparency.

[4] Alloa, 'Magic Concept of Modernity' (n 2) 27.

The Discursification of Transparency

What Is 'Discursification'?

What, in fact, constitutes a discourse? Discourse is a theory-laden concept that can be defined in many ways depending on the academic discipline and the school of thought. Here, I loosely follow the Foucauldian tradition.[5] A discourse can be seen as a way of using language in a particular manner, to make the world appear in a certain way and not in some other. Discourses mean talking about things using a certain vocabulary in a certain modality of language that is connected to a set of other words and the associations they evoke.

Although discourses consist of language, from a Foucauldian perspective they are essentially tied to power and sub-linguistic practices. When we talk about intangible things such as governance, the state, or, say, a production chain, how these things are portrayed in different debates is not just a matter of naming, it is also a matter of association, attribution, and imagination. Whose or which imagination, again, has the potential to label these things most authoritatively, and to connect them with other similar concepts discursively, is a corollary of power. This kind of understanding of discursive power was also briefly discussed in chapter five.

What about the term 'discursification', then? The term is my own. As I define it, it builds on these previously mentioned discursive strategies. It signifies a process of semantic-normative uprooting, or decontextualizing: legal or otherwise normative concepts and ideas become detached from their original system of meaning and potential enforcement mechanisms, and hence become available for strategic language use outside of the original context. As for law, that would mean that discursified legal concepts would lose their connection to legal order and the state monopoly on violence. That violence, which bolsters the effectiveness of the legal order in the state, would cease to guarantee being able to protect individuals from the misuse of power. Normative legal concepts would become sheer expressions for approval or disapproval.

By discursification, I thus mean discursive agendas that utilize semantically diluted but normatively convincing concepts. The described context-detachment that these concepts would have undergone would further enable their strategic use. These agendas may appear neutral but in fact they can be used to further particular plans, such as boosting one's own prestige, legitimacy, reputation, or market share. The agendas would utilize the positive qualities these concepts still represent. When applied to transparency, this would mean talking about transparency in an indeterminate yet convincing way, utilizing its powers as a normative if not a

[5] Michel Foucault discussed his conception of a discourse especially in his book *The Archaeology of Knowledge* (Pantheon Books 1969).

magic concept, to bring about a certain consequence in the world. Legal enforcement mechanisms, however, would be lacking.

The coinage of the term discursification is purely practical, as to my knowledge, no term depicting this process exists so far. This does not mean, however, that discursification would not be associated with larger theoretical developments in the social sciences or not have many neighbouring concepts and approaches. Generally, the term can be argued to be connected to the 'linguistic turn' in the social sciences. The linguistic turn is not a solid theory or movement, but an umbrella term referring to many different approaches and theories focusing on the meaning of words, argument, rhetoric, narrative, and discourse.[6] In the linguistic turn, the overarching theme is the emphasis on the reality-constructing meaning of language: it does not only represent reality, it also creates it by naming things and justifying power.

Pollitt and Hupe's theory of magic concepts—discussed in chapter one—and their emergence are particularly closely connected to the idea of discursification. This why I often refer to the qualities of magic concepts and their applicability to transparency. Although discursification and magic concepts have many overlapping qualities, differences do exist. Most importantly, discursification attempts to describe a process, whereas Pollitt and Hupe are quite reticent in giving a general account of the development of magic concepts. As Tøllefsen argues, the literature on the conceptual history of how concepts become magical remains scarce. Nevertheless, an implied theory of their historical origins can be detected.[7] Moreover, not all discursified concepts are necessarily magic concepts, although in extreme cases—such as transparency—they may be. This constitutes the second important difference between magic concepts and discursification.

As I will explain, there are many drivers to discursification in general and transparency in particular. Among the most important megatrends, I argue, are the changes happening in global power relations from about the 1990s onwards, the neoliberal governmentality they represent, and the related relativization of law they further and rely on. This megatrend can be argued to represent the modernist narrative of progress. To legitimize these changes, it seems that there is a high demand for normative concepts, which would not directly portray any religion, ideology, or political system. Legal discourse, above all, has the potential

[6] See also Christopher Pollitt and Peter Hupe, 'Talking About Government: The Role of Magic Concepts' (2011) 13(5) Public Management Review 641, 642–43 (hereafter Pollitt and Hupe, 'Talking About Government').

[7] T O Tøllefsen, 'Sustainability as a "Magic Concept"' (2021) 64 Deusto Journal of European Studies 29. Tøllefsen (at 36–37) argues that Pollitt and Hupe, in Pollitt and Hupe, 'Talking About Government' (n 6) 653, follow the definition of James C Scott, presented in the book *Seeing Like a State: How Certain Schemes to Improve the Human Condition Have Failed* (Yale University Press 1998); Scott, for one, has adopted his definition of modernism from the noted Marxist scholar: David Harvey, *The Condition of Postmodernity* (Blackwell 1990). See also Anthony Giddens, *Modernity and Self-Identity* (Polity Press 1991).

to supply those concepts however, only if its concepts are understood liberally enough.[8] Interestingly, as Alloa argues, many of those concepts originate from the Enlightenment, although only some of them—such as transparency—are considered worth resurrecting.[9]

Figuratively speaking, in discursification, the 'intellectual rights' of originally specialist concepts have expired, and in consequence, they have been relocated to the 'public domain', free for anyone to use, even in unrecognizable ways. In consequence, specialists no longer have the monopoly to use them in their professional language; the previously internally esoteric nature—knowledge kept protected for the sake of its own integrity—of these concepts is thus banalized by exoteric use. If normative concepts discursify successfully, they become 'floating legitimizers'. When that happens, a word or a symbol of another kind becomes a subject of liberal discursive meaning-making. It becomes the linguistic capital of its user, adopted from the said 'public domain'.

Additionally, I argue that discursification as a process is structurally analogous to the way in which literal meanings make metaphors. The meanings of metaphors and their cognitive foundations were discussed in chapter two. Here, I wish to build on those findings and argue that the way in which literal meaning becomes metaphorical may further help to reveal how specialist meanings can become discursive. If literal meanings lend their inherent understandability to abstractions, discursified meanings lend their inherent legitimacy to strategic talk and behaviour. Thus, a concept that is subject to discursification needs to evoke positive associations with a positive value charge (cf the normative attractiveness of magic concepts).

For example, let us take 'human rights'. It is very easy to be for 'human rights' if they are vaguely defined. That is, as long as it is left vague precisely which rights we are talking about, whose rights, in what context, in what jurisdiction, at the expense of what, and enforced by whom. In a liberal democratic society, it does not cost anything to endorse the current vocabulary of political morality. As Douzinas has put it, 'The right to free speech or to annual holidays can be accompanied by a right to love, to party or to have back episodes of Star Trek shown daily. If something can be put into language, it may acquire rights and can certainly become the

[8] This approach is visible in the preparatory materials of the Council of Europe Code of Good Administration. Recommendation CM/Rec (2007)7, Recommendation of the Committee of Ministers to Member States on Good Administration [2007]. The motivation for including the concept in the code was that the concept had become 'widely known'. See Council of Europe, Project Group of Administrative Law (CJ-DA): Preliminary Draft Report on the feasibility and desirability of preparing a recommendation and/or a consolidated model code of good administration. 17th meeting, Strasbourg 28 February–2 March 2005. Council of Europe (CJ-DA (2005) 4) 9.

[9] cf Alloa, 'Magic Concept of Modernity' (n 2) 37: 'After the end of the Cold War, the Western world presents itself as fundamentally post-ideological. It might not be an accident thus, when among all the shining concepts in the pantheon of Enlightenment, transparency has been chosen as the less controversial and most widely acceptable one.'

object of rights.'[10] At the same time, for lawyers and other experts in the field this discursification can be a source of annoyance. The fact that in law, human rights also have more pronounced specialist meanings does not mean that these meanings would have disappeared along with their discursification.

Another overlapping example—not as established as 'human rights', but perhaps in the process of becoming a human right—is the rainbow flag, the symbol of sexual and gender minorities' rights. Although the flag is a symbol rather than a term, in my view, it is still warranted to talk about its discursification. The flag is symbolic in the sense that a rainbow can be associated with diversity and equality. All seven colours are equally important parts of the rainbow; there is no hierarchy. Together, they make a beautiful totality that depicts the diversity of different genders and sexualities. However, today, the rainbow flag has partially escaped from its original status as a token of resistance to the status quo. Even multinational companies are taking part in Gay Pride parades and are waving rainbow flags. Are sexual minority rights really a particular concern of theirs? Hardly. If public opinion is favourable enough, it does not cost anything for the firm to use the symbol. Instead, it signals that the firm is endorsing a societal good and is implicitly against its opposite. Adopting discursified concepts can thus signal virtue without any suggestion of virtuous action. This is sometimes referred to as 'pink washing'.

To the extent that discursification entails components of (Foucauldian) discourse itself, one could argue that discursification is at least a semi-spontaneous process. Discourses, though connected to power, have no clear agents and agencies; in a way, they are 'in the air', established ways of talking about something. At the same time, the result of discursification is, as mentioned, strategic use and discursive meaning making. Is there, thus, a contradiction between discursification and its relation to agency and conscious attempts to bring about certain consequences in the world? I do not think so. Discursification as such is rarely planned but it can be adopted as a practical solution to an emerged problem of legitimacy. Subsequently, the concept becomes gradually semantically diluted, then the strategic use of the concept in other contexts is enabled. In other words, when the trend has been set, following it, and applying it needs fewer motivations than if that were not the case.

Is discursification such a bad thing? In the end it could be argued that discursification could help in normalizing originally marginal ideas or interests. These ideas could gain more public exposure and endorsement, and in that way

[10] Costas Douzinas, 'The End(s) of Human Rights' (2002) 26(2) Melbourne University Law Review 445. cf Martti Koskenniemi, 'Human Rights Mainstreaming as a Strategy for Institutional Power: Humanity' (2010) 1(1) International Journal of Human Rights, Humanitarianism, and Development 47, 48: 'The language of "rights" contrasts with that of "management" and suggests that there must be some limit to the weighing of costs and benefits—that some requirements are so self-evidently "good" (or some forms of behavior so intrinsically "evil") that they should leave no room for instrumental calculations.'

become gradually societally accepted, like the rainbow flag example. This is a valid point. It is possible that discursified concepts can do useful work. However, it seems that in discursification, the battles over concepts have largely already been fought, their ideological oppositions have faded away, and the ideology or group interests they once represented do not appear as ideology or group interests at all but as sheer societal good. As such, it is easy to favour discursified concepts without paying any price for doing so, so to speak. It is 'safe' to be in favour of them. It can be argued that magic concepts have undergone discursification to the extreme, transparency being one of those concepts.[11]

Discursifying Transparency

I argue that transparency as a legal concept has become discursified. This has happened to the extent that it has even become a magic concept. Transparency has become indeterminate in meaning (broadness) and extensive in use (global marketability). The people and institutions that flag transparency have proliferated, and a growing number of practices are attributed to it (normative attractiveness). Transparency's ideological counterarguments have been marginalized if not evaporated: they sound obsolete and questionable, perhaps even downright immoral (consensus implication).[12] As Christensen and Cornelissen put it, 'transparency has become a taken-for-granted ideal and explanation of how society and its organizations must function'.[13]

Of course, it is also possible to argue that transparency never was 'pre-discursive'. Quite the contrary, it was surely discursive from the very beginning of its role as an ideal for governing, like all important concepts of law and governance. In other words, there was hardly a time when a pristine and original transparency ideal existed, and where a perfect consensus as to its content and correct interpretation prevailed. This is a valid argument, and I have no objections to it. However, something has changed when we entered the 'transparentocene'.[14] Transparency has become the presumption, a default ideology, which, however, does not appear ideological at all, but a cultural signifier of neutrality, as it were. To date, there is no powerful anti-transparency or pro-secrecy movement—such as the *arcana imperii* in the Middle Ages—and even if there was, those who would be endorsing it would have the burden of proof to argue why secrecy is better than transparency.

[11] cf Alloa, 'Magic Concept of Modernity' (n 2).

[12] ibid, 29: 'transparency has no exact antonym, that is, it has no exact counter-concept which would negatively cover all its meanings'.

[13] Lars Thøger Christensen and Joep Cornelissen, 'Organizational Transparency as Myth and Metaphor' (2015) 18(2) European Journal of Social Theory 132, 133.

[14] Alloa, 'Magic Concept of Modernity' (n 2).

Due to its metaphorical nature and accumulated positive connotations, transparency has associative power, which the neighbouring concept of publicity, for example, is lacking.[15] As argued in chapter five, transparency is connected to a democratic governing structure in which the governed monitor the governor. Transparency thus promises that the object of the power, the governed, has the power to affect the governor. Ideationally, the governed is not just a helpless object of power but a part of a social contract. As such, the governed is not merely empowered; she is the very source of that delegated power that the governor is using on behalf of her and her fellow governed. This promise makes transparency normatively attractive. It can be so precisely due to its presupposition of a powerful and rational individual, democratic government, and its legal organization.

Because of these qualities that are peculiar to transparency—its metaphoric nature and its institutionalized positive connotations—transparency is an especially apt concept for discursification. That said, it is important to point out that not all discursified concepts are necessarily metaphors; for example, 'human rights' is not a metaphor. However, the metaphoric nature of the concept to be discursified may make it even more powerful. The legal, well institutionalized meaning of transparency—which, in turn, partially derives its force from the metaphorical meaning that understanding is seeing—helps the discursive meaning to become easily authoritative. Metaphors are powerful because they help us to understand abstractions. Transparency does this both through form (it is a metaphor) and content (it promises seeing and understanding).

In this way, the discursification process is analogous to how the literal meaning functions as the starting point for the metaphor to make sense. That is to say, the virtues of transparency are no longer anchored to any predefined practices or have any enforcement mechanisms. This, in turn, may make transparency a 'Humpty Dumpty concept'—'When I use a word, it means just what I choose it to mean—neither more nor less.' Such concepts have no direct connection to their origins, and thus are subject to endless negotiations of meaning. Thus, when transparency is successfully discursified, its meaning becomes over-inclusive (cf the broad scope of magic concepts). This is because on the one hand, the different normative practices attributed to transparency resemble it as a legal concept in some important way, but do not commit to its enforcement mechanisms, on the other.

The use of transparency rhetoric can thus misleadingly imply the existence of legal obligation and regulation where there is none.[16] This is because to have bearing in the state, transparency has legal and institutional guarantees.

[15] Sandrine Baume, 'Publicity and Transparency: The Itinerary of a Subtle Distinction' in Emmanuel Alloa and Dieter Thomä (eds), *Transparency, Society and Subjectivity: Critical Perspectives* (Palgrave Macmillan 2018).

[16] Monika Zalnieriute, 'Transparency-Washing in the Digital Age: A Corporate Agenda of Procedural Fetishism' (2021) 8(1) Critical Analysis of Law 39 (hereafter Zalnieriute, 'Transparency-Washing in the Digital Age').

Discursified transparency may not have those guarantees, but through association with the legal concept, it is 'as if' it has. As Zalnieriute puts it, transparency rhetoric is both related to ethics but is also an alternative to it. It is an additional discourse because of its connotations to legal normativity—for example, transparency is one of the foundational values of administrative law as well as another fuzzy legal concept, the 'rule of law'.[17]

The discursification of transparency thus implies at least two overlapping things. First, it implies that in today's world, the assumed legitimacy gained through transparency is increasingly desirable. One could claim that before the discursification of transparency, the general legitimacy of power was not that much of a general concern, or, even if it were, it was not framed as a problem of transparency. Second, the connotations associated with transparency are now in high demand. Why those connotations—sincerity, honesty, purity, rationality, understandability, the right to know, objectivity, authenticity, accountability, law-adherence, trust, order, and legitimacy—and not some others? What societal changes gave transparency the boost for discursification? What problem should transparency solve?

To summarize, what I mean by discursification in the context of transparency is that not only transparency's literal meaning but also its connotations may become metaphorical. In other words, if metaphorical meanings borrow understandability from a concrete phenomenon to form an abstraction, discursive meanings borrow the value, normativity, and even institutional guarantees to legitimize strategic behaviour. Transparency as a discursive strategy takes advantage of the many virtues associated with transparency in legal, societal, and moral vocabularies. Discursification, I argue, thus explains at least partially, why transparency has been able to become a cultural signifier of neutrality. In the following, I look at two examples of this process: global governance institutions and multinational technology companies. What work does discursified transparency perform in them?

Discursified Transparency in Global Governance

The Significance of Good Governance

The conceptual building blocks of discursification have been put in place, and it is now time to look at these processes in context. What kind of discursification processes of transparency can be detected in recent decades? I will start by looking at global governance, and the normative discourses that characterize it.[18] As I will

[17] ibid; see also Monika Zalnieriute, Lyria Bennett Moses, and George Williams, 'The Rule of Law and Automation of Government Decision-Making' (2019) 82 Modern Law Review 425.

[18] Global governance lacks a consensual definition and can be approached from many angles. From a legal point of view, it can be seen as referring to the diversifying understanding of international law after the Second World War. A tendency to solve transnational problems—in areas such as peace, the environment, development, finance, food, health, traffic, organized criminality, etc—on a transnational

argue in the following, transparency has become one of the most prominent norms in global governance, due to its connection to the discourse of good governance, and to changing power constellations.

Transparency started to feature in global governance discourses from the 1990s onwards. Why then? One explanation is its intimate connection to another magic concept, which was established in the late 1980s: the concept of *good governance*. The World Bank (WB) gave the first blueprint to the concept in 1989, when it described the problems of Sub-Saharan Africa as 'a crisis of governance'. The problem that this formulation aspired to address was the ineffectiveness of development aid. Even if money was lent to Sub-Saharan developing countries, it did not have the planned effect due to corruption and dysfunctional governmental structures.[19] The WB defined the term governance as 'the manner in which power is exercised in the management of a country's economic and social resources for development'.[20]

Hence, even mere 'governance' without any epithets was a normative term, as it implied a view of a desirable society. The requirement of goodness, however, made the normativity of 'governance' even more pronounced: good governance should be established. Although many definitions and emphases exist, good governance is typically defined as entailing the rule of law, a functioning market economy, the promotion of human rights, democratic government, and a light yet legally defined administration. Additionally, it should reflect procedural principles such as transparency, participation, review, and efficiency.[21]

Governance that was labelled by these characteristics was, by definition, good. Gradually, good governance underwent a metamorphosis of a kind. First, it was a remedy to bad governance or a crisis of governance, then it was a proactive imperative on how a functioning society should be organized. This is visible in the WB's words: 'Good governance requires the power to carry out policies and to develop institutions that may be unpopular among some—or even a majority—of the population.'[22] Thus, although it appeared neutral, merely a compilation of managerial

level emerged, thus transcending the capacities and interests of a single state. The number of intergovernmental organizations, non-governmental organizations (NGOs), and public-private hybrid regimes grew. Global governance is thus a general term for the ways in which different institutions manage transnational or global problems. See, for example, Jan Klabbers, 'Law, Ethics and Global Governance: Accountability in Perspective' (2012) 11 New Zealand Journal of Public and International Law 309; David Kennedy, 'The Mystery of Global Governance' (2008) 34 Ohio Northern University Law Review 827. cf Tero Erkkilä, *Government Transparency: Impacts and Unintended Consequences* (Palgrave Macmillan 2012) 3.

[19] The World Bank, 'Sub-Saharan Africa: From Crisis to Sustainable Growth' (The World Bank, November 1989).

[20] The World Bank, 'Governance and Development' (The World Bank, 30 April 1992).

[21] Jan Wouters and Cedric Ryngaert, 'Good Governance: Lessons from International Organizations' in Deirdre M Curtin and Ramses A Wessel (eds), *Good Governance and the European Union: Reflection on Concepts, Institutions and Substance* (Intersentia 2005).

[22] The World Bank, *World Development Report 2002: Building Institutions for Markets* (Oxford University Press 2002) 99.

best practices, it relied heavily on the power to carry through the suggested reforms. In particular, the relationship between good governance and democracy is strained: good governance should be democratic, yet the reforms necessitated by good governance may be unpopular even among the majority of the population.

The concept of good governance rapidly became popular. Soon after the WB started to use the concept, other international financing institutions (IFIs) such as the International Monetary Fund (IMF) followed, later also the United Nations Development Programme (UNDP) and the EU.[23] Although good governance programmes were directed towards aid-recipient states from the very start, the contemporary use of the term 'governance' was associated with globalization, neoliberal market ideology, and indeed, development.[24] Good governance was something that IFIs required from their aid recipients: paradoxically, it could be seen both as a condition and as an objective of development.[25] At the same time, however, organizations were not that concerned with the quality of their own governance. Neither would they formulate their internal matters according to the vocabulary of good governance. Good governance was designed to be an exportable idea.[26]

How did good governance agendas contribute to transparency becoming a discursive strategy? At least two ways can be identified. First, the definition of the very concept of good governance contributed to the discursification of transparency. For example, according to the WB's definition, 'Good governance is epitomized by predictable and enlightened policy making (that is, transparent processes); a bureaucracy imbued with a professional ethos; an executive arm of government accountable for its actions; and a strong civil society participating in public affairs and all behaving under the rule of law.'[27] That is to say, transparency was one of the key tenets of good governance from its very inception. It could be argued that the aid recipients' policy-making should be comprehensible for the aid lenders.

[23] Ida Koivisto, 'Varieties of Good Governance: A Suggestion of Discursive Plurality' (2014) 27(4) International Journal for the Semiotics of Law 587 (hereafter Koivisto, 'Varieties of Good Governance').

[24] The World Bank, *World Development Report 1991: The Challenge of Development: World Development Indicators* (Oxford University Press 1991) 1 (hereafter World Bank, 'World Development Report 1991'): 'A consensus is gradually forming in favour of a "market-friendly" development.' See also, for example, United Nations Development Programme, 'Governance for Sustainable Human Development' (UNDP policy document, January 1997): '[t]he growing international consensus that good governance and sustainable human development are indivisible.'

[25] Carlos Santiso, 'The Paradox of Governance: Objective or Condition of Multilateral Development Finance?' (2003) SAIS Working Paper Series WP/03/03, 2: 'a fundamental paradox plagues the IFIs' (international financial institutions) approach to governance reform, as the strengthening of governance institutions is conceived both as a condition and an objective of development finance.'

[26] See Beate Rudolf, 'Is "Good Governance" a Norm of International Law?' in Pierre-Marie Dupuy, Bardo Fassbender, Malcolm N Shaw, and Karl-Peter Sommermann (eds), *Völkerrecht als Wertordnung: Festschrift für Christian Tomuschat* (Engel 2006).

[27] World Bank, 'World Development Report 1991' (n 24); The World Bank, *Governance: The World Bank's Experience* (The World Bank, May 1994).

Second, after being a slogan for development, the meaning of good governance—and transparency as part of it—has widened to cover new areas in society. In fact, it seems to have no limits, but its significance is pervasive.[28] Conversely, it is possible to state things such as 'Bad governance is being increasingly regarded as one of the root causes of all evil within our societies'.[29] As Grindle shows, the scope of good governance has steadily widened over the years.[30] Along with this proliferation of areas that good governance covers, as well as the growing number of institutions adopting the concept, transparency also became more widely known. In the 2000s, it has become popular to the extent that its spread has been characterized as 'pandemic'.[31] In consequence, not only has good governance, too, discursified—although admittedly, it was vague from its very coinage—it has also become institutionalized in different specialist discourses, such as ethics, law, and economics.[32]

Transparency's association with something as vague and overarching as the goodness of governance has given it a new sheen of legitimacy, regardless of how it is defined.[33] Nevertheless, the less transparency works as an institutionalized term for certain practices—in addition to transparency's structural functioning logic and its characteristics, discussed in chapters two to four—the easier it is to use discursively to depict almost anything. Transparency's linkage to good governance and other equally uncontestable concepts such as human rights, democracy, and participation, works as a guarantee of its overall legitimacy; it belongs to the group of 'good concepts'. Discursification requires that something has started to signify a societal good with no equally institutionalized objections. This is exactly what has happened to good governance and to transparency as part of it.

[28] Koivisto, 'Varieties of Good Governance' (n 23) 587, 588: '[Good governance] can be used as a panacea for different kinds of problems in exercising societal power. Questions of, for example, decision-making, financial management, institutional design, public spending, administrative law, political co-operation and networking and professional ethics are formulated by using good governance vocabulary. That is to say problems in those areas can be interpreted as problems of good governance or good administration.'

[29] United Nations Economic and Social Commission for Asia and the Pacific, 'What is Good Governance?' (Report by the ESCAP, published 10 July 2009).

[30] Merilee Grindle, 'Good Enough Governance: Poverty Reduction and Reform in Developing Countries' (2004) 17(4) Governance: An International Journal of Policy, Administration and Institutions 525, 527: '[s]ummarizes statements about "what must be done" to achieve good governance that appeared in World Development Reports from 1997 to 2002/2003. These included the characteristics of good governance and the institutions, laws, policies, services, and strategies that are needed to achieve it. In the 1997 report, developing countries were advised to pay attention to 45 aspects of good governance; by 2002, the list had grown to 116 items. Even allowing for considerable overlap among categories in the table, it seems that countries in need of good governance must undertake a great deal to get it—and the longer they wait, the more things they will need to do to get it. Indeed, it may be difficult to identify a desirable condition or action that is not conducive to good governance, suggesting that the underlying agenda is actually a search for a cure to underdevelopment.'

[31] Pollitt and Hupe, 'Talking About Government' (n 6) 646.

[32] Koivisto, 'Varieties of Good Governance' (n 23).

[33] cf Mikkel Flyverbom, 'Sunlight in Cyberspace? On Transparency as a Form of Ordering' (2015) 18 European Journal of Social Theory 168, 169; see also Onora O'Neill, 'Transparency and the Ethics of Communication' in Christopher Hood and David Heald (eds), *Transparency: The Key to Better Governance?* (Oxford University Press 2006) 75, 76.

The 'Transparency Turn'

Good governance thus contributed to normalizing the concept of transparency by associating it with a wider conception of a good and functioning society. At least to some extent, good governance discourse enabled the framing of different problems of governance as problems of transparency, as was visible in the WB's definition of good governance. Along with this process, transparency has become increasingly normative—a good society is a transparent one and pursuing it should be made a priority. For example, the WB and the World Trade Organization (WTO) have compelled their member states or aid-recipients to establish separate transparency policies.[34]

That said, these new transparency demands to the member states have not automatically meant or led to the transparency of those IFIs themselves. Instead, there has been a significant informational asymmetry between the aid-recipients and the IFIs, which has led to allegations of hypocrisy. Over the last couple of decades, the perceived informational gap between the obligors and obligees of transparency has been increasingly recognized. The credibility of global governance institutions insisting on the adoption of good governance programmes and transparency policies has necessitated a more self-reflective attitude towards those concepts.[35] This also means giving up at least some of the institutional-informational asymmetry stemming from unequal transparency requirements.[36]

When the idea of normative transparency outside of state governance and legal articulation was established, it could also be used defensively. Why should not the IFIs and other global governance institutions be transparent themselves if they require that from the member states? In fact, the practice of adopting transparency policies in global governance institutions has indeed become common to the extent to which the term the 'transparency turn' has been used.[37] An illustrative example of this development can be found in the history of the IMF.

During the last couple of decades, transparency as a policy value has made significant inroads at the IMF. It has offered transparency as a common solution to many of the global economic and financial problems it had to face with the Asian financial crisis in the late 1990s. In 2009, after the global financial crisis, transparency was described as 'the new norm' within the IMF. It was expected to increase

[34] Peters, 'Towards Transparency as a Global Norm' (n 3) 557–58. See also Thomas Blanton, 'The Struggle for Openness in the International Financial Institutions' in Ann Florini (ed), *The Right to Know: Transparency for an Open World* (Columbia University Press 2007).

[35] cf Rachel Adams, *Transparency: New Trajectories in Law* (Routledge 2020) 45–48.

[36] Peters, 'Towards Transparency as a Global Norm' (n 3) 557–58.

[37] Gupta, 'Transparency Under Scrutiny' (n 3); Koivisto, 'The IMF and the "Transparency Turn"' (n 3); Megan Donaldson and Benedict Kingsbury, 'The Adoption of Transparency Policies in Global Governance Institutions: Justifications, Effects, and Implications' (2013) 9 Annual Review of Law and Social Science 119, 142–43 (hereafter Donaldson and Kingsbury, 'The Adoption of Transparency Policies in Global Governance Institutions').

the IMF's effectiveness, legitimacy, quality of surveillance and programmes, and to contribute to the public debate. The way in which transparency was adopted in the IMF followed this development: first, it demanded the loan recipients to be transparent, and later, it adopted transparency as a general principle regarding its own policies.[38]

Can we plausibly identify larger trends behind the 'transparency turn' in global governance? Although the emergence of good governance discourse certainly helped discursifying transparency, other explanatory factors can also be named. One important factor is the growing power of global governance institutions.[39] The increasing influence of these, both in national policy-making and in global legal structures, has created a growing concern over their legitimacy. This has raised many questions. Given the power they are using, are they accountable for their actions? Alternatively, is there, as commonly accused, a 'democratic deficit' or an 'accountability deficit'? Do global governance institutions function as global administrative agencies and should they therefore be subject to similar rules? Are they subject to sufficient monitoring and control?[40] In other words, the question is about the legitimacy of the mechanisms in which global problems are governed, and whether discursified transparency can provide such legitimacy without formalized enforcement mechanisms.

Finally, the transparency turn may also be simply a matter of trendy governance buzzwords and institutional imitation, peculiar to discursification (cf the fashionableness of magic concepts). Namely, the popularity of the concept of transparency encourages different institutions to adopt it, not only because of what it is, or can do, but also because of the 'social pressure' coming from other similar institutions. In that way, transparency can function as a tool for impression management and virtue signalling, as was argued to be characteristic of discursification in general.

[38] Koivisto, 'The IMF and the "Transparency Turn"' (n 3). In my article 'The IMF and the "Transparency Turn"', I discussed in more detail how the concept of transparency is understood in the IMF and what could be extrapolated from that understanding. I concluded that within a single institution, the IMF in this case, many varieties of transparency exist, making it a radically indeterminate concept. As the discourse of transparency spills over into all fields of policy, forming standards and soft law, the normative core of the concept inevitably disperses. At the same time, given transparency's performative logic, the adopted transparency policies make power appear in a certain way, whereas other forms may stay undetected. In other words, although I did not use the concept in describing the IMF's conception of transparency, it could well be called discursified transparency.

[39] Similarly, Peters, 'Towards Transparency as a Global Norm' (n 3) 557–58.

[40] Donaldson and Kingsbury, 'The Adoption of Transparency Policies in Global Governance Institutions' (n 37) 142–43: Donaldson and Kingsbury identify some additional drivers to the new fashionableness of adopting transparency policies in global governance institutions. In addition to the growing power of those institutions, they mention the developments in national public law and public international law that impose greater national obligations for disclosure on state governments and public authorities (cf the IMF example). The FOIAs function as a benchmark for those policies. The institutions may also be subject to criticism coming from NGOs, member states, and even from their own staff, who demand those institutions to disclose more of their activities.

As Hood has put it, 'more-transparent-than-thou' has become the secular equivalent of 'holier-than-thou'.[41]

In conclusion, no single clear reason to account for the entire 'transparency turn' in global governance can be detected. Instead, there are several interlocking drivers, as presented. In any case, the pressure for global governance institutions to adopt a transparency policy has significantly increased, as the opinion in international law has started to favour transparency over confidentiality and secrecy.[42] Although the development towards greater transparency has not been linear, all-encompassing, or monocausal, cultural change towards presumptive transparency from presumptive secrecy can be argued to exist.[43] As already mentioned, the way in which discursification works is by metaphorizing the institutionalized functioning mechanisms attributed to the concept. In this case, it would mean using transparency *as if* it were a legal concept, having its intellectual roots in democratic theory and public law. This is clear in global governance institutions in which the adopted transparency policies work *as if* it were a binding legal regulation, and *as if* the FOIA were outside the state.

Discursified Transparency in Technology Companies

Transparency and the Digitalized Society

Global governance is not the only influential context in which the concept of transparency has gained unprecedented rhetorical assets. Another context I would like to look at as a matrix of discursified transparency is multinational technology companies, more specifically the digital platforms[44] they own. As these companies have gained unprecedented power in a short amount of time, their relationship with transparency is important. What are the drivers and effects of discursified transparency in this context?

It is easy to see that transparency as a concept is in strategic use in a growing number of companies, not only technology companies. Indeed, nowadays transparency policies and declarations are to be found on almost any company's website. For example, in fashion retail, transparency policy may mean explaining the

[41] Christopher Hood, 'Transparency in Historical Perspective' in Christopher Hood and David Heald (eds), *Transparency—The Key to Better Governance?* (Oxford University Press 2006) 3.

[42] Andrea Bianchi, 'On Power and Illusion: The Concept of Transparency in International Law' in Andrea Bianchi and Anne Peters (eds), *Transparency in International Law* (Cambridge University Press 2013).

[43] Peters, 'Towards Transparency as a Global Norm' (n 3) 599.

[44] Tarleton Gillespie, *Custodians of the Internet: Platforms, Content Moderation, and the Hidden Decisions that Shape Social Media* (Yale University Press 2018) 18, defines platforms as online sites and services that: 'a) host, organize, and circulate users' shared content or social interactions for them, b) without having produced or commissioned (the bulk of) that content, c) built on an infrastructure, beneath that circulation of information, for processing data for customer service, advertising, and profit'.

process of production, to convince the consumers that no child labour, unethical working conditions, unsustainable materials, or other such things were involved. International coffee shop chains may reveal the details of their coffee production in the name of transparency. An aviation company may explain their CO_2 emissions and strategies to reduce them. This visible endorsement of transparency can be argued both to represent and to further the discursification of transparency.

Transparency can be an outlet for companies to 'tell their story', to govern the way in which they portray themselves in the market. In fact, a survey from 2011 shows that 'transparency' is the most used concept of CEOs' annual addresses along with 'competence' and 'authenticity'.[45] This kind of use of discursified transparency needs to be approached critically. I argue that by sharing information in the name of transparency, companies wish to appear as if they had nothing to hide. At the same time, they can use transparency as a tool for showcasing their values, goals, and accomplishments; in other words, for impression management purposes. By so doing they also show how they are up to par in following institutional trends, which the call for transparency undoubtedly represents. Like the previously mentioned examples of human rights and the rainbow flag, it is easy for companies to be in favour of transparency and against secrecy and opacity, when they themselves can define what transparency might mean. For example, they would hardly disclose their trade secrets in the name of transparency.

However, the call for transparency may have more profound implications in the digitalized society. In addition to the general logic of positive transparency as self-reporting, transparency in the discourses of digital platforms may be indicative of changing societal power constellations, as argued.[46] The so-called data monopolies Google (Alphabet), Facebook (Meta), Apple, Amazon, etc, which are private companies, have gained huge power in governing the entire fabric of the digital society.[47] They offer most of the most popular internet services, such as search engines and social media platforms, while systematically gathering data about their users. This new logic is referred to as the emergence of the digital economy or more pessimistically, surveillance capitalism.[48]

Indeed, data have become increasingly the way to govern; this development is often called datafication. It, in turn, is enabled by the technological developments which have taken place over the last couple of decades.[49] With the internet,

[45] Wei (Vivian) Guo, 'The Power of Plain Language: Executives' Rhetoric in Conference Presentations, Persuasion, and Stock Market Reaction' (Unpublished Doctoral Dissertation, DPhil, University of Maryland 2011) 4.

[46] Mikkel Flyverbom, *The Digital Prism: Transparency and Managed Visibilities in a Datafied World* (Cambridge University Press 2019) 88–92 (hereafter Flyverbom, 'The Digital Prism').

[47] Beata Mäihäniemi, *Competition Law and Big Data: Imposing Access to Information in Digital Markets* (Edward Elgar 2020).

[48] Shoshana Zuboff, *The Age of Surveillance Capitalism: The Fight for a Human Future at the New Frontier of Power* (Profile Books 2019).

[49] Stefan Larsson, *Conceptions in the Code: How Metaphors Explain Legal Challenges in Digital Times* (Oxford University Press 2017). Larsson defines digitalization in the following way at 5: 'Digitalisation

growing computing power, data analytics, artificial intelligence (AI), and so on, modern society has drastically changed. On the one hand, this means that we are more connected to each other than ever before. On the other hand, we are increasingly dependent on technology and the way in which it mediates and alters social life, society, and commerce. This digitalization of society is certainly technological, but it is also socio-material. It makes us dependent on digital intermediaries—platforms and other internet services but also material objects such as computers and mobile phones.

In other words, it would be shortsighted and reductionist to think that the digitalization of society would only be a matter of the changing media of social interaction.[50] Although the media, too, have undoubtedly changed, the ramifications of digitalization run deeper. The data monopolies—in particular, Google and Facebook—function as entry points to many digital services.[51] Their surreptitious and ultimately commercial logic has been pervasive and paradigm shifting to the extent that it has entailed new, overarching characterizations: the black box society,[52] the platform society,[53] platform capitalism,[54] and so on. These terms imply how the power relations in the digitalized society are formed in a different way than in the analogue society.

Instead of governments or even intergovernmental organizations, the main power holders of the digital society are thus these few companies. Although the platforms govern what we can see online, the way in which the curation of visibilities is done often remains in the 'black box': we do not know how algorithms translate inputs into outputs. Consequently, transparency is increasingly demanded of those companies, perhaps partially in compensation for our own forced transparency to them. Increasingly, this inequality of power between the digital platforms and their users has been recognized: as with the discourses of global governance, similar concerns about accountability have been voiced.

Interestingly, also in this context, there are theoretical attempts to bring concepts and rationalities of public law into the discussions of the power used by these companies, to conceptualize the ways in which to hold them accountable. For example, 'digital constitutionalism' and the call for 'public values' have been mentioned.[55] In

can be seen as a sort of ontological revolution in which all sorts of events and artefacts are redefined within a shift and interaction between analogue materiality and digital immateriality.'

[50] See Taina Bucher, *If... Then: Algorithmic Power and Politics* (Oxford University Press 2018).

[51] José van Dijck, Thomas Poell, and Martijn de Waal, *The Platform Society: Public Values in a Connective World* (Oxford University Press 2018) 12 (hereafter van Dijck, Poell, and de Waal, 'The Platform Society').

[52] Frank Pasquale, *The Black Box Society: The Secret Algorithms That Control Money and Information* (Harvard University Press 2015).

[53] van Dijck, Poell, and de Waal, 'The Platform Society' (n 51) 22–26, 139–41.

[54] Nick Srnicek, *Platform Capitalism* (Polity Press 2016).

[55] Nicolas Suzor, *Lawless: The Secret Rules That Govern Our Digital Lives* (Cambridge University Press 2019) 112–13 (hereafter Suzor, 'Lawless'): Suzor argues that digital constitutionalism 'seeks to develop

these discussions, the idea is that the power of technology companies should not be understood through unnegotiable terms of use alone, but through constitutional and administrative principles. The power of these companies should be informed by the rule of law, democracy, and transparency.

The Implications of Transparency Reporting

How is the impression management logic of transparency manifested in the context of digital platforms? Transparency may, for example, be relevant in many practices, such as content moderation. Here, however, I concentrate on 'transparency reports', which technology companies—first Google and then many others—have started to publish from 2010 onwards.[56] Although Google and Twitter were in the forefront of establishing this new practice, an important moment for its more general adoption seems to have been the Snowden revelations in 2013. When the National Security Agency (NSA) surveillance and its magnitude were disclosed, proactive transparency became fashionable in a new way.[57] It seems that by adopting the practice of transparency reporting, the technology companies wanted to distance themselves from government surveillance.

The main idea in transparency reporting is thus to communicate how often and under what authority governments have requested or demanded information, data, or records from the company in question in each period. Transparency reporting is often motivated by human rights rhetoric. As it says in Google's transparency report from 2020, the report aims at: 'Sharing data that sheds light on how the policies and actions of governments and corporations affect privacy, security, and access to information'.[58] Facebook states in their report that 'We're committed to making Facebook a place that's open and authentic, while safeguarding people's private data and keeping our platform safe for everyone. We publish regular reports to give our community visibility into how we enforce policies, respond to data requests and protect intellectual property, while monitoring dynamics that limit access to Facebook products'.[59] Apple, in turn, says that 'We believe our

new guiding principles that can be applied to the unique way the internet is governed in different ways by many different actors'. See also van Dijck, Poell, and de Waal, 'The Platform Society' (n 51).

[56] Google, 'Google Transparency Report' <https://transparencyreport.google.com/about> accessed 5 July 2021 (hereafter Google Transparency Report).

[57] See, for example, Kasmir Hill, 'Thanks, Snowden! Now All the Major Tech Companies Reveal How Often They Give Data to Government' *Forbes* (New York, 14 November 2013) <www.forbes.com/sites/kashmirhill/2013/11/14/silicon-valley-data-handover-infographic/?sh=2dddc9da5365> accessed 5 July 2021.

[58] Google Transparency Report (n 56).

[59] Facebook, 'Facebook Transparency Report' <https://govtrequests.facebook.com> accessed 5 July 2021.

customers have a right to understand how their personal data is managed and protected. Apple's Transparency Report provides information regarding government requests for customer data.'[60]

In the reports, the companies explain the way in which they are using the data in their possession and what kind of problems have followed. For example, Google's transparency report includes a variety of topics under the headlines of Security and privacy, Content removal, and Additional reports. The last category covers, among other things, political advertisements. The aim is to disclose information on the money put into political advertising in selected countries. In a similar way, Facebook has established a library of political ads.[61] Transparency reports thus create an impression of political and ideological neutrality.

Transparency reports are also a good example of what I previously described as institutional imitation. When one company adopts the practice of creating and publishing transparency reports, others follow (cf the global marketability of magic concepts). The practice of transparency reporting has spread rapidly across industry, starting from the most influential companies. Conversely, when the immediate external pressure to adopt the transparency reporting practice after the Snowden revelations had evaporated, the spreading of the practice declined, at least for some time.[62] This demonstrates the effect of institutional social pressure to follow current trends and to adopt policies that are fashionable.

The effectiveness of transparency reports has been subject to criticism. What do they disclose and what does that disclosure mean?[63] Companies choose what they report, and by so doing, carefully curate their public image.[64] It seems that through this curation, they tend to shift the focus from their business model to digital rights, such as freedom of speech and privacy and to the actions of governments.[65] When they distance themselves from government surveillance, the attention is simultaneously deflected from the surveillance they are practising themselves. In this way,

[60] Apple, 'Apple Transparency Report' <www.apple.com/legal/transparency/about.html> accessed 5 July 2021.

[61] Rob Leathern, 'Expanded Transparency and More Controls for Political Ads' (Facebook, 9 January 2020) <https://about.fb.com/news/2020/01/political-ads/> accessed 5 July 2021. The worry about political ads is most probably a response to the Cambridge Analytica scandal. See, for example, Christopher Wylie, *Mindf*ck: Cambridge Analytica and the Plot to Break America* (Random House 2019).

[62] See, for example, Rob Pegoraro, 'Tech Companies Are Quietly Phasing Out a Major Privacy Safeguard' *The Atlantic* (29 September 2019) <www.theatlantic.com/technology/archive/2019/09/what-happened-transparency-reports/599035/> accessed 5 July 2021.

[63] cf Christopher Parsons, 'The (In)effectiveness of Voluntarily Produced Transparency Reports' (2017) 58(1) Business and Society 103.

[64] cf Flyverbom, 'The Digital Prism' (n 46) 131: 'Transparency reports, like other transparency efforts, are forms of visibility management where decisions about what to highlight and what to downplay are central.'

[65] Ryan Budish, 'What Transparency Reports Don't Tell Us' *The Atlantic* (19 December 2013) <<https://www.theatlantic.com/technology/archive/2013/12/what-transparency-reports-dont-tell-us/282529/> accessed 30 March 2022; Rikke Frank Jørgensen, 'What Platforms Mean When They Talk About Human Rights: Platforms and Human Rights' (2017) 9 Policy Internet 280.

they can avoid addressing the legitimacy of their way of using their users' data and concentrate on solving the problems which are secondary to the business model, instead. Therefore, it is fair to assume that transparency reports only shed light on a fraction of the operations of the platforms.

Transparency reporting relies on and further accelerates the discursification of transparency. In technology companies, the concept of transparency is used in a strategic way. This is enabled, as presented, by transparency's connection to other positively charged concepts such as authenticity, trust, and accountability. These concepts often feature together, and one is said to lead to the other. However, discursified transparency does not necessarily lead to greater accountability or understanding; the effect can be obscuring, instead. As Suzor argues, when companies use transparency strategically as a theatre to repel claims for greater accountability, the promised understanding hardly follows from transparency. Instead, the lack of detail in the reports can allow platforms to respond to demands for more information while avoiding accountability.[66]

In consequence, we can ask whether adopting proactive transparency strategies such as transparency reporting is indeed a way for the companies to escape hard regulation, a form of 'ethics washing'.[67] Zalnieriute has even talked about 'transparency washing', namely the ostentatious adoption of transparency practices for companies to strengthen their brand, and to avoid regulation and binding laws.[68] At the same time, transparency remains open to the new practices and meanings that are attributed to it, in other words, for further discursification. As it says in Google's 2017 Transparency Report, 'As the Internet and technology evolves, so, too, does the notion of transparency. Google's Transparency Report continues to evolve, building a foundation to publish more data in the future.'[69]

To conclude, transparency has found its way into the practices of technology companies and their digital platforms as a general corporate value, and, among other things, as a practice of publishing transparency reports. It seems that this trend is a consequence of transparency having a readily available conceptual response to general legitimacy concerns stemming from the laws of the datafied society. As in the case of global governance, also in this context, criticism of secrecy or illegitimate practices has made the key players adopt a more proactive attitude towards transparency.

66 Suzor, 'Lawless' (n 55) 137.

67 cf Ben Wagner, 'Ethics as an Escape from Regulation: From "Ethics-Washing" to Ethics-Shopping?' in Emre Bayamalioglu and others (eds), *Being Profiled: Cogitas Ergo Sum: 10 Years of Profiling the European Citizen* (Amsterdam University Press 2018) 84.

68 Zalnieriute, 'Transparency-Washing in the Digital Age' (n 16).

69 Google Transparency Report (n 56).

Transparency and Discursified Public Law

As I have argued, both in global governance institutions and in digital platforms, a major driver for the discursification of transparency is the emergence of a new and non-democratic power relation and the informational asymmetry that comes with it. In both contexts, the 'governed' have accused the 'governors' of accountability deficit. No wonder: these governors have emerged outside of democratic structures, yet they hold great power. They are disturbingly free to use their power as they see fit.

I argue that this is one of the reasons why transparency has become so popular: it both reveals and hides power. It reveals power by its very existence as an institutionalized legitimation tool. If one can find declarations of transparency, one can assume that they are there to justify the unequal use of power. These declarations hide power by creating an illusion of symmetry: I am transparent to you, and you are transparent to me. However, the governed have less choice about whether and how to be transparent due to their dependent position on the governor: transparency can be a condition for the governed to get what the governor can offer. The governor, instead, can well adopt a Humpty Dumpty version of transparency.

Let me illustrate. In global governance, IFIs have first required aid-recipient countries to become more transparent, namely to adopt transparency policies, to follow good governance recommendations, and to become more legible for the monitoring IFIs. Later, this asymmetry has led to accusations of opacity against the IFIs themselves, which further contributed to them adopting transparency policies as well. In digital platforms, a roughly similar trajectory can be detected. Technology companies have made their users transparent by collecting massive amounts of data on them. However, the ways in which this was done remained undisclosed. Later, the users and governments started to demand more transparency concerning their black box operations. This, in turn, has influenced the adoption of the practice of transparency reporting as well as framing the question of legitimacy as a question of transparency.

In both contexts, the underlying factor is a 'take-it-or-leave-it' logic. In both, there is a highly unequal power relationship at play in which the governed want or need something from the governor, making the governed dependent on the governor. This means that the governed have no choice other than to obey the conditions set by the governor: If you want our development aid, adopt transparency policies. If you want to use our digital platform, consent to the terms of use. This kind of overt inequality, however, seems to have become less publicly acceptable. That is why the mutual adoption of the language of transparency has the potential to create an illusion of equality. That power imbalance feeds into the discursification of transparency; it hides the existence of the power imbalance.

Difficulty in detecting new power relations is exacerbated by the crumbling of the public-private divide. This is largely due to digitalization but it is not restricted to it. In global governance, there are even private associations, which resemble public agencies, such as the Internet Corporation for Assigned Names and Numbers (ICANN). New power constellations in global governance and especially in digital society have affected the ways in which the classical divide between public and private spheres is conceived. The effects of this are remarkable. As Harcourt argues, the digital economy has torn down the traditional boundaries between governing, commerce, and private life. The customary lines between politics, economics, and society are quickly disappearing, and these spheres are melding into one. That one totality consists of a 'gigantic trove of data, one colossal data market that allows corporations and governments to identify and cajole, to stimulate our consumption and shape our desires, to manipulate us politically, to watch, surveil, detect, predict, and, for some, punish'. In the same process, 'we turn more and more into marketized malleable subjects who, willingly or unwittingly, allow ourselves to be nudged, recommended, tracked, diagnosed, and predicted by a blurred amalgam of governmental and commercial initiatives'.[70]

Indeed, in the globalized and digitalized environment, it is difficult to demarcate the public sphere from the private.[71] For example, in the fabric of the digital economy, our privacy is constantly under jeopardy due to the aggressive commercial use of our personal data and internet behaviour. At the same time, social media platforms—private companies—are increasingly expected to make sure that people's digital rights are fulfilled, or, at least, that they are not violated by the companies themselves, governments, or other users. This has influenced, in turn, the discursification of transparency; the originally public law principle has also spread to traditionally private and hybrid contexts.

The discursification of transparency can thus be argued to overlap and intersect with another megatrend: the spread of procedural public law as a cure-all normative framework. In Alloa's words, 'In an allegedly postideological era, it is telling that the highest, uncontroversial value is a principle pretending to regulate only the form, not the content, of social interactions: a principle that purports to be neutral, all the while imposing a morality upon both public and private life.'[72] In the context of global governance, several normative theories (such as global constitutionalism, global administrative law) aim at reconstructing the problems of global governance in the language and rationality of public law. In internet governance, as mentioned, 'digital constitutionalism' or 'public values' are called for.[73]

[70] Bernard Harcourt, *Exposed: Desire and Disobedience in the Digital Age* (Harvard University Press 2015) 187.

[71] Frieder Vogelmann, 'Transparency's Trap: Problems of an Uncontested Norm' in Stefan Berger and Dimitrij Owetschkin (eds), *Contested Transparencies, Social Movements and the Public Sphere: Multi-Disciplinary Perspectives* (Palgrave Macmillan 2019) 44–45.

[72] Alloa, 'Magic Concept of Modernity' (n 2) 47; see also Flyverbom, 'The Digital Prism' (n 46) 121.

[73] Suzor, 'Lawless' (n 55) 128–49; van Dijck, Poell and de Waal, 'The Platform Society' (n 51) 22–26, 139–41.

Yet, this kind of public law is discursified public law: it is lacking constitutive norms, and clear articulation of rights and execution mechanisms. Rather, this kind of discursified conception of public law would be a moral demand manifested in codes of conduct, recommendations, policy papers, and other soft law instruments. Such demands formulated as *as-if* law would thus be considered better than other options. All this is, however, macro-legitimation through micro-critique: transparency or other procedural principles do not regulate the goals but only the processes.[74]

As is typical of magic concepts—concepts discursified to the extreme—transparency is also closely connected to other magic concepts. As Pollitt and Hupe argue, 'Frequently, magic concepts are used in an interactive and mutually supportive way. Better governance is said to require more accountability, for instance, or networked approaches are claimed to be more conducive to innovation.'[75] When we are talking about transparency in particular, these neighbouring concepts—such as good governance, accountability, participation and democracy—also happen to feature in public law doctrines. In a way, this is exactly why the discursification of transparency has been possible in the first place: through the association with legality and legitimacy that public law vocabulary provides.

This connection between magic concepts and the current popularity of public law as a vocabulary is hardly a coincidence.[76] It seems that public law in general is becoming more of a mindset than a formal structure; much of public law vocabulary going beyond transparency seems to have discursified. The trendiness of public law as a mindset is not necessarily a harmless phenomenon, but it does signal the enmeshing of the private and the public, and obscures the meaning of law. As Cohen exemplifies:

> To be sure, there are differences between platform usership and citizenship: Citizenship is constitutive of juridical identity, whereas platform usership is not. Nation states make citizenship difficult to attain and easy to relinquish, while for digital platforms the reverse is true. The logic of platform membership is a network logic that relies on lock-in, and it persistently undercuts the strategies of exit and voice through which users police more ordinary commercial relationships. The increasingly indispensable nature of the services that platforms provide makes exit practically infeasible for many users.[77]

Discursified public law cannot grant rights and legal statuses.

[74] cf Zalnieriute, 'Transparency-Washing in the Digital Age' (n 16) 139, 150–53.

[75] Pollitt and Hupe, 'Talking About Government' (n 6) 653.

[76] Ida Koivisto, 'From Moral Rules to Individual Rights—and Beyond? The Institutionalization of Good Administration in Finland and in Europe' (2018) 1 Förvaltningsrättslig tidskrift 71.

[77] Julie E Cohen, *Between Truth and Power: The Legal Constructions of Informational Capitalism* (Oxford University Press 2019) 235.

This conceptualization of the legitimacy of power as a matter of public law principles has both a normative and a heuristic dimension, both justifying and explaining power. It helps to formulate the questions of legitimacy in circumstances in which power use is asymmetrical. In consequence, if public law is successfully discursified, all kinds of institutions can be subject to its requirements. The implication is that if some institution—be it public, private, or hybrid—in fact uses power analogously to a governor, it should therefore be subject to public law principles. Perhaps, following Harcourt, the entire divide between private and public needs to be rethought in the age of the globalized and digitalized society. Instead of the public/private divide, we might encounter a new watershed in legal thought and regulation: the equal/unequal power relation.[78]

Summing Up: Transparency for the Sake of Transparency

In this chapter, I have discussed the phenomenon I coined the discursification of transparency. It has enabled transparency to function as a 'floating legitimizer'. One of the main characteristics of discursification is the relativization—or metaphorization, or analogization—of law. As argued, discursification comes close to the development of magic concepts. Along with this process, transparency has become increasingly devoid of the normative guarantees presented in chapters five and six; there are hardly any effectively enforceable legal rights and obligations when transparency is used as a discursive strategy. Instead, different practices named transparency have emerged, practices that are not binding, at least not in a legal sense.

I argued that metaphorization and discursification are analogous processes. What I meant by that was that if metaphors borrow the literal meaning of a thing or a phenomenon to make an abstraction understandable, discursification borrows the cultural value and the normative guarantees for discursive practices in order to use power in an effective way. By discursified transparency, an institution may govern its visibility by calling it transparency. As such, discursified transparency is performative, and functions as an especially effective tool for impression management. This performativity implies intentionality: 'Transparency is what *I* mean by it', and yet, regardless, of this haphazard definition, it sounds plausible, due to the cultural value accumulated to the concept.

I illustrated the discursification of transparency with two examples: those of global governance and multinational technology companies. I showed how

[78] cf Suzor, 'Lawless' (n 55) 113: on digital constitutionalism: 'Unlike regular constitutions, which just have to articulate how power is shared between different parts of a single government, digital constitutionalism requires us to develop new ways of limiting abuses of power in a complex system that includes many different governments, businesses, and civil society organizations.'

transparency requirements are a corollary of changing power constellations, whereby the illusion of symmetry is of key importance. In global governance, I argued that transparency is closely connected with the rise of good governance ideology as well as with the 'transparency turn', a change in the general attitude towards transparency in international law. In the context of technology companies, I discussed how transparency works as a general impression management strategy but also as a defensive concept to avoid hard regulation. I argued that both contexts represent a wider megatrend whereby public law has started to be portrayed in a post-ideological vocabulary of legitimacy. Discursified transparency thus mirrors a wider discursification of public law.

When we compare modern discursified transparency with a more theoretically robust understanding of it (chapter five), we can assume that the main collateral damage of discursification is the democratic rationality of transparency. Although it is exactly this promise that has enabled transparency to spread outside the context of a state, there are no established democratic structures that would enable the effective collective influencing of the fundaments of the power exercised. Of course, consumers can cease to use the services of a particular technology company, for example, but they cannot overthrow the governor and vote in a new one. Moreover, due to the companies' function as the main entry points—virtually, monopolies—of many services in our digitalized society, not using Google's services, for instance, would make life difficult.

In conclusion, the way in which transparency is assumed to cure the lamented democratic deficit or accountability deficit is less than clear, although it most certainly offers a fruitful soil for the discursification of transparency and other concepts of public law. With discursification, transparency's normative attractiveness has become unprecedented, leading to radically over-inclusive meaning. This being the case, the rise of transparency implies new conceptions and possibly also new functioning mechanisms of global power, whereby tools for creating legitimacy are increasingly distanced from their role as tools. Instead, these tools are becoming self-standing emblems of legitimacy. Transparency is not only valuable because it would, as the narrative goes, make power visible and as such controllable, but also, because assumedly, transparency is valuable for its own sake.

8

The Future of Transparency

From Representation to Simulation?

Plato's Cave Revisited

In the previous chapters, I discussed the conceptual and structural characteristics of transparency as an ideal, and the connections between power and transparency. Much of these discussions rely on the epistemology of seeing. Different arrangements of visibility make it possible to see some parts of the governor, at least in theory. In addition, the discussion has built on the idea of the performativity of showing; transparency is essentially a social practice of constructed or allowed visibilities. In this chapter, the approach is different: I will challenge the potency of these premises in our current circumstances. I ask whether this epistemology of seeing and performativity of showing can have a bearing in the digitalized society, and if so, how. The goal is thus to map out some critical aspects of transparency's potential future.

To answer this epistemological question, we need to return to the questions of representation that were discussed in chapter two. We need to ask what is it that inspires the different arrangements of visibility that transparency is to show. If we follow Plato's famous allegory of the cave, we can formulate the question in the following manner: what is the reality, the 'ground truth' that the theatre of shadows imitates?[1] In the digitalized world, the question of reality and its representation becomes increasingly complicated. To quote Christiane Paul: 'If one would update Plato's allegory for the age of cinema, one might replace the cave with a movie theatre, the fire with a projector, and the wall in front of the prisoners with a screen. In the age of digital media and "digital light", the relationships between light, shadow, screen, and projection have become more complex: light is generated by electronic

[1] Plato presented the allegory of the cave in his *Republic*. Plato, *The Republic of Plato* (translated with notes and an interpretive essay by Allan Bloom, 2nd ed, Basic Books 1991), 514a–520a. Its idea is to compare 'the effect of education and the lack of it on our nature'. In the allegory, Plato uses shadows, which are reflected on the walls of the cave, as an example of human sensing. People, who have been captive in the cave their entire lives, can only see shadows. The shadows are, however, caused by puppets when a fire, which is behind the prisoners, silhouettes the puppets. These shadows constitute the reality of the prisoners. If one of the prisoners were to be set free, he would learn that the reality he previously experienced was nothing but shadows, and the puppets were more real. If he stepped out from the cave, he would learn that there are things of which the puppets were only representations. This is to depict how opinion is slowly replaced with knowledge, and a person will gradually gain a greater knowledge of reality.

The Transparency Paradox. Ida Koivisto, Oxford University Press. © Ida Koivisto 2022.
DOI: 10.1093/oso/9780192855466.003.0008

"on and off states", shadows can be "read" and recoded to "move" elements projected on a screen, and the relationship between screen and projection has shifted.'[2]

This emergence of 'digital light' is of crucial importance for the representational potency of transparency in the digitalized society. It leads one to ask: if not only shadows but also light become digital constructs, what would happen to the representable reality, the thing in itself? How does the digital environment alter the laws of representation? These questions are important as they have the potential to relativize the very reality principle, the ideological core assumption of transparency. They inform my discussion in this chapter.

In the following, I will deepen the discussion on the representability of governance through transparency practices in the digital environment. Especially under the condition of so-called hyperreality—reality, in which the laws of representation no longer hold valid—questions of representation become more multifaceted. Hyperreality can be argued to be manifested fully in the digital era and in the form of digital practices, although the concept was coined well before digitalization and the emergence of the internet. Regardless of whether there can be any truth-value in digital representations, the illusion of such truth-value seems to be important. If we were to forfeit it, transparency would have difficulties in justifying itself.

As transparency is inherently social, the veracity of representation also extends to the users of transparency. The way in which the world portrays us in the digital if not hyperreal environment cannot but affect how we act in it. Therefore, it is important to discuss the ways in which hyperreality and the digital production of the real affects us as digital subjects and blurs the divide between the frontstage and the backstage. It calls us to question the nature of truth as revelation and the realist or materialist truth conception it presupposes. Should truth be sought, in Žižek's words, within the illusion, not behind it? To illuminate the potency of transparency in the digital environment, I also discuss algorithmic transparency. It can be seen as an attempt to use transparency in addressing the surreptitiousness of digital reality production. How can such digital curation of the real be made transparent, and what would follow from that?

The chapter is organized as follows. First, I discuss Baudrillard's idea of hyperreality, in which reality no longer follows the rules of representation but simulation. I also consider hyperreality in the context of digitalization. How will it affect transparency? Second, I look at algorithmic transparency: what is its object of representation, and what kind of understanding can result from it? Third, I shift the focus somewhat, and delve into digital subjects and the ways in which impression management can work in the digital environment. What is the frontstage and what is the backstage in the digital environment? Fourth, I ask whether there is a tension between hyperreality and performativity. I conclude that the very core of

[2] Christiane Paul, 'Mediations of Light: Screens as Information Surfaces' in Sean Cubitt, Daniel Palmer, and Nathaniel Tkacz (eds), *Digital Light* (Open Humanities Press 2015) 179, 180.

icono-ambivalence may be a product of hyperreality in itself. If this is the case, it needs to be asked whether transparency can sustain its legitimating function in the future.

Towards Hyperreality

Before delving into the digital challenges of transparency, it is necessary to recognize that the roots of questions of representation and representability reside in epistemology and phenomenology. Representation and representability go back a long way and can be traced from Plato to Immanuel Kant and on to postmodern philosophy. Acknowledging this, I do not attempt to focus on their philosophical roots in general but instead ask this specific question: what is governance like as an object of representation in the digitalized world?

This question has already been touched upon in chapters two and five in the contexts of icono-ambivalence and the successfulness of the legitimating promise of transparency. I also discussed it with the help of the concept of 'the hand at work', the human mediator between the thing itself and the thing for us. The opposite to this was conceptualized as acheiropoieton, 'made without hands'. That means spontaneous representations of the real are without any human influence. For example, a shadow on the wall would be an acheiropoietic image, whereas a drawing on the wall would be a product of the hand at work.

As explained in chapters six and seven, over the last couple of decades, our society has become digitalized. Technology companies have become the governors of the internet. Along with that development, data cannot be reduced to the raw material of more elaborate information any longer, and instead data have become a way of governing in their own right. In addition, digitalization also extends to state governance, in which less emphasis is put on traditional documents, and more on data, information repositories, and automated decision-making (ADM). If humans were not to directly control the emergence of those data and their use, the iconophilic practices of transparency might well become more complex. It seems plausible that the relationship between governance reality and its representation may need to be rethought.

What would this mean? Would we then be entering *hyperreality*? Hyperreality is a term coined by philosopher Jean Baudrillard in his famous treatise *Simulacra and Simulation* (1981). Baudrillard himself was a media and culture critic who saw problems in the mass media and in mass consumption and their effect on society. The concept of hyperreality was created as a criticism towards structural semiotics and the correspondence conception of truth it represented. Although the term is no longer new, it is still worth discussing as it succeeds in conceptualizing the deepening crisis of representation in contemporary society, and is relevant for assessing the future of transparency. The significance of hyperreality can be argued to have grown and diversified in the era of the internet, although it preceded that.[3]

In his treatise, Baudrillard theorizes questions of hyperreality to explore the ways in which reality and its representation are becoming mixed. Some representations are not really representations of anything actual, but are simulacra, in which the representation becomes disconnected from its object. Baudrillard defines hyperreality in the following way: it is 'real without origin or reality'. The epigram to the treatise, attributed (fallaciously) to Ecclesiastes is: 'The simulacrum is never that which conceals the truth—it is the truth which conceals that there is none. The simulacrum is true.' Instead of representation, hyperreality is based on simulation, producing—instead of representations—simulacra, copies without an original.

Hence, simulation may be opposed to representation, in which good images are accurate copies (mimesis1), as Sherwin puts it.[4] According to Baudrillard, representation is based on the principle that the sign (representation) and the real are equivalent. Simulation, conversely, considers the principle of equivalence to be utopian. While representation attempts to absorb simulations and portrays them as false representations, simulation envelops the entire edifice of representation as itself a simulacrum.[5]

To illustrate the nature of hyperreality, Baudrillard uses the famous example of Disneyland. Disneyland is a materialized dream world, embodying cultural meaning, which does not have an actual, original reference in reality. What makes it politically dangerous is precisely its overtly fictional nature. For just by existing, it indirectly suggests that the surrounding reality (the world outside Disneyland) would be more real. Simulated reality, however, infiltrates everywhere, both Disneyland and the world outside. For Baudrillard, trying to save the reality principle is a futile endeavour in a society that is saturated by media. He argues that 'real' can only produce its opposite and exacerbated experience of hyperreality.[6]

The logic of simulation is particularly illustrative when we talk about images as a form of representation. Baudrillard argues that an image would have successive phases of correspondence with reality: 1) it is a reflection of basic reality; 2) it masks and perverts basic reality; 3) it masks the absence of a basic reality; 4) it bears no relation to any reality whatsoever, it is its own simulacrum. Each of these

[3] Interestingly, the treatise also makes an appearance in the film *The Matrix*, which is about the nature of reality and its simulated character. Lana Wachowski and Lilly Wachowski, 'The Matrix' (Warner Bros Pictures 1999).

[4] Richard K Sherwin, 'What Authorizes the Image? The Visual Economy of Post-Secular Jurisprudence' in Desmond Manderson (ed), *Law and the Visual: Transitions and Transformations* (University of Toronto Press 2017) 334.

[5] Jean Baudrillard, *Simulations* (Paul Foss, Paul Patton, and Philip Beitchman trs, Semiotext(e) 1983) 11 (hereafter Baudrillard, 'Simulations'). See also 146: '[t]he real is not only what can be reproduced, but *that which is always already reproduced*. The hyperreal' (emphasis in original).

[6] ibid, 12–14.

representational relations implies different things. In the first case, the image is a *good* appearance, in terms of the religious analogy (or origin), the representation is of the order of a sacrament. In the second case, it is an *evil* appearance, in the order of malefice. In the third case, the image plays at being an appearance, as such it is of the order of sorcery. In the fourth, the image is no longer in the order of appearance at all, it is a simulation.[7]

Baudrillard argues that the transition from signs that dissimulate something, to signs which dissimulate that there is nothing, represents a significant turning point. Namely, the former implies a theology of truth and secrecy. Baudrillard also includes ideology in that category. The latter initiates an age of simulacra and simulation in which it is no longer possible to distinguish true from false, real from artificial. Subsequently, myths of origin and signs of reality proliferate. The true and lived experience escalates, which leads to a resurrection of the figurative where the object and substance have vanished. Baudrillard states that there is a panic-stricken production of the real and the referential, above, and parallel to, the panic of material production. In this way simulation is the phase that concerns us, a strategy of the real, neo-real, and hyperreal whose universal double is a strategy of deterrence.[8]

If Baudrillard is correct in his analysis, we need to ask how extensive hyperreality is. Has governance, too, become hyperreal? Can we apply the ideas of simulation and simulacra to analyse the phenomenology of governance? If we could, the consequences would be dramatic. We would need to reassess the realist conception of truth, and all that comes with it, or perhaps, keep it as a useful illusion. Baudrillard recognizes this and compares simulation with feigning. As he defines it, 'To dissimulate is to feign not to have what one has. To simulate is to feign to have what one hasn't.' Importantly, 'feigning or dissimulating leaves the reality principle intact: the difference is always clear, it is only masked; whereas simulation threatens the difference between "true" and "false", between "real" and "imaginary"'.[9]

Hyperreality thus means no less than the very crumbling of the reality principle, the correspondence between reality and its representation. According to the reality principle, by unmasking the hidden, secret, or veiled reality, the actual truth is there to be discovered. This is the assumption on which the ideological iconoclasm of transparency is based, as I have argued throughout the book. In a similar vein, Baudrillard refers to religious iconoclasts and argues that: 'One can live with the idea of a distorted truth. But their metaphysical despair came from the idea that the images concealed nothing at all, and that in fact they were not images, such as

[7] ibid, 11–12.
[8] ibid, 12–13.
[9] ibid, 4–5.

the original model would have made them, but actually perfect simulacra forever radiant with their own fascination. But this death of the divine referential has to be exorcised at all cost.'[10]

Astonishingly, Baudrillard wrote his book before the rise of the internet and digitalization. The theory was thus not, and could not have been, inspired by the digitalization of our lifeworld, but the mass media of the time. However, even if we were to discard Baudrillard's vocabulary and thinking, the question of the reality principle and its future would nonetheless remain relevant. Just by following some of the recent twists and turns in world politics, we can see how the reality principle has lost at least some of its privileged position in public discourses. For example, we can mention discussions of post-truth politics, 'alternative facts' and 'fake news' characteristic especially of the previous Trump administration.[11] Brexit enthusiasts had had 'enough of experts'.[12] In the wake of the COVID-19 pandemic, we have witnessed an overflow of disinformation and conspiracy theories.[13] The war in Ukraine is described very differently in the Russian media and in the West. These phenomena may not be digital simulacra as such, but they discard objective reality as a guarantee of believability.[14] Although they are partially independent from digitalization, partially they are exacerbated by it, as the internet had democratized the production and dissemination of (dis) information.

What enables the reality principle to crumble in the contemporary world? Is it a question of plausibility and what feels true? So long as a message—or representation of another kind—is seemingly sincere, does it have to correspond to reality?[15] Perhaps the world has become too complex for the objective reality to serve as an accessible enough reference point of believability. It is not clear how this affects the sustainability of transparency. I discuss some implications of hyperreality and digitalization in relation to transparency in the following.

[10] ibid, 8–9.

[11] Mark Fenster, 'A "Public" Journey Through COVID-19: Donald Trump, Twitter, and the Secrecy of U.S. Presidents' Health' (2021) 8(1) Critical Analysis of Law 25 (hereafter Fenster, 'A "Public" Journey Through COVID-19'); Mikkel Flyverbom and Juliane Reinecke, 'The Spectacle and Organization Studies' (2017) 38(11) Organization Studies 1625, 1634 (hereafter Flyverbom and Reinecke, 'The Spectacle and Organization Studies').

[12] Before Brexit, a British politician Michael Gove stated, 'People in this country have had enough of experts'. See, for example, Henry Mance, 'Britain has had enough of experts, says Gove', *Financial Times* (3 June 2016) <https://www.ft.com/content/3be49734-29cb-11e6-83e4-abc22d5d108c> accessed 14 July 2021.

[13] Md Saiful Islam et al, 'COVID-19–Related Infodemic and Its Impact on Public Health: A Global Social Media Analysis' (2020) 1 American Journal of Tropical Medicine and Hygiene 1621. The authors show how as much as 82% of pandemic information disseminated in social media is false.

[14] cf Clare Birchall, 'Interrupting Transparency' in Emmanuel Alloa and Dieter Thomä (eds), *Transparency, Society and Subjectivity: Critical Perspectives* (Palgrave Macmillan 2018) 343, 356; also Mark Fenster, 'Transparency in Trump's America' (2017) 30 Governance 173.

[15] Fenster, 'A "Public" Journey Through COVID-19' (n 11).

Hyperreality, Digitalization, and Transparency

The theory of hyperreality is radical, as it questions the very fundaments of how we are accustomed to approach reality. However, everyday life would become impossible if we could never rely on what we see to represent reality. As mentioned, Baudrillard's theory dates to the early 1980s, when a digitalized world was nothing but a sci-fi utopia. Nevertheless, today, hyperreality has been manifested in a new way. In a digital environment—or, cyberspace, if you will—copies without an original suddenly make sense. When everything consists of zeros and ones, what, indeed, is the original, what is a copy? Whether we think of hyperreality as a postmodern fantasy or something uncannily characteristic of our everyday experience, there is no doubt that we need to talk about digitalization as a context.[16]

The example of Disneyland mentioned above may seem far-fetched in the digital era. However, there are also many more topical and daunting examples in the modern world that align with the ideas of hyperreality and simulacra: think of reality TV, virtual reality, sex dolls, or cosmetic surgery, to mention but a few. In them, the result is real without any origin in reality; they are copies of something that does not have a basis in reality. They simulate reality without representing it. Nevertheless, we often recognize their nature as simulacra, and do not mix them up with reality. We might just think of them as tokens of our contemporary condition.

However, artificial intelligence (AI) also generates constructs in which representations and simulacra cannot be separated. For example, through advanced machine learning techniques, researchers have created photorealistic images of people who do not exist. These images look so realistic that one could not tell the difference between them and pictures of strangers. Another example would be so-called deepfake videos. Those are computer-generated videos, which enmesh the representation of an actual person with fictitious activities. We might find a president's very real-seeming speech recording on the internet, though the recording never took place. We might find a famous Hollywood actor engaged in a porn movie that never took place. In other words, feigning and dissimulation can be interwoven with actual people's representations so that it may become impossible to say whether the video represents an actual event or not.

These uncertainties question our reliance on visual representations on the internet: verisimilitude no longer guarantees its status as a representation. Like the photograph, video footage is also slowly losing some of its privileged power to

[16] Richard K Sherwin, *Visualizing Law in the Age of the Digital Baroque: Arabesques and Entanglements* (Routledge 2012) 154: Sherwin brings the ideas of simulation and simulacra into the age of digitalization. He argues that digital simulation may encode physical reality, but the encoded reality leaves no trace in the image that is digitally produced. In the digital regime, the authenticating function of the original ceases to operate. The meaning of digital signs does not depend on originals or make a difference between the original and copies. In the realm of digital simulation, everything is equally susceptible to transportation, recombination, and change.

represent reliably the real thing. The epistemological intuition of 'understanding is seeing' or 'seeing is believing' is forced to unravel, unless, of course, we recognize that we are in the world of fiction and its established laws of make-believe.

Hyperreality, however, specifically mixes fact and fiction, which may cause anxiety. It is increasingly difficult to know what is true. As Sherwin argues, we are today witnessing expressions of profound mistrust in the simulacrum. This is also visible in popular culture, in which iconophobic anxiety can be detected, for example, in the forms of computer games (*the eXistenz, Dark City*) and movies (*The Matrix, Inception, Memento, Eternal Sunshine of a Spotless Mind*). They question our immediate experience of living in circumstances which we call and experience as 'reality'.[17] This iconophobia cannot but also affect the way in which transparency can function through its iconophilic practices. Can transparency reveal simulation, or is it adopting the simulation principle instead of the reality principle?

Baudrillard also recognizes the pertinence of transparency and its struggle in hyperreality, although naturally, not in the digital context. Interestingly, he predicts—before the entire expansion of contemporary transparency discourse—the decline of the panoptic rationality and its effects: 'The eye of TV is no longer the source of an absolute gaze, and the ideal of control is no longer that of transparency. The latter still presupposes an objective space (that of the Renaissance) and the omnipotence of a despotic gaze. This is still, if not a system of confinement, at least a system of scrutiny. No longer subtle, but always in a position of exteriority, playing on the opposition between seeing and being seen, even if the focal point of the panopticon may be blind.'[18] In other words, for Baudrillard, the objective space for democratic surveillability would no longer exist.[19]

However, the relationship between transparency and hyperreality can be more complex than that. For example, Han refutes Baudrillard's prediction of the death of transparency in hyperreality. Instead, he suggests that instead of panoptic rationality being exhausted, it has been transformed into something new: an a-perspectival panopticon. Han argues that this twenty-first century digital panopticon is a-perspectival in the sense that no central tower exists with the omnipotence of the 'despotic gaze'. Instead, the structure of centre and periphery, crucial to the Benthamite idea of the all-seeing institution, is dismantled. A-perspectival penetrating illumination becomes more efficient, for it means, according to Han, the utter illumination of everyone from everywhere, which can be performed by anyone.[20] Brought into the context of today, in Thomä's words, 'As the users of

[17] ibid, 121.
[18] Baudrillard, 'Simulations' (n 5) 52.
[19] Compare Rachel Adams, *Transparency: New Trajectories in Law* (Routledge 2020) 56.
[20] Byung-Chul Han, *The Transparency Society* (Stanford University Press 2015) 45 (hereafter Han, 'The Transparency Society').

social media act as observers and are being observed at once, they become hybrid figures or observed observers. The panopticon is transformed into a polyopticon.'[21]

An a-perspectival panopticon or polyopticon would also question the role of the beholder and her point of view. If vantage point no longer plays a role, it makes one wonder whether any view whatsoever is possible. Does it make one nonchalant about the views witnessed or even blind to them? Or do we need to reimagine the idea of the 'view from nowhere', as Thomas Nagel has coined it? Therefore, in an a-perspectival panopticon, by definition, all gazes would be controlling in nature, there would be no revelations, no projections, or no looking awry. An a-perspectival panopticon could mean the end of privacy and transparency based on impression management and created appearances.[22] Rousseau's utopia of reciprocal gazes would thus turn into a dystopia of despotic gazes.

This all suggests that transparency is somehow turning into its antonym, an interactive theatre of shadows with no object casting them and no audience viewing them. Han argues that the society of transparency is a society of information, and that information is increasingly hyperreal. Unlike in Plato's allegory of the cave, when it comes to modern transparency, no transcendent light works as the medium to make the shadows appear. In the society of transparency, light would be replaced by lightless, suffusing radiation, making everything see-through and penetrating its objects. Han suggests that not only does the society of transparency lack truth, it also lacks symbolic appearance, neither of which is see-through. Only emptiness is totally transparent—to avert this emptiness, mass information is brought into circulation. More information and communication do not illuminate the world. In Han's poetic words, hyper-information and hyper-communication bring no light into darkness.[23]

To conclude, hyperreality may have profound effects on the way in which we experience reality in the digital environment. This also extends to transparency.[24] There are many examples of the crumbling of the reality principle as well as changes in the constellations of the beholder and the object. Although it is possible to argue, as Han does, that there is no 'central tower' in the panopticon of the digital

[21] Dieter Thomä, 'Seeing It All, Doing It All, Saying It All: Transparency, Subject, and the World' in Emmanuel Alloa and Dieter Thomä (eds), *Transparency, Society and Subjectivity: Critical Perspectives* (Palgrave Macmillan 2018) 57, 76; compare Clare Birchall who uses the term "shareveillance": '"Shareveillance" is intended to capture the condition of consuming shared data and producing data to be shared in ways that shape a subject who is at once surveillant and surveilled. To phrase it with a slightly different emphasis, the subject of shareveillance is one who simultaneously works with data and on whom the data works.' Clare Birchall, *Shareveillance: The Dangers of Openly Sharing and Covertly Collecting Data* (University of Minnesota Press 2018).

[22] Compare Vincent Kaufmann, 'Transparency and Subjectivity: Remembering Jennifer Ringley' in Emmanuel Alloa and Dieter Thomä (eds), *Transparency, Society and Subjectivity: Critical Perspectives* (Palgrave Macmillan 2018) (hereafter Kaufmann, 'Transparency and Subjectivity').

[23] Han, 'The Transparency Society' (n 20) 39–41.

[24] cf Dieter Mersch, 'Obfuscating Transparency' in Emmanuel Alloa and Dieter Thomä (eds), *Transparency, Society and Subjectivity: Critical Perspectives* (Palgrave Macmillan 2018) 259, 268–70 (hereafter Mersch, 'Obfuscating Transparency').

society, in my view, the theatre and the audience of transparency have not completely disappeared in the digital environment. Instead, as argued in chapter seven, transparency has found its way into the discourses of the big technology, the power holders of the digital society. Perhaps this implies that transparency is, in fact, also becoming hyperreal: it no longer needs to have a reference point in real practices. I will come back to the themes of the subject in the digital environment and the relationship between performativity and hyperreality.

Algorithmic Transparency

Given hyperreality and the wavering status of the reality principle, one could assume that the call for transparency would also be in crisis, as discussed. At least at the level of discourse, however, this does not seem to be the case, regardless of whether transparency can live up to its promise or not. In fact, quite the opposite is true—in the digital environment, the call for transparency is perhaps stronger than ever. Transparency as an ideal does not seem to have suffered from digitalization but has become even more prevalent along with it. We can notice that the popularity of transparency in normative discourses on AI ethics, ADM, and algorithmic governance is beyond doubt.[25] At least partially, this can be attributed to the discursification of transparency. Perhaps the wish is that the way in which digital (hyper)reality is coded could be revealed with transparency.[26] At best, this could save the reality principle.

The main drivers in digitalization are technology companies, as already discussed in chapter six. They have revolutionized commerce and communication in innumerable ways. However, digitalization does not end there. As mentioned, already now, governance—like so many other societal practices—is becoming digitalized. For example, ADM and algorithmic modelling are increasingly employed.[27] The technological developments of the recent decades have enabled this. Computer programs have become so sophisticated that they can replace human labour in a growing number of tasks and functions. The use of AI in state governance is, however, a legally thorny issue, and regulation is so far not well fitted to tackle

[25] The number of different codes of conduct (AI ethics) have skyrocketed over the years 2018–19. As shown by an independent non-governmental organization (NGO), Algorithm Watch, the number is staggering. These codes of conduct are of various kinds and given by different institutions. Almost all of them include a call for transparency. Algorithm Watch, 'AI Ethics Guidelines Global Inventory' (2019) <https://algorithmwatch.org/en/project/ai-ethics-guidelines-global-inventory/> accessed 30 June 2021.

[26] Riikka Koulu, 'Crafting Digital Transparency: Implementing Legal Values into Algorithmic Design' (2021) 8(1) Critical Analysis of Law 81.

[27] See, for example, Algorithm Watch, 'Automating Society: Taking Stock of Automated Decision-Making in the EU: A Report by Algorithm Watch in Cooperation with Bertelsmann Stiftung, supported by the Open Society Foundations' (1st ed, January 2019) <https://algorithmwatch.org/de/wp-content/uploads/2019/02/Automating_Society_Report_2019.pdf> accessed 30 June 2021.

that.[28] Although the current academic discussion about algorithmic transparency is extensive, here, however, I concentrate only on some of the theoretical preconditions of algorithmic transparency and not on the current legal issues concerning it.

The call for transparency has been formulated in a novel way in digitalized governance. Instead of the traditional technocratic translations of transparency (access to documents, the presence of the public, proactive communication), in digitalized governance, the object of transparency is somewhat different. Often, transparency adopts the epithet of 'algorithmic', pointing to its object of exposure. Algorithm as a term refers to a detailed description or a set of rules and commands to perform a particular task, typically in the form of a computer code. The main problem that is sought to tackle with algorithmic transparency is the following: we do not really know how these algorithmic models operate and reach the decisions and outcomes they do. This difficulty is often referred to as 'the black box problem', as mentioned in chapter seven. In that way, by opening or x-raying the black box, this problem should be solved. We encounter the call for the iconoclastic aspect of transparency.[29]

On the one hand, this is well in line with more traditional constellations of transparency. Black boxes are, in a way, digital chambers of power. Whether the decision-maker is a human, an institution, or a machine, we want to know how power is exercised upon us. This was previously called the public law rationality of transparency. We want to make sure that the grounds of our subjection to that power are justified. On the other hand, however, something fundamentally changes when the object of knowledge is no longer human action. If governance starts running through algorithmic modelling and machine learning, the basic functioning logic of transparency may change.

Regardless of the impressive technological development of our time, machines are only capable of restricted functions. However, according to the most radical visions of singularity, once created by human beings with human desires, algorithms may become increasingly independent from their makers.[30] This would cause problems of predictability, fairness, and legitimacy, thus forming, in Danaher's words, 'the threat of algocracy'.[31] In this process, humans could lose their monopoly to control and understand algorithms. Algorithms could become independent to the extent that they themselves create new algorithms, even audit other

[28] See, however, the EU's AI Act proposal. Commission, 'Proposal for Regulation of the European Parliament and of the Council Laying Down Harmonised Rules on Artificial Intelligence (Artificial Intelligence Act) and Amending Certain Union Legislative Acts' COM/2021/206 final. Transparency is one of the key principles of the proposed regulation.

[29] Ida Koivisto, 'Thinking Inside the Box: The Promise and Boundaries of Transparency in Automated Decision-Making' (2020) Academy of European Law Working Papers 2020/01 <http://hdl.handle.net/1814/67272> accessed 14 July 2021 (hereafter Koivisto, 'Thinking Inside the Box').

[30] cf Nick Boström, *Superintelligence: Paths, Dangers, Strategies* (Oxford University Press 2014).

[31] cf John Danaher, 'The Threat of Algocracy: Reality, Resistance and Accommodation' (2016) 29(3) Philosophy and Technology 245.

algorithms. If that were the case, what happens to the performative, human-faced logic of transparency? The question is important for two reasons.

First, the covert human logic of transparency may become jeopardized; algorithms should not be anthropomorphized. This is because there is no reason to assume that algorithms would necessarily 'think' like humans, and consequently, would interpret the ideal of transparency in a similar way.[32] It would be hard to imagine that algorithms would desire other algorithms' approval, or would want to be in contact with them and belong to the community of other algorithms. Nor is there a reason to assume that they would want to be seen in a favourable light by other algorithms, to have high status in the algorithmic community, and avoid being shamed in front of other algorithms. Just by this little thought experiment, our own humanity, having a core of a social animal, becomes sufficiently clear. It is easy to see how transparency practices work through our human way of thinking and acting. Would this be lost if humans were no longer to oversee transparency practices?[33]

Second, it is unlikely that even if we could see the inner workings of the black box, we would understand them. The revelation through the iconoclastic mechanism—removing the obstacles of visibility (cf opening the box approach)—would not necessarily communicate anything to an average person. That revealed information would be highly esoteric, comprehensible only to experts, perhaps not even to them. The underlying promise of transparency, 'understanding is seeing', would thus be jeopardized, the only gazes we could aim at them would be observing and projecting. As Ananny and Crawford argue, transparency may privilege seeing over understanding.[34] In algorithmic modelling, seeing seldom constitutes immediate understanding to a layperson. Instead, it leaves one puzzled with confusing information, comparable perhaps to a text in a foreign language.

Therefore, it is likely that so long as transparency is directed to a human audience, human mediation is needed. The hand at work is necessary in the process of 'translating' the inner workings of the black boxes into human (layman) understandable form. In fact, if we look at algorithmic transparency from the viewpoint of reality production and hyperreality, we can notice that transparency inevitably adopts a second layer of mediation. Transparency is not only a medium itself, but in the digital environment, algorithms serve as a medium for transparency. The way in which transparency discourse participates in digital reality

[32] cf Burrell, 'How the Machine 'Thinks': Understanding Opacity in Machine Learning Algorithms' (2016) Big Data and Society <https://journals.sagepub.com/doi/pdf/10.1177/2053951715622512> accessed 14 July 2021; see also John Zerilli, Alistair Knott, James Maclaurin and Colin Gavaghan, 'Transparency in Algorithmic and Human Decision-Making: Is There a Double Standard?' (2018) 32 Philosophy and Technology 661.

[33] Koivisto, 'Thinking Inside the Box' (n 29).

[34] Mike Ananny and Kate Crawford, 'Seeing Without Knowing: Limitations of the Transparency Ideal and its Application to Algorithmic Accountability' (2018) 20(3) New Media and Society 973, 981–82.

production makes it even more difficult to decipher the represented reality, if indeed there is one.[35] Because digital transparency builds on a two-fold mediation of reality—transparency as a medium itself and algorithms as a medium of digital transparency—seeing with one's own eyes no longer guarantees a privileged access to reality.[36] Transparency's iconoclastic ideology may start to unravel.

Whether seen as simulation or as a representation of computer logic, for most of us, understanding will not follow from seeing these operations. This observation is not only of a theoretical kind. In addition to transparency, other similar conceptualizations have lately emerged into the normative discourses on AI ethics and ADM: *explainability, interpretability, intelligibility, explicability, understandability,* and *comprehensibility*.[37] These concepts intimate that the assumption that transparency would be an easy overall solution is false. Transparency is not enough to guarantee understandability, it needs other components to complement it.[38] This may be problematic because ideologically, transparency specifically privileges immediate seeing over mediated human explanations, as I have argued throughout this book. If transparency becomes a synonym for explanation, it inevitably loses something from its legitimating power. The core promise of transparency 'do not believe what I say, see for yourself' would thus be transformed into its antonym, 'do not believe what you see, let me explain, instead'.[39]

Thus, iconophily—transparency that requires constructs to create a visible appearance—together with the intentionality of transparency, enables one to consider human understanding and its limitations. On the one hand, it may produce information, which is meaningful from an average person's point of view and has the potential to create legitimacy in that way. On the other hand, however, it is a forum of impression management logic. The more human mediation there is, resulting in carefully managed visibilities, the more legitimacy may be produced. At the same time, this may also mean truncated reality, as the exposed intricacies of the black box cannot necessarily communicate anything.

[35] cf Emmanuel Alloa and Dieter Thomä, 'Transparency: Thinking Through an Opaque Concept' in Emmanuel Alloa and Dieter Thomä (eds), *Transparency, Society and Subjectivity: Critical Perspectives* (Palgrave Macmillan 2018) 9: 'Digital transparency is far from being neutral and generates a social and political sphere subject to its logic.'

[36] Ida Koivisto, 'The Digital Rear Window: Epistemologies of Digital Transparency' (2021) 8(1) Critical Analysis of Law 64 (hereafter Koivisto, 'The Digital Rear Window').

[37] In the EU's General Data Protection Regulation, transparency is one of the key principles. In addition to transparency, it calls for disclosing 'meaningful information of the logic involved' in the automated decision-making to its subject. On the debate, see, for example, Gianclaudio Malgieri and Giovanni Comandé, 'Why a Right of Legibility of Automated Decision-Making Exists in the General Data Protection Regulation' (2017) 7(4) International Data Privacy Law 234. This indirectly separates transparency from understandability.

[38] See, for example, Henrik Palmer Olsen, Jacob Livingston Slosser, Thomas Troels Hildebrandt, and Cornelius Wiesener, 'What's in the Box? The Legal Requirement of Explainability in Computationally Aided Decision-Making in Public Administration' (2019) University of Copenhagen Faculty of Law Research Paper 2019-84, iCourts Working Paper Series no 162 <https://static-curis.ku.dk/portal/files/235473618/WorkingPaper_SSRN_id3402974.pdfz> accessed 14 July 2021.

[39] Koivisto, 'Thinking Inside the Box' (n 29).

It is important to note that also in the digital environment, impression management logic cannot take place effortlessly. It requires assessing the effects of the information release. ADM and algorithms lack the sense of common decency and the understanding of when to interpret things to the letter and when more liberally. They do not have the human capability to steer through varying contexts with a compass such as the law or, indeed, transparency; in other words, they lack practical wisdom. This, in turn, may bifurcate the two realms of what happens in the black boxes and what is conceivable to us. It seems that we want to both go beyond a human understanding of technological development and to keep it as the guiding principle. In consequence, there may be less and less use for the ideal of transparency, or it will be reduced to its iconophilic aspect.[40]

Impression Management in the Digital Environment

Frontstage Self: Digital Masks

So far, in this chapter, I have discussed some of the conditions that may question transparency as an ideal in the digitalized environment and hyperreality more widely. I also discussed the promise of algorithmic transparency and whether it can reveal the way in which this digital (hyper)reality is created. This is to say, I have only discussed one side of the power relation, the governor—although it is still uncertain how the governor will change. As explained previously, transparency is an essentially social practice whereby the position of its user needs to be addressed, in particular in the digital environment. Therefore, it is necessary to look at our own visibility in the digital environment.

A digital governor implies a digital governed.[41] I mentioned in chapter seven that due to the digital economy, people, the governed, have become increasingly transparent to the governor, although their transparency lacks symbolic expression and concomitant normative practices. How has this happened, and how does it affect transparency as an ideal? In this section, I change the focus of the discussion somewhat: I look at some of the ways in which we humans, denizens of the digital world, form subjects under digitalized circumstances.[42] How does hyperreality affect us as social agents in the digital environment?

[40] ibid.

[41] See, for example, Oana B Albu and Hans Krause Hansen, 'Three Sides of the Same Coin: Datafied Transparency, Biometric Surveillance, and Algorithmic Governmentalities' (2021) 8(1) Critical Analysis of Law 9.

[42] For recent analysis of privacy as a correlate of power in the context of data protection, see Susanna Lindroos-Hovinheimo, *Private Selves: Legal Personhood in European Privacy Protection* (Cambridge University Press 2021).

To address these themes, it is necessary to examine the ways in which the performative logic of human social action can function in the digital environment. This raises important questions. How can impression management work if the division between the backstage and frontstage selves is altered or has partially disappeared? What kinds of frontstage and backstage mechanisms are available? These questions are at the heart of how we can make digital social subjects. First, I discuss our digital frontstage self by framing the question in terms of digital masks. Second, I delve into digital backstage operations and ask whether that backstage has been lost in the wake of the datafied economy. Also in this context, the relationship between transparency and the reality principle remains pertinent; what is revealed, what is performed?

Although debates about transhumanism and post-humanism exist, at least for now, we humans remain humans. We cannot erase our species-specific features of a social animal. Even though the means have partially changed, the ends ultimately have not: we still seek community, connection, approval, and status.[43] We want legitimacy from the power that is exercised upon us. Even if that power were to lose its theatrical functioning logic, we humans are bound to the idea of a theatre in our social relations. Rousseau's festival never existed, as we cannot read each other's minds. This is not to say, however, that changes could not happen in the culture of self-presentation.[44] On the contrary, more than ever, our current culture is labelled by the ethos of curated confession, of managed self-exposure.

Along with the emergence of the social media, we have become our online makers. Media production has democratized, and we have much agency on how we present ourselves. Again, however, we waver between belief and suspicion in the spirit of postmodernism and hyperreality. Can we trust our own eyes in the digital environment; to what extent are people's digital self-presentations believable? Hildebrandt has stated that we have—apart from our social and legal persona—a digital persona.[45] The digital persona is concerned with questions of how we are represented online. Instead of strictly following Hildebrandt's conception of a digital persona, I will analyse whether the impression management logic, peculiar to our social life, is altered in our current online habitat, and if so, how. The main point that I make is that although the online environment gives us unprecedented opportunities for performativity and impression management, our

[43] Mathew Zaia and Randy K Lippert, 'Review of Harcourt's *Exposed: Desire and Disobedience in the Digital Age*' (2017) 15(2) Surveillance and Society 354; Bernard E Harcourt, *Exposed: Desire and Disobedience in the Digital Age* (Harvard University Press 2015) 18 (hereafter Harcourt, 'Exposed'). Harcourt explains, how the twenty-first-century 'homo digitalis' craves for social recognition through 'likes', 'retweets', and 'shares' on social media. To get such digital recognition, people are persuaded to virtually express themselves in ways that deliver them as subjects of surveillance.

[44] cf Mikkel Flyverbom, *The Digital Prism: Transparency and Managed Visibilities in a Datafied World* (Cambridge University Press 2019) 5 (hereafter Flyverbom, 'The Digital Prism').

[45] Mireille Hildebrandt, 'Profiling and the European Citizen' in Mireille Hildebrandt and Serge Gutwirth (eds), *Profiling the European Citizen* (Springer 2008) 303.

backstage self is not fully protected. This means that we are represented (or simulated) in the digital world in different ways than in the analogue one.

The age of the internet could also be called the age of performativity. Previously, we have not been able to construct such personas, whose connection to our physical makeup would be so distant, if not at least seemingly non-existent. On the one hand, this has the potential to be liberating. Finally, to exaggerate a little, we can be the way we choose to be, and not how we physically are. We no longer have limitations of age, culture, gender, sexuality, appearance, social status, religious expectations, peer pressure, and so on. A middle-aged Asian woman, for example, can quite plausibly pretend to be a young man from Russia—not to mention more imaginative identities even freed from the constraints of time (why cannot I be a denizen of the Bronze Age?) and species (why cannot I choose to be a mythical creature?). The internet with all its chat rooms, social media platforms, dating apps, and gaming communities, forms an endless playing field for different identities.

However, it can be argued that these performed digital identities are as 'authentic' selves as the physical, natural person. They are our creations, products of our creative spirit. In a way, they make us 'hyperauthentic'.[46] In Oscar Wilde's famous words, 'Man is least himself when he talks in his own person. Give him a mask and he will tell the truth.' Indeed, in some ways, these identities include more authenticity than our spontaneous habitus: we have more agency over ourselves than we do in the physical world, in which our freedom of mind clashes with the limitations mentioned above.[47] Our physicality cannot but disprove those imaginative identities.

On the other hand, the freedom of 'identity-shopping' can provoke anxiety. One may lose oneself in the constant masquerade of changing identities. Additionally, if anyone can be whoever they want, it is difficult to form relations transcending short encounters. We can never really know for sure with whom we are communicating online. This ignorance can lead to many negative consequences ranging from subtle disappointment to downright crime and abuse. Nor can we form any physical relations with avatars, pseudonyms, and online personas. In this sense, they are fundamentally restricted: they escape all materiality.

However, some big social networking companies, such as Facebook, specifically urge us to use our actual identities. Most of the users appear with their birth name. Superficially, we are representations of our natural person. Nonetheless, we can present ourselves in a better light than in the analogue world and filter out more negative information. This selectivity and performativity may boost our self-esteem, whereas a view of the self with no curation, such as a mirror image, may

[46] cf Bernard E Harcourt, 'Virtual Transparency: From the Panopticon to the Expository Society and Beyond' in Emmanuel Alloa and Dieter Thomä (eds), *Transparency, Society and Subjectivity: Critical Perspectives* (Palgrave Macmillan 2018) 380 (hereafter Harcourt, 'Virtual Transparency').

[47] Mersch, 'Obfuscating Transparency' (n 24) 272–75.

worsen it.[48] However, culture based on seeking digital approval may make us more willing to expose ourselves than we would in the analogue world. As Harcourt explains, people are giving themselves up 'in a mad frenzy of disclosure'. This disclosure may extend all the way to the most intimate things of personal life—from love life and everyday habits to political views—to become ourselves.[49]

That said, we know perfectly well that people's online personas are curated; we know that nobody's life consists only of beach holidays, Michelin star restaurants, or opening nights. We cannot know, however, to what extent they do. As Flyverbom argues, as digital platforms move closer to the core of cultural and social life, we need to ask new questions. How do these digital transformations affect how we see, know, and govern social life?[50] We easily assume that at least a part of people's 'real' self oozes into those self-presentations. This glimpse of reality seems to have an intoxicating effect. Although we know that our friend does not dine solely in Michelin star restaurants, it seems that at least sometimes they do. We might feel admiration or envy.

However, it is quite possible that the friend has downloaded the picture of their succulent dish from the internet and has never even been in the mentioned restaurant. There is no way of knowing. Iconoclash makes an appearance once again. Perhaps due to this uncertainty, we seem to want more 'real' reality than before. We are tormented by reality hunger. We binge on autobiographies and blog posts, assess social media profiles, and watch reality TV and vlogs.[51] We are surprisingly comfortable with the concept of auto-fiction. We want to peek into the backstage and yet manage our own impression. Is there an original and not just copies? We want to escape from hyperreality.

Backstage Self: Digital Footprints

Regardless of this wild performativity, the digital persona, however, is not as curated as we would like it to be. There is more to it than postings on our websites, different comment fields, or social media profiles—let alone in anonymous digital playing fields. Dauntingly, in the internet environment, it seems that we have partially lost our ability to manage our impression. Our backstage self is increasingly difficult to keep hermetically protected. This becomes apparent when we think about our different online habits. We readily confess to Google things we used to confess to our diary or a trusted friend—or to no one. We do this because we do

48 Harcourt, 'Exposed' (n 43) 231; Amy L Gonzales and Jeffrey T Hancock, 'Mirror, Mirror on My Facebook Wall: Effects of Exposure to Facebook on Self- Esteem' (2011) 14(1–2) Cyberpsychology, Behavior, and Social Networking 79.

49 Harcourt, 'Virtual Transparency' (n 46) 386.

50 Flyverbom, 'The Digital Prism' (n 44) 12.

51 Kaufmann, 'Transparency and Subjectivity' (n 22).

not think it cares, judges, or defames us. However, Google, or other big technology company, does not forget, it does not let us spontaneously go into oblivion. This was already briefly touched upon in chapter seven.

Conversely, we seldom consider ourselves performing online. We think that probably happens primarily when we comment on a social media post or upload a carefully selected photograph. Of course, this may happen quite often, but if we compare the amount of it with our other online behaviour, it hardly forms a substantive amount. We do not think we perform when we search for symptoms of an awkward malady, or when we visit political or religious webpages, or when we use hours and hours playing online games or watching cat videos. We think that no one is watching or caring and therefore we can safely be as private or embarrassing as we want.[52]

However, we leave digital footprints everywhere, we leak information. Before long, targeted advertisements follow. If anything, it is surveillance capitalism that really cares about our deepest desires and fears. This makes our backstage selves vulnerable to manipulation and economic seduction. As Harcourt puts it, 'We want to believe the information will not be seen or used. That we are only giving the information to machines. But we know, we've read, that this is not really true. We know far too well that humans are behind the machines.'[53] In fact, Facebook, for example, knows us better than our spouses do.[54]

This is also why we call for data protection, respect for privacy, and a right to be forgotten. These desires conversely communicate the hazard of an eternal, uncontrollable internet presence, which is potentially endlessly replayed by search engines. It does not let our foolishness evaporate or be excluded from our persona. Our past behaviour follows us like a constantly lengthening train dress. Even when we do not log in to a certain service, or we enjoy the sense of complete anonymity, our undetectability is a dangerous illusion. Our online behavior is constantly tracked and stored—even on official government webpages—into enormous databases and used for different, often commercial, purposes.[55] In a way, we pay with our personal data for many services, and that concerns us surprisingly little. We have a hard time seeing its value.

[52] Compare Harcourt, 'Exposed' (n 43) 181.

[53] ibid, 182.

[54] Wu Youyou, Michal Kosinski, and David Stillwell, 'Computer-Based Personality Judgments Are More Accurate Than Those Made by Humans' (2015) 112(4) Proceedings of the National Academy of Sciences of the United States of America 1036.

[55] cf Cookiebot, 'Ad Tech Surveillance on the Public Sector Web: A Special Report on Pervasive Tracking of EU Citizens on Government and Health Service Websites' (Cookiebot with policy recommendations by EDRi, March 2019) <https://www.cookiebot.com/en/cookiebot-report/> accessed 14 July 2021. According to the abstract of the report, 'when EU citizens visit their governments online, or when they access public health service resources about sensitive issues such as pregnancy, sexual health, cancer or mental illness, more than 100 commercial companies are systemically and invisibly tracking them'.

What is more, we cannot know what happens to the collected data. Our online behaviour is used to reproduce it. In consequence, the online reality is not the same for everyone. Instead, customized online realities are created, leading to phenomena such as filter bubbles and echo chambers. We are as if in a room full of mirrors, surrounded by numerous copies of ourselves. Our personal data can be used for data mining and profiling, whereby we are translated into a collection of predicted behaviours. Through profiling, we become less curated selves than we otherwise would be. Our age, gender, and social status, and so on, are inferred from our behaviour, after all. We are pushed towards revealing our most private backstage persona, regardless of our myriad digital masks.[56]

We are thus tormented by ambivalence. On the one hand, we want to be able to manage our impression and be who we choose to be. On the other hand, we also want access to the vast repository of information that technology companies govern. We want to be able to find answers to the questions that haunt us privately, those that are easy to search for online. We are not ready to give up on either of these desires. It can be, however, be that these two things are mutually exclusive, and we struggle to recognize this. We are not sure how much information we are leaking, and how that affects us. What we might think of as the backstage, can be, in fact, an unnoticeable frontstage. It is just that the audience is eerily invisible, silent, and unresponsive. If we do not know when we are exposed to a revelatory gaze, we cannot control over our self-presentation.

In other words, technology companies have access to the backstage. The implications of this are huge and manifold, and subject to expanding literature, largely concentrating on data protection and privacy. As Hildebrandt and Gutwirth state, 'The risks and opportunities of profiling derive from the transparency of the personality, life-style, habits, desires and preferences of individual citizens'.[57] As mentioned previously, involuntary transparency is something that we tend to abhor. If we approach the digital persona from a Goffmanian point of view, it is hardly a persona at all. It is not that because it does not allow us to have full control over the backstage of the self.[58] We would be reduced to our animality, bereft of what defines our very dignity in social life.[59]

Of course, some people are more aware of their transparency online than others. They may prevent tracking, decline cookies, or just simply act as if they were in a panopticon or the mentioned polyopticon (the so-called chilling effect). In other words, the online environment mixes up the frontstage and the backstage, and this makes the subject more transparent than ever. We may mistake a frontstage for a backstage. In that case, the gaze of the technology companies is not transformative

[56] Koivisto, 'The Digital Rear Window' (n 36).

[57] Mireille Hildebrandt and Serge Gutwirth, 'Concise Conclusions: Citizens out of Control' in Mireille Hildebrandt and Serge Gutwirth (eds), *Profiling the European Citizen* (Springer 2008) 365, 366.

[58] Harcourt, 'Exposed' (n 43) 221.

[59] cf Kaufmann, 'Transparency and Subjectivity' (n 22) 311.

but revelatory, at worst voyeuristic and abusive. They feel no shame about peeking. We do not always know when we are watched or when we can be watched. The companies do not have anything against us not adjusting our behaviour. On the contrary, the less we censor our behaviour, the more backstage information we leak, and the more vulnerable we are in the face of capitalist forces. That is why, contrary to the panoptic modality of power, we encounter power based on revealed desires. Not because we would want to give up on the principle of control but because we cannot separate a private place from a public one.

However, to flourish, we need at least an illusion of a backstage. Total transparency—a dystopian version of Rousseau's festival, as it were—would probably extinguish our humanity as we know it. With the loss of our control to our backstage self we would no longer be able to uphold a social persona and thus manage our impression. As Žižek exemplifies, there would be no more flirtation, as our thought would be transparent: 'I want to sleep with you'. No more politeness and social niceties because our thoughts would expose us: 'I am not really happy to see you and I am not interested how you are'. We would lose much of our social agency.[60] At worst, total transparency would mean social suicide. Instead of choice and volition, we would and could respond to immediate desires as there would be no encouragement to hide them. At the same time, transparency would lose its legitimating function, because we could not control what we release. If the theatrical logic of social life came to an end, we would lose our motivation to control our animality.

How to Reconcile Hyperreality and Performativity?

In this chapter, I have discussed the ways in which transparency can provide what is promised in a digitalized environment that struggles with questions of hyperreality. I have approached this question from two directions, the digital representability of governance on the one hand, and the laws of digital impression management of the governed on the other. In other words, the reality principle, on which the ideal of transparency ideologically builds, has been questioned. However, it is not quite clear whether the ideas of hyperreality—the crisis of representation—and performativity, which builds on careful mechanisms of curated representation, can be reconciled. Are they in fact mutually exclusive?

Thus, to the extent that transparency is or is becoming hyperreal, we still need to return to the question of the human-faced agent who is concerned about her representation to her audience or community, whatever that is. What would it imply

[60] 'Mind-reading AI may spell end to humanity as we know it, but not because it will enslave us—Zizek' *RT* (7 September 2019) available at <https://www.rt.com/news/468228-mind-reading-computer-humanity-zizek/> accessed 5 July 2021.

from the perspective of transparency's legitimating promise if humans were removed from the equation and an automatic, a-perspectival theatre of shadows was established? Under these conditions, what is the meaning of intentionality and impression management? Would the performativity of transparency be demolished with hyperreality and the simulacra it produces? Would acheiropoietic representation of governance also become impossible, as there would be no reality to spontaneously reveal itself?

I approach the theme with the help of Mikkel Flyverbom and Juliane Reinecke's article 'The Spectacle and Organization Studies' (2017).[61] In the article, the authors seek to introduce Guy Debord's critical theory and in particular the concept of a spectacle into analysing organizations. In Debord's thinking, spectacle means a condition of intentional visibility, stemming from capitalism and commodity fetishism. It has started to replace human relationships: 'The spectacle is not a collection of images; it is a social relation between people that is mediated by images.'[62] Although in Flyverbom and Reinecke's article Debord's thinking forms a crucial point of departure, I am not discussing the spectacle outside the context of that article. Instead, I use the categorization presented in the article as analogous to my own thinking.

Flyverbom and Reinecke's reading of the spectacle resembles remarkably the wide conception of performativity that I have presented in this book: 'The manifestations of the spectacle are thus manifold. They range from the theatrical and fantastic to the mundane and banal: Ritual. Circus. Carnival. Show. Performance. News. But also accounts. Reports. Certificates. Labels. They can be a tool of asserted transparency and dispassionate information disclosure, or one of playful imagery. Organizing increasingly resides in the production of "spectacular" reality claims which outplay the material-physical presence of material objects, formal structures or relationships. Organizations may seem more "real" if they have a website and recognizable brand rather than a physical building and employees.'[63]

In particular, Flyverbom and Reinecke are interested in how the relationship between the spectacle and reality can be understood in organizations. Does the spectacle showcase, mask, or construct reality—or is there a relationship between the two at all? The authors analyse three ways in which the spectacle may relate to reality: fetish, hyperreality, and performativity. Interestingly, these three ways to approach the spectacle-organization nexus are very similar to how I approach the transparency-reality nexus in this and some other chapters of this book. This is why Flyverbom and Reinecke's analysis is pertinent to my reasoning.

[61] Flyverbom and Reinecke, 'The Spectacle and Organization Studies' (n 11).

[62] Guy Debord, *The Society of the Spectacle* (translated and annotated by Ken Knabb, Bureau of Public Secrets 2014) 4 §.

[63] Flyverbom and Reinecke, 'The Spectacle and Organization Studies' (n 11) 1627.

First, the fetishizing of the spectacle departs from the Marxist idea that things are often not as they seem, but appearances may mask some more fundamental reality. Its ontology is thus multilayered and is based on material realism. Although organizations' spectacles can be loyal representations of reality, they can also hide an ugly reality; the spectacle may thus be a false representation. For example, a flashy strategy of a company may conceal the fact that the working conditions in the company are abusive. Fetishizing the spectacle thus builds on ideological obfuscation and false consciousness; spectacle has the potential to conceal the real. This being the case, the spectacles can also be debunked, and the 'real' reality behind them exposed. Consequently, fetishized spectacles should be approached critically and suspiciously.

Second, performativity, for one, is generative. It builds on constructive ontology, which relies on humans' capacity to create new things and meanings in the world. In a strict sense, such creation is neither a representation of something more fundamental, nor is it a lie, masking such a reality. It can consist both of material and verbal practices. Performativity suggests that all kinds of representations need be thought as 'intricate and inseparable processes of meaning making involving subjects, objects, artefacts and material forces'.[64] The reality-representation relation in the performativity approach builds on the idea that representation is a part of what makes up the real. Its politics entail multiplicity, engaged intervention, and critique.

Third, as presented, the ontology of hyperreality is postmodern. In hyperreality, representation—simulacra—have no bearing in reality, as I have argued previously. That is to say that the real and the unreal are folded into one another and become indistinguishable. When trying to puncture the surface level, there is nothing to reach but endless circulation of impressions and images. Indeed, as Flyverbom and Reinecke put it, 'Maybe there is no outside reality that the spectacle disguises; and the search for a backstage reality will circle around an endless series of frontstages?'[65] Hyperreality results in a suspicious attitude towards the spectacles: people waver between belief and doubt. I have previously referred to this duality with Latour's concept of iconoclash. Due to this uncertainty, the politics of the spectacle, seen from the hyperreality point of view, is tainted by cynicism, sarcasm, and indifference.

As mentioned, Flyverbom and Reinecke's categorization of the different relationships between spectacle and organization is helpful in the attempt to clarify the relationship between transparency and reality. We might think that what Flyverbom and Reinecke call fetish is, in fact, structurally like the iconoclastic ideology of transparency. They both share the same ontology of material realism and the potentially false representations it enables. It makes it possible to formulate

[64] ibid, 1636.
[65] ibid, 1633.

the question of the quality of the correspondence between the representation and the real: is it good or bad, accurate or inaccurate, correct or false? This resembles what Baudrillard argued about the first two steps in representation: 1) representation is a reflection of basic reality; 2) it masks and perverts basic reality. Therefore, the reality principle remains untouched.

The performativity of the spectacle, in turn, corresponds to the iconophilic aspect of transparency. Something is brought to the realm of the visible, and the value and the effects of that something can be assessed. Unlike fetish and the material realism it presupposes, iconophilic practices (performativity) rely on the human production of meaning. Humans generate visibilities, material objects, and verbal practices whose relation to reality is difficult to frame as a matter of representation. The social, the material, and the normative are intertwined. As I have explained, the iconophilic practices of transparency need to derive their inspiration from an invisible source—from law and the literal, metaphorical and discursive meanings of transparency—as well from the social context in which the expected consequences of transparency are carefully assessed. Performativity resembles Baudrillard's third step: it masks the absence of a basic reality in which the image plays at being an appearance.

As I have argued in this chapter, hyperreality and transparency make the most problematic conjunction. Hyperreal transparency could not falsify (fetish; iconoclasm) nor construct content (performativity; iconophily). It just frequents normative discourses neither revealing nor creating anything. As pointed out, this would make transparency a floating signifier, which has no basic reality to correspond to, and perhaps not even iconophilic expressions, which would anchor it into the materiality of the world. This is already visible in the discursification of transparency, which was discussed in chapter seven. In the digital environment, the assumption of 'understanding is seeing' has started to crumble, as the realms of the visible and the understandable have started to separate from each other. Transparency has become partially hyperreal.

Are these different relationships between transparency and reality in an unbridgeable tension with each other? Not necessarily. I do not think that the legitimating ideology of transparency would go away even if it were tainted by obfuscation or false consciousness. So long as people are producing and crafting transparency practices to other people, the performativity and theatrical logic remain. As I have argued, these two ontologies of transparency, the truth is behind the mask (iconoclasm) and the truth is what is created (iconophily), cannot really be permanently reconciled, but they coexist and intertwine. Thus, it can be argued that hyperreality is at the heart of icono-ambivalence and the concomitant chagrin over mediation. It underpins the oscillation between debunking and constructing practices. The fact that transparency has been able to discursify and become a floating legitimizer, builds on this confusion.

Summing Up: What Happens to the Reality Principle?

In this chapter, I have established how fragile and indeterminate the entire question of governmental phenomenology—underpinning the theme of transparency—is, especially in the era of the digitalized society. This is due to various reasons, which have been elaborated above. Let me now summarize.

First, I discussed the general question of the representability of governance: to what extent can transparency deliver a truthful image of governance? How can an abstraction be represented, anyway? In chapter two, I discussed this theme using the concept of iconophily. On many occasions, transparency needs created appearances to serve its purpose of allowing visibility. To illustrate the question, I used Plato's allegory of the cave as a reference point. I argued that when it comes to governance, it is not often clear whether there is a distinction between the thing in itself and the thing for us—the representation would thus be as good as it gets, if not the very same thing. I deepened this analysis by discussing Baudrillard's concept of hyperreality and the crises of representation it entails. As Baudrillard argues, simulation and simulacra have come to replace representation and the reality principle. If representation means a copy of the original, a simulacrum would be copy without an original.

Second, in the age of digitalization and the information society, the representation of governance has become an acute issue, although, as argued, the theory of hyperreality preceded the emergence of the internet, digitalization, and datafication. In the digitalized world, hyperreality questions the very reality principle that transparency ideologically presupposes. How can transparency deliver a plausible representation of governance if governance increasingly consists of zeros and ones? Through transparency, are we to encounter hyperreality and simulacra instead of unveiled, 'more real' reality? I presented some of the criticisms targeted towards transparency's promise in the age of hyperreality.

Third, regardless of whether the reality principle is broken along with the emergence of hyperreality, it seems that transparency has not lost its popularity and productivity. Quite the contrary, in debates on AI ethics, and attempts to regulate ADM, transparency discourse is, perhaps, stronger than ever. This is often manifested as demands for algorithmic transparency. It is called for to open black boxes, to make visible the inner workings of algorithmic models. However, often this iconoclastic wish is futile. Even if the black boxes were made transparent, we would encounter technical, esoteric information, understandable only to experts, perhaps not even to them. Along with the development of AI and machine learning, the information in the black boxes may even be essentially esoteric, something that does not submit to human understanding at all. Consequently, the call for transparency has partially been complemented with calls for understandability or explicability. This, in turn, turns the promise of transparency upside down. Understanding would no longer be seeing but being explained to.

Fourth, I discussed some of the effects of digitalization on subjects and the ways in which the logic of impression management can work in the digitalized environment. What happens to the performative logic of social life? I explained how the theatrical structure is in place also on the internet. On the one hand, it creates countless opportunities for imaginative impression management; it is often hard to verify the identity behind the person represented in different internet fora. On the other hand, however, we often mistake the internet for an anonymous place. Subsequently, we leak information continuously, by our clicks, likes, and searches. Technology companies are collecting, storing, and often commodifying our data for their economic benefit. In the digital environment, we have lost some of our backstage self, and become involuntarily transparent.

Lastly, I brought these themes together by asking whether hyperreality as an idea can be reconciled with the performative, human-faced logic I have theorized in this book. By looking at iconoclasm (fetish), iconophily (performativity), and hyperreality as alternative ways to analyse the relationship between reality and representation, I concluded that they do not seem to be mutually exclusive, but all of them feature in contemporary transparency practices. However, the very fact that we often cannot be quite sure which of those, in fact, is at play, can be a sign of the emergence of hyperreal transparency in itself. It can be argued that transparency may also have been starting to adopt hyperreal forms and is thus becoming a simulacrum.

In the end, it seems that we are not willing to let the reality principle go as a regulative ideal. In the face of post-truth politics, alternative facts, and fake news, transparency is discursively presented as the last bastion of neutrality and reliability. Although critical transparency studies argue otherwise, in public discourse, transparency still represents the realist conception of truth. We need to recognize that the rise of normative transparency discourse has coincided with the rise of hyperreality and the relativization if not implosion of the reality principle. That implies that during this postmodern call for transparency, the hyperreal was already there. The answer to this contemporary call for transparency might be available if we think of its reactivity. As the world seems to be becoming increasingly complex, and the hand at work so subtle that its curating effect can be very difficult to recognize, we want sobering plain truth. However, that truth is not what it used to be: it is possible that we are departing from the epistemology of seeing and entering the epistemology of feeling, as feeling is even more immediate than seeing. This would mean that the ocular-centric undertone of transparency would cease to be a guarantee of veracity.

9
The Truth-Legitimacy Trade-off

What Does the Truth-Legitimacy Trade-off Mean?

A fundamental critique of the functioning logic of transparency has largely been missing in the academic literature so far. This is especially true in the field of law, from whence the term transparency could be said to have originated as a tool for legitimacy. My goal has been to fill that gap. As I have argued in this book, self-evidently good concepts such as transparency tend to be turned into tools of power and control. I hope this work will contribute to giving both academics and practitioners a more nuanced view of the ideal of transparency, its promise, its perils, its attraction, and its future.

The overarching question I have attempted to answer in this book is this: *why is transparency not working as it is commonly assumed it should?* I am not alone in asking this question. The entire interdisciplinary field of critical transparency studies can be argued to have grappled with it in one way or another. The very emergence of critical transparency studies is, perhaps, a symptom of a cresting of the growing wave of modern transparency discourse. This discourse is, I argue, driven by a narrative of empowerment: to fix what is wrong, we have a right to see the evidence. By fixing what is wrong, we will make the world a better place.

However, transparency does not and cannot work in this way. At its best, transparency works like a camera. It only gives the illusion of unvarnished reality: It can give us a polished impression like in a fashion shoot as easily as it can give us the brutal exposé of a crime photo. Given that what is shown is up to the operator and his camera, how much more real is a photo than a naturalistic painting or a map or a graph? What can be said is that transparency promises firsthand knowledge over curated secondhand knowledge about how things 'really are'. But how objective is the reality painted by this selected firsthand information?

In the first chapter, I presented the more detailed research questions of the book. These questions have guided my analysis throughout, although I have not addressed all of them directly. Rather, they have enabled me to keep the discussion coherent, and to build a multifaceted yet straightforward overall argument. The questions were the following: What is the problem to which transparency is the solution? Why specifically do we use the metaphor of transparency? How does law regulate the visibility of governance? Is firsthand knowledge about governance possible? The first question was particularly pertinent in chapters two, four, five, and six. The second one informed the discussion in chapters two, three, and five.

The Transparency Paradox. Ida Koivisto, Oxford University Press. © Ida Koivisto 2022.
DOI: 10.1093/oso/9780192855466.003.0009

The third, in turn, was a specific concern in chapter six, and to some extent, chapters seven and eight. The fourth was the underlying question in chapters two, three, and eight.

Although the questions are complex and hard to answer in a concise manner, I will nonetheless attempt to do so here. As for the first answer, I argue that the problem to which transparency is the solution are the changes in global power constellations together with a declining belief in truth and facts. The more intricate ways that power adopts, the less we understand it. This makes transparency a balancing act: regardless of this intricacy of power, transparency promises that we can see and understand what is happening. This brings us to the second answer: we use the metaphor of transparency because of its cognitive and cultural promise of accessing unmediated reality. For that reason, the term has proven to be more normatively attractive than its competitors. Third, law regulates the visibility of governance in many ways by allowing certain visibilities to emerge while hiding others. Law gives democratic weight to these practices. At the same time, law functions as a benchmark for the discursification of transparency. Fourth, firsthand knowledge of governance is possible on limited occasions, but it is seldom desired. Counterintuitively, we tend to prefer secondhand knowledge.

Informed by these answers, the main overall conclusion of this book is the argument of *the truth-legitimacy trade-off in transparency*, which I briefly introduced in the first chapter. For the sake of clarity, I will recapitulate it here. With the argument of the truth-legitimacy trade-off, I question the promise of transparency that connects legitimacy with access to truth. I argue that transparency is tacitly but inherently a social practice. The key principle in transparency practices is that of intentionality and the attempt to manage an impression. For an entity—be it a person, a state, an organization, or a company—to be considered in high regard (legitimacy) in the eyes of its audience—be it other people in the community, citizens of the state, customers of a company, or other organizations—transparency needs to be intentional to be esteemed.

That means transparency must be named as such. By naming its information release practices transparency, the entity in question can control its visibility to its audience and create an image as if it had nothing to hide, and all its information were available. However, if we subscribe to the idea of the social self, and the impression management aspirations it entails, we can assume that this allowed or created visibility is curated and designed to show the entity in a positive light. At the same time, potentially compromising information is omitted from that visibility. This is how transparency can guarantee legitimacy, through intentionally curated visibilities; visibilities that the audience would wish to see.

However, if transparency is unintentional, and the entity is revealed to be transparent (the negative connotation of transparency)—for example, through an information leak, or through the experience of being 'seen through'—the audience can gain more information about it than through intentional transparency practices. The audience would have access to a richer, more multifaceted truth because the curation of visibility could not take place; instead, failed impression management bypasses it. Under these conditions, the entity is thus subject to the revelatory gaze. This means, nevertheless, that disconcerting information about the entity—which could be hidden with intentional transparency practices—would also become visible, and the audience would end up seeing 'too much'. Through this unintentional transparency, the entity would lose its possibility to show itself in a positive light.

In consequence, there is access to more truth, and transparency ideologically privileges this truth. However, because this truth is not filtered through impression management practices, legitimacy hardly follows from it. Instead, it has the potential to disappoint the audience when the discrepancy between the apparent and the actual is revealed. Therefore, the audience can 1) access either legitimacy through intentional transparency and curated visibilities, or 2) truth through unintentional transparency practices and unfiltered visibilities. In conclusion, contrary to the promise of transparency, the audience cannot access legitimacy of the entity and the 'naked truth' about it at the same time; depending on the intentionality, these two values of truth and legitimacy of transparency are subject to an either-or logic. This is what I mean by the truth-legitimacy trade-off in transparency.

What Truth?

If there is, indeed, a trade-off between truth and legitimacy in transparency, as I argue, I need to say more about how I have conceived truth in this book. Truth is without a doubt a contested concept. The attempt to theorize something as philosophically loaded as 'truth' is risky. In public discourse, we tend to talk about truth in conjunction with reality, something that corresponds with the facts in the world. Consequently, questions of epistemology, reality, realism, and materialism follow, all subjects of hundreds of years of philosophical inquiry. I have no wish to resolve these philosophical questions once and for all, but it is necessary to recognize them as a focal point in the quest for truth.

It seems that truth is conceivable through its opposites: if something is true, something else must be false, erroneous, or untruthful. Although this holds true in all meaning-making in a strict sense, it is not clear, however, whether there are alternative ways of approaching truth except for binary oppositions such as true/false, real/fake, the real thing/representation, or revelation/concealment. Although these oppositions seem to be a natural way of approaching the issue, are they sustainable? For example, are hyperreality and truth alternative conceptualizations? As argued in this book, many of the discussed themes are phenomenological. With these points in mind, I have approached truth, reality, and their relativization from three angles.

First, I have approached these themes by questioning realism and revelation as necessary preconditions of truth. I argued that we should not succumb to naïve realism or naïve iconoclasm; truth is not just a matter of opening the curtain and exposing material reality. With the notion of the iconoclastic aspect of transparency, I have referred to the hostility towards mediation and representations and to the idea of removing obstacles that hinder visibility. I have asked instead whether truth can be immaterial, abstract, conceptual, ineffable, or even unrepresentable. If the answer is affirmative, how can abstractions be made visible, or is transparency blocked? Can truth be invisible in the sense that it would refer to social constructions and collective imagining? I have argued that this is the case. Otherwise, we could not talk about the iconophilic aspects (reliance on mediation and representation; constructed visibilities to represent abstractions) of transparency, but we would need to succumb to a radically material conception of truth and reality. Nor could we talk about truth about governance, truth about social relations, truth about power, or truth about the content of the mind.

Arguing this point—that the requirement of truth needs to extend to abstractions if transparency is to make sense, even though talking about them in any clear way is difficult—has led to the development of the theoretical toolkit of this book. If this were not the case, there would be no point in discussing and applying such concepts as the hand at work, acheiropoieton, chagrin over mediation, icono-ambivalence, etc). Developing and using these concepts imply that truth and access to it cannot be approached merely from a material point of view. The endeavour to commit to the threefold understanding of truth—its materiality, its performativity, its hyperreality—has led to dedicating numerous pages to these conceptual exercises.

Second, truth and reality are—at least discursively—related to the binary distinction of frontstage and backstage operations. However, the truth implications of the concomitant performativity of transparency are complex. Intuitively, it is easy to think that the backstage would be truer than the frontstage; the backstage would mean unvarnished reality, because it does not consider the preferences of the viewer, or indeed, considers him, but with wishes of being hidden from the viewer. When the 'real thing' undoubtedly exists, why do we need representation and mediation, which a managed impression inevitably entails? Although we mostly accept this logic of the theatre, it may even lead to ontological paranoia: if no one sees—or can see—to the backstage, does it even exist? Is there anything behind the curtain; or is the curtain the border or the truth? Whatever is happening backstage, that behaviour is uncommunicative if it does not attempt to reach anyone's sensorium.

Although the legitimacy promise of transparency uses the vocabulary of truth, this intersection of truth and legitimacy brings about a call for considering the audience. We are often ambivalent about this: managed visibilities mean that we are subject to iconophilic practices (performativity on the frontstage) when iconoclasm (access to the backstage)—which transparency ideologically privileges—would also be possible. Some behaviour is designed to be seen; other behaviour is not. Is the 'designed' element of the impression less true because we are dealing with the hand at work and concomitantly, with chagrin over mediation? Theoretically, we could reach beyond the mediation, and access the 'real thing', yet we mostly do not want the 'real thing' unless it is also something that we appreciate. Often, we prefer mediation.

Third, to the extent that our life and society has become digitalized, the representation of the 'real thing' has become even more questionable, if not a useful fiction. We need to ask: Is the reality principle dead? As argued in the previous chapter, along with digitalization, the premediated existence of the thing represented has become tangibly questionable. Fake news, alternative facts, post-truth politics, and disinformation flourish in the digitalized environment. If transparency is a medium, what happens to the representation if transparency becomes digital? As argued, the 'medium-ness' of transparency adopts a second layer. The representation is mediated not only through transparency, but also through the algorithms that govern it in the digital environment.

The internet is a site of simulacra and distorted representations on the one hand, and a ruthless, a-perspectival panopticon on the other. In this environment, the ways in which we perceive reality and other people cannot help but change. Truth cannot be reduced to a matter of representation and its loyalty to its object, but perhaps to the illusions these representations provide. We may need to jettison the 'depth metaphor', which privileges the unseen over the apparent in the quest for truth. It is possible that to the extent that we must approach simulacra as real without an origin, we also need to reimagine the laws of icono-ambivalence. If neither iconoclasm nor iconophily has any bearing on hyperreality, the core mechanism of transparency implodes.

With these clarifications, I have used the word 'truth' for heuristic reasons, to describe the dynamic of the transparency-truth nexus. In the context of the truth-legitimacy trade-off, by truth I mean the unmediated, uncurated visibility of reality, the object of the revelatory gaze. This means if we want the unmediated truth, the acheiropoietic representation of governance, it cannot be accessed through intentional transparency techniques. In hyperreality, it cannot be accessed at all. As I have argued, the ideal of transparency is based on the idea of the reality principle, sometimes even on naïve realism and naïve iconoclasm. Although the concept of truth can mean many other things too, it has proven difficult to talk about truth without the vocabulary of concealment and revelation when arguing for the existence of the trade-off.

What Legitimacy?

As I have argued throughout this book, the legitimacy of power seems to be both a permanent and paradoxically, an intensifying concern. It seems that traditional power structures are in flux, and the widening transparency discourse can be seen as a token of this. This observation has led to the following questions: How and when do we call for legitimacy? What kind of legitimacy? Although legitimacy can be theorized in a myriad of ways, in this book I have approached the transparency-legitimacy nexus from three different, partially overlapping, perspectives.

First, I approached transparency as a value judgement in social interaction: in interpersonal relations, transparency is not only a neutral affair of being able to see through. Instead, it can be considered good or bad as a function of perceived intentionality. When transparency is deemed good, a particular kind of ethics, the ethics of confession, becomes relevant. In the ethics of confession, truth is revealed for the greater good ('they deserve to know the truth'), or for individual emancipation ('I have to get this out of my system'). Thus, it further builds on the ideals of authenticity and sincerity, and the generally beneficial effect of knowing the truth. A good person is sincere. Transparency is thus good for individual wellbeing, and it is good for the community.

When truth is seen as a matter of the binary oppositions such as concealment/revelation, that revelation inevitably raises questions about the worthiness of its receiver. What follows from the revelation? Is the receiver worthy of knowing the truth, or is he better off if he is ignorant about it? This is essentially tied to the idea of transparency as a value judgement, as discussed in chapter four. I argued that legitimacy through transparency would be communicating the content of the mind in the most loyal way—transparently—without distortion, concealment, or half-truths, thus diminishing possible chagrin over mediation. At its core, telling the truth or speaking one's mind is a social matter. Through analogy, I argued that this general mechanism also extends to states, companies, organizations, and other such entities.

Second, transparency embodies the Enlightenment ideal of rational actors, and their role as informed citizens. The legitimacy question is tied to the way in which democracy is conceived. As a governance ideal, transparency is connected not only to confession, but also to a structurally similar question of the truthfulness of representation, and the worthiness of the recipients. Instead of the content of the mind, the 'real' content of governance should be either represented through transparency practices (intentional transparency) or be normalized under the panoptic gaze of the governed. Furthermore, transparency is needed for the functionality of democracy and the justification of executive power. As discussed in chapter five, democratic and public law rationalities create different kinds of legitimacy structures. The uniting question is this: Why should we accept the unequal power exercised on us when we are ultimately the source of that power?

Third, transparency represents a legal understanding of legitimacy. The legitimacy promise of democratic oversee-ability of power thus becomes a function of law and legal regulation. Although law does not necessarily mean legitimacy in the spirit of legal positivism (in John Austin's famous words, 'the existence of law is one thing, its merit or demerit another one'), legality often implies it nonetheless. At its strongest, transparency may be guaranteed with judicial forms, whereby transparency has exceeded its most direct logic of impression management. Legality as a form entails its own legitimacy concerns in addition to those that relate to transparency. Legality implies legitimacy through the democratic process that precedes it. In this context, the additional legitimacy that legal form provides is thus procedural. Its enforceability, however, relies on the monopolized violence of the state.

That said, the legal conception of legitimacy has widened its scope and has become relativized. It is no longer only anchored to democratic, legislative processes and the exclusivity of the state enforcement mechanisms. It has become a matter of 'best practices' or 'good governance'. Seen in this way, the legitimacy of transparency would not necessarily be strictly legal, let alone ideological, but managerial. It would entail morality, which is technocratic, and whose connection to revelation and concealment is based on functionality rather than deontic rationalizations. As explained, transparency can be seen as a token of the discursification of transparency, and even the discursification of procedural public law more widely. However, as I have discussed in chapter seven, when we talk about discursification, this legality becomes easily 'as if' legality, or 'legality light'.

All these different ways of approaching the transparency-legitimacy nexus have a somewhat different view as to why transparency is desirable. Is it good because it is deferential to the receiver ('they deserve to know the truth'; 'I need to get this out of my system'), because it enables one to influence the power one is subject to, or because it creates structures in society that fortify and enforce such influencing? All these sub-narratives of the legitimacy of transparency have been discussed in the pages of this book. Despite their differences, I would maintain that these sub-narratives share a common background assumption: that it is possible to access the truth about the object of transparency—be it content of mind, modes of power, or operations of governing—and that access to truth is essential for legitimacy to work. As I have demonstrated, this access is often merely a useful fiction. Nonetheless, whether that truth is fictional or symbolic, it is desperately needed for transparency's legitimizing promise to have a bearing.

The Transparency Myth Revisited

The transparency narrative presupposes that reality, even the truth about governance out there, is accessible through transparency. Committing to the truth-legitimacy trade-off suggests the opposite, namely giving up on the fallacious fantasies of accessing reality through transparency. These fantasies, however, are alive and well. We may not want to give them up as they serve an important purpose, protecting us from a fundamental epistemological anxiety and a concomitant feeling of powerlessness.

As van de Port explains, our sensations of immediacy are sought and produced by different fantasy scripts. Some of these scripts attempt to undo media-awareness. They conceal or deny the involvement of the hand at work. They suggest the sensation that one's own imagination is not of human origin but is immanent to the world. Other scripts, nonetheless, ostentatiously reveal the mediation process and the workings of the hand in it. However, on closer examination, the latter scripts often throw into relief the moment where—all awareness of the medium aside—the mediation process is transcended. What is the place of the medium in 'the cultural production of the really real?'[1] It can be argued that this is exactly what transparency as a medium attempts to do—producing fantasies of the really real.

The fantasy scripts that buttress the transparency ideal have become influential to the extent that transparency can be considered a myth. In today's parlance, myth is false; it can be a conviction that is false yet tenacious.[2] Whenever myth is at play, concepts and ideas are transformed from representations and their indirect meanings into their instant appearance.[3] Even though myth is metaphorical in nature, it creates a tension towards its representative character. It denies its nature as presenting a part of the whole and instead presents itself as a totality. In this way, a myth is like dogma, a set of beliefs, which go together as a totality, and posits itself beyond doubt.[4] Seen like this, transparency is clearly myth-like; it is firmly believed in, yet its problems remain overlooked. In the transparency myth, access to information is not seen as a token of transparency but is instead seen as transparency itself; or, 'as if' turns into 'as'.[5]

The myth, however, may need to change. We can assume that as long as transparency has been a governance ideal, performative structure has also been there, although the expectations regarding the quality of the performance have changed over time. In this sense, the functioning mechanism of transparency has not changed. Reality, however, is not what it used to be. We may have entered the age of the hyperreal, in which the separation between the original and the copy is questioned. In the wake of digitalization and the development of artificial intelligence

[1] Mattijs van de Port, '(Not) Made by the Human Hand: Media Consciousness and Immediacy in the Cultural Production of the Real' (2011) 19(1) Social Anthropology 74,

[2] Robert A Segal, *Myth: A Very Short Introduction* (2nd ed, Oxford University Press 2015) 5.

[3] Lars Thøger Christensen and Joep Cornelissen, 'Organizational Transparency as Myth and Metaphor' (2015) 18(2) European Journal of Social Theory 132, 136.

[4] ibid.

[5] ibid, 138, also Byung-Chul Han, *The Transparency Society* (Erik Butler tr, Stanford University Press 2015) viii: 'Transparency is an ideology. Like all ideologies, it has a positive core that has been mystified and made absolute. The danger of transparency lies in such totalization. If totalized, it yields terror.'

(AI), the entire reality principle has become more complex. It is less and less warranted to argue that the truth-transparency nexus can survive.

If the truth-transparency nexus ceases to be valid, the metaphorical promise of transparency may implode. If seeing as a privileged way of knowing no longer holds true, why would we use such a misleading concept as transparency? In the context of algorithmic governance, there are already weak signals of recognizing this problem: new ideals such as understandability and explicability have emerged into normative discourses, and partially questioned the concept of transparency. What is the use of immediate information, which we cannot make sense of, when understanding no longer guarantees seeing, if it ever did?

Much is at play. Transparency is not just a politically innocent, managerial discourse, based on the cognitive metaphor of understanding is seeing. In addition, people are governed by managing what and how they can see and how transparency is talked about. As explained, transparency has reached the status of a magic concept. It has started to mean so many things that it is hard to be critical towards it: although it is not conceptually necessary, its desirability has become self-explanatory. Hence, instead of emancipating people to influence power, transparency is a form of power itself.

Perhaps a somewhat gloomy picture of transparency is presented in this book. However, it has the potential to create a matrix for future research and socio-legal imagining. Should we replace the term transparency with some other? Should we conclude that there is nothing wrong with legitimacy tied to performance, and truth, whatever it may be, has no bearing so long as it does not interrupt transparency? Is there a way to resolve the trade-off? Is the 'transparentocene' ultimately a self-obsessed era? These questions may fuel further research.

The main contribution of this book is in its encouragement to make connections between our current time labelled by both the call for transparency, and the simultaneously declining belief in facts and truth. Perhaps the legitimacy produced by transparency practices is enough to enable public debate and democratic control of power, and no access to more fundamental truth is necessary. That said, the truth-legitimacy trade-off is not a trade-off if we reformulate how truth is conceived. Controlled transparency provides truth but in a different way than it promises. It provides truth of the ways in which the controller of transparency wants to be seen. This image tells its own truth.

References

Abazi V and Tauschinsky E, 'Reasons of Control and Trust: Grounding the Public Need for Transparency in the European Union' (2015) 11(2) Utrecht Law Review 78

Ackerman J and Sandoval-Ballesteros I, 'The Global Explosion of Freedom of Information Laws' (2006) 58(1) Administrative Law Review 85

Adams R, *Transparency: New Trajectories in Law* (Routledge 2020)

Albu O A and Hansen H K, 'Three Sides of the Same Coin: Datafied Transparency, Biometric Surveillance, and Algorithmic Governmentalities' (2021) 8(1) Critical Analysis of Law 9

Alemanno A, 'Unpacking the Principle of Openness in EU Law: Transparency, Participation and Democracy' (2014) 39(1) *European Law Review* 72

Alloa E, 'Transparency: A Magic Concept of Modernity' in E Alloa and D Thomä (eds), *Transparency, Society and Subjectivity: Critical Perspectives* (Palgrave Macmillan 2018)

Alloa E and Thomä D, 'Transparency: Thinking through an Opaque Concept' in E Alloa and D Thomä (eds), *Transparency, Society and Subjectivity: Critical Perspectives* (Palgrave Macmillan 2018)

Ananny M and Crawford K, 'Seeing Without Knowing: Limitations of the Transparency Ideal and Its Application to Algorithmic Accountability' (2018) 20(3) New Media and Society 973

Aristotle, *The Poetics of Aristotle* (S H Butcher tr, The Project Gutenberg EBook, release date 3 November 2008, last updated 22 January 2013)

Atkin A, *Peirce's Theory of Signs* (E N Zalta ed, The Stanford Encyclopedia of Philosophy 2010) <https://plato.stanford.edu/entries/peirce-semiotics/> accessed 14 July 2021

August V, 'Theorie und Praxis der Transparenz: Eine Zwischenbilanz' (2018) 21 *Berliner Blätter* 129

August V and Osrecki F, *Der Transparenz-Imperativ: Normen – Praktiken – Strukturen* (Springer 2019)

Bacon F, *The Advancement of Learning and New Atlantis* (A Johnston ed, Clarendon Press 1974)

Barish J, *The Anti-Theatrical Prejudice* (University of California Press 1981)

Barney D, 'Politics and Emerging Media: The Revenge of Publicity' (2008) 1(1) Global Media Journal 89

Baudrillard J, *Simulations* (Semiotext(e) 1983)

Baudrillard J, *Simulacra and Simulation* (University of Michigan Press 1994)

Baume S, 'Publicity and Transparency: The Itinerary of a Subtle Distinction' in E Alloa and D Thomä (eds), *Transparency, Society, Subjectivity: Critical Perspectives* (Palgrave Macmillan 2018)

Baume S and Papadopoulos Y, 'Transparency: from Bentham's Inventory of Virtuous Effects to Contemporary Evidence-based Skepticism' (2018) 21(2) Critical Review of International Social and Political Philosophy 169

Benjamin W, 'On the Mimetic Faculty' in W Benjamin (ed), *Reflections: Essays, Aphorisms, Autobiographical Writings* (Schocken Books 1986)

Benjamin W, *The Origin of German Tragic Drama* (Verso Books 1998)

Benjamin W, 'Goethe's Elective Affinities' in M Bullock and M Jennings (eds), *Walter Benjamin: Selected Writings, 1: 1913–1926* (Harvard University Press 2004)

Bentham J, *Panopticon: Postscript: Part II: Containing a Plan of Management for a Panopticon Penitentiary-house* (T Payne 1791)

Bentham J, *Tactique des Assemblées législatives* (J J Paschoud 1816)

Bentham J, *Panopticon Writings* (M Božovič ed, Verso Press 1995)

Bentham J, *The Collected Works of Jeremy Bentham: Writing on the Poor Laws*, vol 1 (M Quinn ed, Oxford University Press 2001)

Bentham J, *Panopticon, or the Inspection-House* (Dodo Press 2008)

Berger S and Owetschkin D (eds), *Contested Transparencies, Social Movements and the Public Sphere: Multi-Disciplinary Perspectives* (Palgrave Macmillan 2019)

Bianchi A, 'On Power and Illusion: The Concept of Transparency in International Law' in A Bianchi and A Peters (eds), *Transparency in International Law* (Cambridge University Press 2013)

Birchall C, 'Introduction to 'Secrecy and Transparency' The Politics of Opacity and Openness' (2011) 28(7–8) Theory, Culture and Society 7

Birchall C, 'Radical Transparency?' (2014) 14(1) Cultural Studies ↔ Critical Methodologies 77

Birchall C, 'Interrupting Transparency' in E Alloa and D Thomä (eds), *Transparency, Society and Subjectivity: Critical Perspectives* (Palgrave Macmillan 2018)

Birchall C, *Shareveillance: The Dangers of Openly Sharing and Covertly Collecting Data* (University of Minnesota Press 2018)

Birkinshaw P, *Freedom of Information: The Law, the Practice and the Ideal* (Cambridge University Press 2010)

Blanton T, 'The Struggle for Openness in the International Financial Institutions' in A Florini (ed), *The Right to Know: Transparency for an Open World* (New York, Columbia University Press 2007)

Bloomfield R and O'Hara M, 'Market Transparency: Who Wins and Who Loses?' (1999) 12(1) The Review of Financial Studies 5

Boltanski L, *Mysteries & Conspiracies: Detective Stories, Spy Novels and the Making of Modern Societies* (Polity Press 2014)

Boström N, *Superintelligence: Paths, Dangers, Strategies* (Oxford University Press 2014)

Brandeis L, *Other Peoples' Money and How the Bankers Use It* (Frederick A Stokes Company 1914) <www.law.louisville.edu/library/collections/brandeis/node/196> accessed 22 June 2021

Brevini B, Hintz A, and McCurdy P, 'Amy Goodman in Conversation with Julian Assange and Slavoj Žižek' in B Brevini, A Hintz, and P McCurdy (eds), *Beyond WikiLeaks: Implications for the Future of Communications, Journalism and Society* (Palgrave Macmillan 2013)

Brighenti A M, *Visibility in Social Theory and Social Research* (Palgrave Macmillan 2010)

Brin D, *The Transparent Society: Will Technology Force Us to Choose Between Privacy and Freedom?* (Perseus Books 1998)

Brown A J, Vandekerckhove W, and Dreyfus S, 'The Relationship between Transparency, Whistleblowing, and Public Trust' in P Ala'i and R G Vaughn (eds), *Research Handbook of Transparency* (Edward Elgar 2014)

Brubaker R and Cooper F, 'Beyond "Identity"' (2000) 29 Theory and Society 1

Bucher T, *If... Then: Algorithmic Power and Politics* (Oxford University Press 2018)

Burrell J, 'How the Machine "Thinks": Understanding Opacity in Machine Learning Algorithms' (2016) 3(1) Big Data and Society 1

Canetti E (1960) *Masse und Macht* (English edn, *Crowds and Power*, New York, Seabury Press 1973)

Carpi D, 'Crime Evidence: "Simulacres et Simulations", Photography as Forensic Evidence' in L Dahlberg, K Stierstorfer, and D Carpi (eds), *Visualizing Law and Authority: Essays on Legal Aesthetics* (De Gruyter 2012)

Christensen L T and Cornelissen J, 'Organizational Transparency as Myth and Metaphor' (2015) 18(2) European Journal of Social Theory 132

Cohen J, *Between Truth and Power: The Legal Constructions of Informational Capitalism* (Oxford University Press 2019)

Comaroff J and Comaroff J, 'Transparent Fictions; or, the Conspiracies of a Liberal Imagination: An Afterword' in H G West and T Sanders (eds), *Transparency and Conspiracy: Ethnographies of Suspicion in the New World Order* (Duke University Press 2003)

Crary J, *Techniques of the Observer: On Vision and Modernity in the Nineteenth Century* (MIT Press 1990)

Cubitt S, Palmer D, and Tkacz N, 'Introduction: Materiality and Invisibility' in S Cubitt, D Palmer, and N Tkacz (eds), *Digital Light* (Open Humanities Press 2015)

Cubitt S, Palmer D, and Tkacz N (eds), *Digital Light* (Open Humanities Press 2015)

Curtin D and Leino P, 'In Search of Transparency for EU Law-making: Trilogues on the Cusp of Dawn' (2017) 54(6) Common Market Law Review 1673

Curtin D and Meijer A, 'Does Transparency Strengthen Legitimacy? A Critical Analysis of European Union Policy Documents' (2006) 11(2) Information Polity 109

Da Vinci, L, *The Notebooks of Leonardo da Vinci* part 1 vol 1, compiled and edited from the original manuscripts by Jean-Paul Richter (S Low, Marston, Searle and Rivington 1883)

Danaher J, 'The Threat of Algocracy: Reality, Resistance and Accommodation' (2016) 29(3) Philosophy and Technology 245

Dean M, *Governmentality: Power and Rule in Modern Society* (SAGE Publications 2010)

Debord, G, *The Society of the Spectacle* (K Knabb tr and an, Bureau of Public Secrets 2014)

Den Boer M, 'Steamy Windows: Transparency and Openness in Justice and Home Affairs' in V Deckmyn and I Thomson (eds), *Openness and Transparency in the European Union* (Maastricht European Institute of Public Administration 1998)

van Dijck J, Poell T, and de Waal M, *The Platform Society: Public Values in a Connective World* (Oxford University Press 2018)

Docherty T, *Confessions: The Philosophy of Transparency* (Bloomsbury Publishing 2014)

Donaldson M and Kingsbury B, 'Ersatz Normativity or Public Law in Global Governance: The Hard Case of International Prescriptions for National Infrastructure Regulation' (2013) 14(1) Chicago Journal of International Law 1

Donaldson M and Kingsbury B, 'The Adoption of Transparency Policies in Global Governance Institutions: Justifications, Effects, and Implications' (2013) 9 Annual Review of Law and Social Science 119

Douzinas C, 'The End(s) of Human Rights' (2002) 26(2) Melbourne University Law Review 445

Dreyfus H and Rabinow P, *Michel Foucault: Beyond Structuralism and Hermeneutics* (University of Chicago Press 1983)

van der Dries L, 'The Pleasure of Looking Behind Curtains: Naked Bodies from Titian to Fabre and LeRoy' in G Rodothenous (ed), *Theatre as Voyeurism: The Pleasures of Watching* (Palgrave Macmillan 2015)

Eco U, 'Not Such Wicked Leaks' in E Alloa and D Thomä (eds), *Transparency, Society and Subjectivity: Critical Perspectives* (Palgrave Macmillan 2018)

Engelke M, 'Text and Performance in an African Church: The Book, "Live and Direct"' (2008) 31(1) American Ethnologist 76
Erkkilä T, *Government Transparency: Impacts and Unintended Consequences* (Palgrave Macmillan 2012)
Esty D C, 'Good Governance at the Supranational Scale: Globalizing Administrative Law' (2006) 115(7) Yale Law Journal 1490
Etzioni A, 'The Limits of Transparency' in E Alloa and D Thomä (eds), *Transparency, Society and Subjectivity: Critical Perspectives* (Palgrave Macmillan 2018)
Etzioni A, 'Is Transparency the Best Disinfectant?' (2010) 18(4) The Journal of Political Philosophy 389
Fenster M, 'The Opacity of Transparency' (2006) 91 Iowa Law Review 885
Fenster M, 'Seeing the State: Transparency as Metaphor' (2010) 62(3) Administrative Law Review 617
Fenster M, 'Transparency in Search of a Theory' (2015) 18(2) European Journal of Social Theory 150
Fenster M, *The Transparency Fix: Secrets, Leaks, and Uncontrollable Government Information* (Stanford University Press 2017)
Fenster M, 'Transparency in Trump's America' (2017) 30(2) Governance 173
Fenster M, 'A "Public" Journey Through COVID-19: Donald Trump, Twitter, and the Secrecy of U.S. Presidents' Health' (2021) 8(1) Critical Analysis of Law 25
Fernandez J, *Transparent Minds: A Study of Self-Knowledge* (Oxford University Press 2013)
de Fine Licht J, *Magic Wand or Pandora's Box? How Transparency in Decision Making affects Public Perceptions of Legitimacy* (University of Gothenburg 2014)
Fischer-Lescano A and Teubner G, 'Regime-Collisions: The Vain Search for Legal Unity in the Fragmentation of Global Law' (2004) 25(4) Michigan Journal of International Law 999
Fisher E, 'Exploring the Legal Architecture of Transparency' in P Ala'i and R G Vaughn (eds), *Research Handbook of Transparency* (Edward Elgar 2014)
Florini A, 'Introduction: The Battle Over Transparency' in A Florini (ed), *The Right to Know: Transparency for an Open World* (Columbia University Press 2007)
Flyverbom M, 'Sunlight in Cyberspace? On Transparency as a Form of Ordering' (2015) 18(2) European Journal of Social Theory 168
Flyverbom M, 'Transparency: Mediation and the Management of Visibilities' (2016) 10(1) International Journal of Communication 110
Flyverbom M, *The Digital Prism: Transparency and Managed Visibilities in a Datafied World* (Cambridge University Press 2019)
Flyverbom M and Albu O A, 'Organizational Transparency: Conceptualizations, Conditions, and Consequences' (2019) 58(2) Business and Society 268
Flyverbom M and Reinecke J, 'The Spectacle and Organization Studies' (2017) 38(11) Organization Studies 1625
Foucault M, *Archaeology of Knowledge* (Pantheon Books 1969)
Foucault M, *Power/Knowledge: Selected Interviews and Other Writings* (C Gordon ed, Pantheon Books 1980)
Foucault M, *Discipline and Punish: The Birth of Prison* (Penguin Books 1991)
Foucault M, *Security, Territory, Population: Lectures at the Collège de France 1978–1979* (M Senellart ed, Palgrave Macmillan 2007)
Foucault M, *The Government of Self and Others: Lectures at the Collège de France 1982–1983* (A I Davidson ed, Palgrave MacMillan 2010)
Freud S, *Civilization and its Discontents* (W W Norton and Company Inc 1966)
Fung A, Graham M, and Weil D, *Full Disclosure: The Perils and Promise of Transparency* (Cambridge University Press 2007)

Galloway A, 'Are Some Things Unrepresentable?' (2011) 28(7–8) Theory, Culture and Society 85

Gaonkar D P and McCarthy J R, 'Panopticism and Publicity: Bentham's Quest for Transparency' (1994) 6(3) Public Culture 547

Garsten C and Lindh de Montoya M, 'In Retrospect: The Play of Shadows' in C Garsten and M Lindh de Montoya (eds), *Transparency in a New Global Order: Unveiling Organizational Visions* (Edward Elgar 2008)

Gibbs D N, 'Sigmund Freud as a Theorist of Government Secrecy' (2011) 19 Research in Social Problems and Public Policy 5

Giddens A, *Modernity and Self-Identity* (Polity Press 1991)

Gilead A, 'Can Brain Imaging Breach Our Mental Privacy?' (2015) 6 Review of Philosophy and Psychology 275

Gillespie T, *Custodians of the Internet: Platforms, Content Moderation, and the Hidden Decisions that Shape Social Media* (Yale University Press 2018)

Gilovich T, Medvec V H, and Stravisky K, 'The Illusion of Transparency: Biased Assessments of Others' Ability to Read One's Emotional States' (1998) 75(2) Journal of Personality and Social Psychology 332

Gitelman L (ed), *Raw Data is an Oxymoron* (MIT Press 2013)

Gitelman L, *Paper Knowledge: Toward a Media History of Documents* (Durham N C 2014)

Grimmelikhuijsen S G and Meijer A J, 'Effects of Transparency on the Perceived Trustworthiness of a Government Organization—Evidence from an Online Experiment' (2014) 24(1) Journal of Public Administration Research and Theory 137

Goffman E, *Interaction Ritual—Essays on Face-to-Face Behavior* (Pantheon Books 1982)

Goffman E, *The Presentation of Self in Everyday Life* (Penguin Books 1990)

Gonzales A L and Hancock J T, 'Mirror, Mirror on My Facebook Wall: Effects of Exposure to Facebook on Self- Esteem' (2011) 14(1–2) Cyberpsychology, Behavior, and Social Networking 79

Gordon N, 'On Visibility and Power: An Arendtian Corrective of Foucault' (2002) 25(2) Human Studies 125

Green J E, *The Eyes of the People: Democracy in the Age of Spectatorship* (Oxford University Press 2010)

Grindle M, 'Good Enough Governance: Poverty Reduction and Reform in Developing Countries' (2004) 17(4) Governance: An International Journal of Policy, Administration and Institutions 525

Guo W, 'The Power of Plain Language: Executives' Rhetoric in Conference Presentations, Persuasion, And Stock Market Reaction' (31st Annual International Conference of the Strategic Management Society, Miami, Florida, 6–9 November 2011) <https://journals.aom.org/doi/10.5465/AMBPP.2012.18185abstract > accessed 3 August 2021

Gupta A, 'Transparency under Scrutiny: Information Disclosure in Global Environmental Governance' (2008) 8(2) Global Environmental Politics 1

Halbertal M, *Concealment and Revelation: Esotericism in Jewish Thought and Its Philosophical Implications* (Princeton University Press 2007)

Han B-C, *The Transparency Society* (Stanford University Press 2015)

Hansen H, 'Numerical Operations, Transparency Illusions and the Datafication of Governance' (2015) 18(2) European Journal of Social Theory 203

Hansen H K, Christensen L T, and Flyverbom M, 'Introduction: Logics of Transparency in Late Modernity: Paradoxes, Mediation and Governance' (2015) 18(2) European Journal of Social Theory 117

Harcourt B, *Exposed: Desire and Disobedience in the Digital Age* (Harvard University Press 2015)

Harcourt B, 'Virtual Transparency: From the Panopticon to the Expository Society and Beyond' in E Alloa and D Thomä (eds), *Transparency, Society and Subjectivity: Critical Perspectives* (Palgrave Macmillan 2018)

Harvey D, *The Condition of Postmodernity* (Blackwell 1990)

Heald D, 'The Varieties of Transparency' in C Hood and D Heald (eds), *Transparency—The Key to Better Governance?* (Oxford University Press 2006)

Hildebrandt M, 'Profiling and the European Citizen' in M Hildebrandt and S Gutwirth (eds), *Profiling the European Citizen* (Springer 2008)

Hildebrandt M and Gutwirth S, 'Concise Conclusions: Citizens out of Control' in M Hildebrandt and S Gutwirth (eds), *Profiling the European Citizen* (Springer 2008)

Hildén J, 'The Politics of Datafication: The Influence of Lobbyists on the EU's Data Protection Reform and its Consequences for the Legitimacy of the General Data Protection Regulation' (Doctor of Philosophy, University of Helsinki 2019)

Hood C, 'Transparency in Historical Perspective' in C Hood and D Heald (eds), *Transparency—The Key to Better Governance?* (Oxford University Press 2006)

Hood C, 'Beyond Exchanging First Principles: Some Closing Comments' in C Hood and D Heald (eds), *Transparency—The Key to Better Governance?* (Oxford University Press 2006)

Hood C, 'Accountability and Transparency: Siamese Twins, Matching Parts, Awkward Couple?' (2010) 33(5) West European Politics 989

Ippolito A, 'The Panopticon is Leaking' in S Cubitt, D Palmer and N Tkacz (eds), *Digital Light* (Open Humanities Press 2015)

Islam M S et al, 'COVID-19–Related Infodemic and Its Impact on Public Health: A Global Social Media Analysis' (2020) 103(4) American Journal of Tropical Medicine and Hygiene 1621

Jay M, *Downcast Eyes: The Denigration of Vision in Twentieth-Century French Thought* (University of California Press 1994)

Jung C G, *Two Essays on Analytical Psychology* (Princeton University Press 1972)

Jørgensen R F, 'What Platforms Mean When They Talk About Human Rights: Platforms and Human Rights' (2017) 9(3) Policy Internet 280

Kahn P, *The Cultural Study of Law: Reconstructing Legal Scholarship* (University of Chicago Press 1999)

Kahneman D, *Thinking, Fast and Slow* (Farrar, Straus and Giroux 2013)

Kaufmann V, 'Transparency and Subjectivity: Remembering Jennifer Ringley' in E Alloa and D Thoma (eds), *Transparency, Society and Subjectivity: Critical Perspectives* (Palgrave Macmillan 2018)

Keane W, 'Sincerity "Modernity", and the Protestants' (2002) 17(1) Cultural Anthropology 65

Kennedy D, 'The Mystery of Global Governance' (2008) 34 Ohio Northern University Law Review 827

Kennedy D, *A World of Struggle: How Power, Law and Expertise Shape Global Political Economy* (Princeton University Press 2016)

Kerby A P, *Narrative and the Self* (Indiana University Press 1991)

Khawaja N 'Unbounded Confession' in E Alloa and D Thomä (eds), *Transparency, Society and Subjectivity: Critical Perspectives* (Palgrave Macmillan 2018)

Kingsbury B, Krisch N, and Stewart R B, 'The Emergence of Global Administrative law' (2005) 68(3–4) Law and Contemporary Problems 15

Klabbers J, 'Law, Ethics and Global Governance: Accountability in Perspective' (2012) 11(2) New Zealand Journal of Public and International Law 309

Koivisto I, 'Varieties of Good Governance: A Suggestion of Discursive Plurality' (2014) 27(4) International Journal for the Semiotics of Law 587

Koivisto I, 'The IMF and the "Transparency Turn"' (2016) 25(2) Minnesota Journal of International Law 381

Koivisto I, 'The Anatomy of Transparency: The Concept and its Multifarious Implications' (2016) Max Weber Programme 2016/09 Working Paper < http://hdl.handle.net/1814/41166> accessed 14 July 2021

Koivisto, I, 'Towards Critical Transparency Studies': A book review on Emmanuel Alloa and Dieter Thomä (eds) Transparency, Society and Subjectivity: Critical Perspectives' (2019) 25(3) Res Publica 439

Koivisto I, 'From Moral Rules to Individual Rights—and Beyond? The Institutionalization of Good Administration in Finland and in Europe' (2018) 1 Förvaltningsrättslig tidskrift 71

Koivisto I, 'Thinking Inside the Box: The Promise and Boundaries of Transparency in Automated Decision-Making' (2020) Academy of European Law working papers 2020/01 <http://hdl.handle.net/1814/67272> accessed 14 July 2021

Koivisto I, 'Transparency in the Digital Environment' (2021) 8(1) Critical Analysis of Law 1

Koivisto I, 'The Digital Rear Window: Epistemologies of Digital Transparency' (2021) 8(1) Critical Analysis of Law 64

Koskenniemi M, 'Human Rights Mainstreaming as a Strategy for Institutional Power: Humanity' (2010) 1(1) International Journal of Human Rights, Humanitarianism, and Development 47

Koskenniemi M and Leino P 'Fragmentation of International Law? Postmodern Anxieties' (2002) 15 Leiden Journal of International Law 553

Koulu R, 'Crafting Digital Transparency: Implementing Legal Values into Algorithmic Design' (2021) 8(1) Critical Analysis of Law 81

Lakoff G and Johnson M, *Metaphors we Live By* (University of Chicago Press 1980/2003)

Larsson S, *Conceptions in the Code: How Metaphors Explain Legal Challenges in Digital Times* (Oxford University Press 2017)

Larsson S, Jensen-Urstad A, and Heintz F, 'Notified but Unaware: Third-Party Tracking Online' (2021) 8(1) Critical Analysis of Law 101

Latour B, *The Making of Law: An Ethnography of the Conseil d'État* (Polity Press 2010)

Latour B, 'What is Iconoclash?' in B Latour and P Weibel (eds), *Iconoclash: Beyond Image Wars in Science, Religion, and Art* (MIT Press 2002)

Leino P, 'Secrecy, Efficiency, Transparency in EU Negotiations: Conflicting Paradigms?' (2017) 5(3) Politics and Governance 6

Leino P, 'Disruptive Democracy: Keeping EU Citizens in a Box' in I Govare, S Garben, and P Nemitz (eds), *Critical Reflections on Constitutional Democracy in the European Union* (Hart Publishing 2019)

Lindroos-Hovinheimo S, *Private Selves: Legal Personhood in European Privacy Protection* (Cambridge University Press 2021)

Lukes S, *Power: A Radical View* (Palgrave Macmillan 2005)

Mäenpää O, *Julkisuusperiaate* (TalentumPro 2020)

Mäihäniemi B, *Competition Law and Big Data: Imposing Access to Information in Digital Markets* (Edward Elgar 2020)

MacFarlane J, 'Aristotle's Definition of "Anagnorisis"' (2000) 121(3) The American Journal of Philology 367

Malgieri G and Comandé G, 'Why a Right of Legibility of Automated Decision-Making Exists in the General Data Protection Regulation' (2017) 7(4) International Data Privacy Law 243

Mansbridge J, 'A "Selection Model" of Political Representation' (2009) 17(4) The Journal of Political Philosophy 369

Mazzarella W, 'Culture, Globalization, Mediation' (2004) 33 Annual Review of Anthropology 345

McLuhan M, *Understanding Media: Extensions of a Man* (MIT Press 1964)

Mersch D, 'Obfuscating Transparency' in E Alloa and D Thomä (eds), *Transparency, Society, Subjectivity: Critical Perspectives* (Palgrave Macmillan 2018)

Mitchell W T J, *What do Pictures Want? The Lives and Loves of Images* (University of Chicago Press 2005)

Morris E, *Believing is Seeing: Observations of the Mysteries of Photography* (Penguin Books 2011)

Nagel T, *Concealment and Exposure and Other Essays* (Oxford University Press 2002)

Naurin D, *Deliberation Behind Closed Doors: Transparency and Lobbying in the European Union* (ECPR Press 2007)

Oklopcic Z, *Beyond the People: Social Imaginary and Constituent Imagination* (Oxford University Press 2018)

Olsen H P, Slosser J L, Hildebrandt T, and Wiesener C, 'What's in the Box? The Legal Requirement of Explainability in Computationally Aided Decision-Making in Public Administration' (2019) 162 iCourts Working Paper Series <https://staticcuris.ku.dk/portal/files/235473618/WorkingPaper_SSRN_id3402974.pdfz> accessed 14 July 2021

O'Neill O, 'Transparency and the Ethics of Communication' in C Hood and D Heald (eds), *Transparency—The Key to Better Governance?* (Oxford University Press 2006)

Parsons C, 'The (In)effectiveness of Voluntarily Produced Transparency Reports' (2019) 58(1) Business and Society 103

Pasquale F, *The Black Box Society: The Secret Algorithms That Control Money and Information* (Harvard University Press 2015)

Paul C, 'Mediations of Light: Screens as Information Surfaces' in S Cubitt, D Palmer, and N Tkacz (eds), *Digital Light* (Open Humanities Press 2015)

Peirce C, *Collected Writings*, vol 8 (C Hartshorne, P Weiss, and A W Burks eds, Harvard University Press 1958)

Peters A, 'Towards Transparency as a Global Norm' in A Peters and A Bianchi (eds), *Transparency in International Law* (Cambridge University Press 2013)

Plato, *The Republic of Plato* (translated with notes and an interpretive essay by Allan Bloom, 2nd edn, Basic Books 1991)

Pollitt C and Hupe P, 'Talking About Government: The Role of Magic Concepts' (2011) 13(5) Public Management Review 641

van de Port M, '(Not) Made by the Human Hand: Media Consciousness and Immediacy in the Cultural Production of the Real' (2011) 19(1) Social Anthropology 74

Power M, *The Audit Society: Rituals of Verification* (Oxford University Press 1999)

Pozen D, 'Deep Secrecy' (2010) 62(2) Stanford Law Review 257

Pozen D, 'Leaky Leviathan: Why the Government Condemns and Condones Unlawful Disclosure of Information' (2013) 127 Harvard Law Review 512

Pozen, D, 'Transparency's Ideological Drift' (2018) 128(1) The Yale Law Journal 100

Pozen, D, 'Seeing Transparency More Clearly' (2020) 80(2) Public Administration Review 326

Preuβ U, 'Transparency in International Law' (2014) 12(3) International Journal of Constitutional Law 820

Reimer M and Camp E, 'Metaphor' in E Lepore B C Smith (eds), *The Oxford Handbook of Philosophy of Language* (Clarendon Press 2006)

Richmond S D, Rees G, and Edwards S J L (eds), *I Know What You're Thinking: Brain Imaging and Mental Privacy* (Oxford University Press 2012)

Riles A, 'Introduction: In Response' in A Riles (ed), *Documents: Artifacts of Modern Knowledge* (University of Michigan Press 2006)

Ringel L, 'Boundaries of Visibility in the Age of Transparency: an Integrative Conceptualization' in L Ringel, P Hiller, and C Zietsma (eds), *Toward Permeable Boundaries of Organizations? Research in the Sociology of Organizations* (Emerald 2018)

Ringel L, 'Unpacking the Transparency-Secrecy Nexus: Frontstage and Backstage Behavior in a Political Party' (2019) 40(5) Organization Studies 705

Roberts A, *Blacked Out: Government Secrecy in the Information Age* (Cambridge University Press 2006)

Roberts J, 'Organizational Ignorance: Towards a Managerial Perspective on the Unknown' (2012) 44(3) Management Learning 215

Rodosthenous G, 'Introduction: Staring at the Forbidden: Legitimizing Voyeurism' in G Rodothenous (ed), *Theatre as Voyeurism: The Pleasures of Watching* (Palgrave Macmillan 2015)

Rose N, *Powers of Freedom: Reframing Political Thought* (Cambridge University Press 1999)

Rousseau J-J, *Politics and the Arts: Letter to M d'Alembert on the Theatre* (A Bloom tr, Cornell 1968)

Rousseau J-J, *The Social Contract and the Discourses* (G D H Cole ed, Dent 1988)

Rousseau J-J, *Confessions and Correspondence, Including the Letters to Malesherbes*, vol 5 (C Kelly tr, Collected Writings of Rousseau, Hanover New England 1995)

Rowe C and Slutzky R, 'Transparency: Literal and Phenomenal' (1963) 8 Perspecta 45

Sanders T and West H (eds), *Transparency and Conspiracy: Ethnographies of Suspicion in the New World Order* (Duke University Press 2003)

Santiso C, 'The Paradox of Governance: Objective or Condition of Multilateral Development Finance?' (2003) SAIS Working Paper Series WP/03/03 <https://citeseerx.ist.psu.edu/viewdoc/download?doi=10.1.1.122.9087&rep=rep1&type=pdf> accessed 14 July 2021

Saunders D, 'The Making of Law: An Ethnography of the Conseil d'État' (2012) 5(1) Journal of Cultural Economy 125

Sartre J-P, *Being and Nothingness: A Phenomenological Essay on Ontology* (Philosophical Library 1956)

Schneider M, *Transparenztraum: Literatur, Politik, Medien und das Unmögliche* (Matthes and Seitz Berlin 2013)

Schneider M, 'The Dream of Transparency: Aquinas, Rousseau, Sartre' in E Alloa D and Thomä (eds), *Transparency, Society and Subjectivity* (Palgrave Macmillan 2018)

Schudson M, *The Rise of the Right to Know: Politics and Culture of Transparency, 1945–1975* (The Belknap Press of Harvard University Press 2015)

Schwarze J, 'The Convergence of the Administrative Laws of the EU Member States' (1998) 4(2) European Public Law 191

Scott J C, *Seeing Like a State: How Certain Schemes to Improve the Human Condition Have Failed* (University Press 1998)

Segal R A, *Myth: A Very Short Introduction* (Oxford University Press 2015)

Sherwin R K, *Visualizing Law in the Age of the Digital Baroque: Arabesques and Entanglements* (Routledge 2012)

Sherwin R K, 'What Authorizes the Image? The Visual Economy of Post-Secular Jurisprudence' in D Manderson (ed), *Law and the Visual: Transitions and Transformations* (University of Toronto Press 2017)

Sifry M L, *WikiLeaks and the Age of Transparency* (Preface by Andrew Rasiej, New York, OR Books 2011)

Simmel G, 'The Sociology of Secrecy and Secret Societies' (1906) 11(4) American Journal of Sociology 441

Solove, D, *The Digital Person: Technology and Privacy in the Information Age* (NYU Press 2004)

Srnicek N, *Platform Capitalism* (Polity Press 2016)

Starobinski J, *Jean-Jacques Rousseau: Transparency and Obstruction* (University of Chicago Press 1988)

Stelkens U and Andrijauskaitė A (eds), *Good Administration and the Council of Europe: Law, Principles, and Effectiveness* (Oxford University Press 2020)

Stokes P, 'Kierkegaard's Mirrors: the Immediacy of Moral Vision' (2007) 50(1) Inquiry 70

Suzor N, *Lawless: The Secret Rules That Govern Our Digital Lives* (Cambridge University Press 2019)

Taussig M, *Defacement: Public Secrecy and the Labor of the Negative* (Stanford University Press 1999)

Teurlings J and Stauff M, 'Introduction: The Transparency Issue' (2014) 14(1) Cultural Studies ↔ Critical Methodologies 3

Thomä D 'Seeing It All, Doing It All, Saying It All: Transparency, Subject, and the World' in E Alloa and D Thomä (eds), *Transparency, Society and Subjectivity* (Palgrave Macmillan 2018)

Treiber H, *Reading Max Weber's Sociology of Law* (M Philpotts tr, Oxford University Press 2020)

Trilling L, *Sincerity and Authenticity* (Harvard University Press 1972)

Tøllefsen T O, Sustainability as a 'Magic Concept' (2021) 64 Deusto Journal of European Studies 29

Tsoukas H, 'The Tyranny of Light: The Temptations and the Paradoxes of the Information Society' (1997) 29(9) Futures 827

Turner M, *Literary Mind* (Oxford University Press 1996)

Vasselau, C, 'Simulated Translucency' in S Cubitt, D Palmer, and N Tkacz (eds), *Digital Light* (Open Humanities Press 2015)

Vattimo G, *The Transparent Society* (Polity Press 1992)

Vaughn R, 'The Associations of Judicial Transparency with Administrative Transparency' in P Ala'i and R Vaughn (eds), *Research Handbook of Transparency* (Edward Elgar 2014)

Vismann C, *Files: Law and Media Technology* (Stanford University Press 2008)

Vogelmann F, 'Transparency's Trap: Problems of an Uncontested Norm' in S Berger and D Owetschkin (eds), *Contested Transparencies, Social Movements and the Public Sphere: Multi-Disciplinary Perspectives* (Palgrave Macmillan US 2019)

Wagner B, 'Ethics as an Escape from Regulation: from "Ethics-Washing" to Ethics-Shopping?' in E Bayamalioglu, I Baraliuc, L Janssens, and M Hildebrandt (eds), *Being Profiled: Cogitas Ergo Sum: 10 Years of Profiling the European Citizen* (Amsterdam University Press 2018)

Watt G, 'Law Suits: Clothing as the Image of Law' in L Dahlberg, K Stierstorfer and D Carpi (eds), *Visualizing Law and Authority: Essays on Legal Aesthetics* (Walter de Gruyter 2012)

Weber M, *Economy and Society* (G Roth and C Wittich eds, University of California Press 1978)

Wilson T, *Strangers to Ourselves: Discovering the Adaptive Unconscious* (Harvard University Press 2002)

Wouter J and Ryngaert C, 'Good Governance: Lessons from International Organizations' in D M Curtin and R A Wessel (eds), *Good Governance and the European Union: Reflection on Concepts, Institutions and Substance* (Intersentia 2005)

Wyatt D, 'The Anaemic Existence of the Overriding Public Interest in Disclosure in the EU's Access to Documents Regime' (2020) 21 German Law Journal 686
Wylie C, *Mindf*ck: Cambridge Analytica and the Plot to Break America* (Random House 2019)
Youyou W et al, 'Computer-Based Personality Judgments Are More Accurate Than Those Made by Humans' (2015) 112(4) Proceedings of the National Academy of Sciences 1036
Zaia M and Lippert R K, 'Review of Harcourt's Exposed: Desire and Disobedience in the Digital Age' (2017) 15(2) Surveillance & Society 354
Zalnieriute M, 'Transparency-Washing in the Digital Age: A Corporate Agenda of Procedural Fetishism' (2021) 8(1) Critical Analysis of Law 139
Zalnieriute M, Bennett Moses L, and Williams G, 'The Rule of Law and Automation of Government Decision-Making' (2019) 82(3) Modern Law Review 425
Zerilli J, Knott A, Maclaurin J, and Gavaghan C, 'Transparency in Algorithmic and Human Decision-Making: Is There a Double Standard?' (2019) 32(4) Philosophy and Technology 661
Zerubavel E, *Hidden in Plain Sight: The Social Structure of Irrelevance* (Oxford University Press 2015)
Žižek S, *For They Know Not What They Do—Enjoyment as a Political Factor* (Verso Books 1991)
Žižek S, *The Plague of Fantasies* (Verso Books 1997)
Žižek S, 'Nature and its Discontents' (2008) 37(3) SubStance 37
Zuboff S, *The Age of Surveillance Capitalism: The Fight for a Human Future at the New Frontier of Power* (Profile Books 2019)

Cases

Case C-57/16 P *ClientEarth v European Commission* [2018] ECLI:EU:C:2018:660
Case T-540/15 *Emilio De Capitani v European Parliament* [2018] ECLI:EU:T:2018:167
Case C-280/11 P *Council of the European Union v Access Info Europe* [2013] ECLI:EU:C:2013:671
Cases C-39/05 P and C-52/05 P *Kingdom of Sweden and Maurizio Turco v Council of the European Union* [2018] ECLI:EU:C:2008:374
Delcourt v Belgium App no 2689/65 (ECtHR, 17 January 1970)
Supreme Administrative Court of Finland, KHO 2018:164, ECLI:FI:KHO:2018:164

Other sources

Abazi V, 'New EU Directive on Whistleblower Protection' (23 April 2019) <http://eulawanalysis.blogspot.com/2019/04/new-eu-directive-on-whistleblower.html?m=1> accessed 14 July 2021
Algorithm Watch, 'Automating Society: Taking Stock of Automated Decision-Making in the EU: A report by Algorithm Watch in cooperation with Bertelsmann Stiftung, supported by the Open Society Foundations' (January 2019) <https://algorithmwatch.org/en/automating-society/> accessed 14 July 2021
Algorithm Watch, 'AI Ethics Guidelines Global Inventory' (9 April 2019) <https://algorithmwatch.org/en/project/ai-ethics-guidelines-global-inventory/> accessed 14 July 2021
Apple, 'Apple Transparency Report' <www.apple.com/legal/transparency/about.html>

Assange J, 'Don't shoot messenger for revealing uncomfortable truths' *The Australian* (7 December 2010) <https://www.theaustralian.com.au/in-depth/wikileaks/dont-shoot-messenger-for-revealing-uncomfortable-truths/news-story/43b912ca277c90355fab12cc83cd4e69> accessed 14 July 2021

Budish R, 'What Transparency Reports Don't Tell Us' *The Atlantic* (Boston, 19 December 2013) <www.theatlantic.com/technology/archive/2013/12/what-transparency-reports-dont-tell-us/282529/> accessed 14 July 2021

Commission, 'Proposal for a Directive of the European Parliament and of the Council on the protection of persons reporting on breaches of Union law' COM (2018) 218 final

Commission, 'Proposal for Regulation of the European Parliament and of the Council Laying Down Harmonised Rules on Artificial Intelligence (Artificial Intelligence Act) and Amending Certain Union Legislative Acts' COM/2021/206 final

Consolidated Version on the Treaty on Functioning of European Union [2012] C326/47

Consolidated Version of the Treaty on European Union [2012] OJ C326/01

Cookiebot, 'Ad Tech Surveillance on the Public Sector Web: A Special Report on Pervasive Tracking of EU Citizens on Government and Health Service Websites' (Cookiebot with policy recommendations by EDRi, March 2019) <https://www.cookiebot.com/en/cookiebot-report/> accessed 14 July 2021

Council Directive 2019/1937 on the protection of persons who report breaches of Union law [2019] OJ L305/17

The Council of Europe, Recommendation CM/Rec(2007)7 Recommendation of the Committee of Ministers to Member States on Good Administration [2007]

The Council of Europe Project Group on Administrative Law (CJ-DA 2005(4))

Edwards S, 'Leaked UN Staff Survey Shows Fears over Whistleblowing, Ethical Accountability' *Devex* (1 March 2018) < https://www.devex.com/news/leaked-un-staff-survey-shows-fears-over-whistleblowing-ethical-accountability-92234 > accessed 14 July 2021

Facebook, 'Facebook Transparency Report' <https://govtrequests.facebook.com> accessed 3 August 2021

Google, 'Google Transparency Report' <https://transparencyreport.google.com/about> accessed 5 July 2021

Heikkilä M, 'Europe Eyes Strict Rules for Artificial Intelligence' *Politico* (14 April 2021) <www.politico.eu/article/europe-strict-rules-artificial-intelligence/> accessed 14 July 2021

Hill K, 'Thanks, Snowden! Now All The Major Tech Companies Reveal How Often They Give Data To Government' *Forbes* (New York, 14 November 2013) <www.forbes.com/sites/kashmirhill/2013/11/14/silicon-valley-data-handover-infographic/?sh=2dddc9da5365> accessed 14 July 2021

Leathern R, 'Expanded Transparency and More Controls for Political Ads' (Facebook, 9 January 2020) <https://about.fb.com/news/2020/01/political-ads/> accessed 5 July 2021

Mance H, 'Britain has had enough of experts, says Gove' *Financial Times* (3 June 2016) <https://www.ft.com/content/3be49734-29cb-11e6-83e4-abc22d5d108c> accessed 14 July 2021

Maroni M, 'Some Reflections on the Announced Facebook Oversight Board' *Robert Schuman Centre* (Helsinki, 17 October 2019) < https://cmpf.eui.eu/some-reflections-on-the-announced-facebook-oversight-board/ /> accessed 14 July 2021

Ministry of Justice of Finland, 'Julkisuuslain ajantasaistaminen' (Public Release 9 February 2021) <https://oikeusministerio.fi/julkisuuslain-ajantasaistaminen> accessed 24 June 2021

Pegoraro R, 'Tech Companies Are Quietly Phasing Out a Major Privacy Safeguard' *The Atlantic* (Boston, 29 September 2019) <www.theatlantic.com/technology/archive/2019/09/what-happened-transparency-reports/599035/> accessed 14 July 2021

Richter M, 'A Police Gadget Tracks Phones? Shhh! It's Secret' *New York Times* (New York, 15 March 2015) <www.nytimes.com/2015/03/16/business/a-police-gadget-tracks-phones-shhh-its-secret.html> accessed 14 July 2021

RT, 'Mind-reading AI may spell end to humanity as we know it, but not because it will enslave us – Zizek' *RT* (7 September 2019) <https://www.rt.com/news/468228-mind-reading-computer-humanity-zizek/> accessed 14 July 2021

Statute of the International Court of Justice (San Francisco Conference 26 June 1945)

Stolton S, 'A Leaky Commission' *Brussels Times* (9 Feb 2020) <www.brusselstimes.com/brussels-behind-the-scenes/94244/a-leaky-commission/> accessed 14 July 2021

Svensk Tryckfrihetsförordningen (1949:105)

Svensk Yttrandefrihetsgrundlagen (1991:1469)

United Nations Development Programme, 'Governance for sustainable human development' (UNDP policy document, Published January 1997)

United Nations Economic and Social Commission for Asia and the Pacific, 'What is Good Governance?' (Report by the ESCAP, published 10 July 2009)

UN Secretariat Survey Results, 'United Nations Staff Engagement Survey' (February 2018) <https://pages.devex.com/rs/685-KBL-765/images/UN-Secretariat-Survey-Results-February-2018.pdf> accessed 14 July 2021

Wachowski L and Wachowski L, 'The Matrix' (Warner Bros Pictures 1999)

World Bank, *Sub-Saharan Africa: From crisis to sustainable development: A Long-Term Perspective Study* (Washington D C, The International Bank for Reconstruction and Development/ The World Bank 1989)

World Bank, *World Development Report 1991: The Challenge of Development: World Development Indicators* (Oxford University Press 1991)

World Bank, *Governance and Development I* (Washington D C, The International Bank for Reconstruction and Development/ The World Bank 1992)

World Bank, *Governance: The World Bank's Experience* (Washington D C, The International Bank for Reconstruction and Development/ The World Bank 1994)

World Bank, *World Development Report 2002: Building Institutions for Markets* (Oxford University Press 2002)

Index

For the benefit of digital users, indexed terms that span two pages (e.g., 52–53) may, on occasion, appear on only one of those pages.